JOHN HUME

JOHN HUME

A BIOGRAPHY

Paul Routledge

HarperCollins*Publishers*

HarperCollins*Publishers*
77–85 Fulham Palace Road,
Hammersmith, London w6 8jb

Published by HarperCollins*Publishers* 1997
1 3 5 7 9 8 6 4 2

Copyright © Paul Routledge 1997

The Author asserts the moral right to
be identified as the author of this work

A catalogue record for this book
is available from the British Library

ISBN 0 00 255670 7

Set in Janson by
Rowland Phototypesetting Ltd,
Bury St Edmunds, Suffolk

Printed and bound in Great Britain by
Caledonian International Book Manufacturing Ltd, Glasgow

*This book is dedicated to all those
who have suffered and lost in the struggle to
achieve a just and democratic society in
Northern Ireland.*

Contents

List of Illustrations

ONE

DECISION TIME

SHORTLY AFTER ELEVEN O'CLOCK on the night of 2 January 1997, the telephone rang in John Hume's country retreat in Greencastle, County Donegal, just inside the Irish Republic. The leader of Northern Ireland's Social Democratic and Labour Party (SDLP), and acknowledged architect of the peace process in his unsettled land, was idly flicking through the teletext versions of a New Year's appeal he had made that day to the Irish Republican Army to heed the wishes of the people and put away their guns. Only then, he insisted, could political negotiations begin on his dream – and theirs – of 'a new Ireland'.

The caller was a friendly journalist at the BBC. Did Hume know that most of the national broadsheet newspapers in London were carrying on the front pages of their next day's editions a story proclaiming that he was about to give up his Westminster parliamentary seat of Foyle? And that this dramatic move was probably a prelude to his running for the presidency of the Irish Republic in November, when the much-admired President Mary Robinson might step down after only one term? No, he did not know. How could he? The newspapers had not yet been printed, but their front pages had been faxed to the studios of the BBC's *Newsnight*, and the stories of his imminent political demise were read out on air.

Hume was grateful for the tip-off, though by turns dismayed, angry and mystified. None of the Belfast-based correspondents of *The Times*, the *Guardian* or the *Daily Telegraph* had contacted him. The newspapers had relied on a throwaway line at the end of his long radio interview earlier that day with RTE, the Irish state broadcasting system. After a discussion on the political and military situation in

Ulster, Hume had been asked if he could confirm whether he would stand again in the Westminster seat he had represented since 1983. Hume replied tersely, 'No.' He meant that no decision had been taken. The SDLP would determine its electoral strategy, and he would not discuss his own situation in a radio interview.

Then, perhaps unwisely, he added: 'I am of course heavily burdened with the work that I have in terms of the European Parliament, the British Parliament, the leadership of my party and, of course, the local work one has to do in politics.' This confession, together with the single word 'No', was enough to set the hares running. There must be a plot, thought reporters. On that slight evidence, the whole case for the existence of his presidential ambitions was built. Hume telephoned the startled night news desks of the papers within minutes to deny that he was a candidate for the presidency. Publicly, he said in a statement that the stories were the product of 'silly season journalism'. Privately, he growled, 'It's a load of crap.' He would not elaborate on his plans as an MP.

The surprising thing is that anyone in the know was surprised. It had been common knowledge in Westminster circles for months that John Hume was weary of the adversarial politics of 'the mother of Parliaments'. He preferred the calmer atmosphere of the European Parliament, of which he had been a member since 1979. Even more, he was at home in the settings of modern politics: the corridors and lobbies, the television studios, the quiet conversations at glittering social occasions, the prepared speeches before select audiences and the private offices of the powerful. Hume is a lobbyist *par excellence*.

Yet, in their own over-excited way, the journalists had put the spotlight on a critical question in John Hume's life. As he reached the age of sixty on 18 January 1997, he was also reaching a personal and political watershed. Since the outbreak of the Troubles in his native Derry almost thirty years previously, he had devoted his whole life to a campaign to take the gun out of Irish politics. 'There is nothing left in his life except the peace process,' observed one commentator. 'I have no outside interests,' Hume himself admits. Nevertheless, three decades of battling to persuade British governments of every hue to find a new accommodation for the predominantly Nationalist Catholics and the Unionist Protestants of Northern

Ireland, staying out of range of the Provo petrol-bombers while in direct contact with their political spokesmen, have exhausted him. Hume has been hospitalized several times for stress-related illnesses. He gave up his eighty-a-day smoking habit, and swore off alcohol for months at a time, taking only an occasional glass of white wine. Yet still he suffered from chronic anxiety. He had pushed himself to the limit for peace. Now, perhaps, he had reached the limits of peace.

Something had to give. His doctors told him so, and his wife and political partner, Pat, had also been urging him to cut down on his workload. He had been considering how to reorganize his sometimes chaotic public life for some time, though he told friends he wanted 'to see this thing [the peace process] through'. His mind had been working on another tack.

Many months before, on a quiet afternoon in the Stranger's Bar at the House of Commons, Hume beckoned Lord Gerry Fitt to a discreet corner adjacent to the terrace that overlooks the Thames. As private conversations go, it was an unlikely affair. Hume had never exhibited much respect for the political judgement of his predecessor as leader of the SDLP. Admittedly, there was a cultural gulf between the two. Hume is a Derryman from the west of Northern Ireland where Catholics predominate, a product of educational emancipation and the civil rights movement of the 1960s. Fitt is a self-taught socialist of the old school, who sailed in the merchant navy's Arctic convoys to the Soviet Union in wartime. A colourful, street-wise operator from Protestant-ruled Belfast, he was the first leader of the SDLP, but had quit years before over the direction of the party. Now, Hume was seeking his advice.

First, a little flattery. 'You know, Gerry,' said Hume, 'that when the history of this period is written, it will be very kind to you. You lifted the veil on Northern Ireland, and broke the parliamentary convention that Unionist rule could not be questioned here.' There was more in this vein, and Fitt listened with growing incredulity, eventually asking with his usual direct humour: 'John, what were you drinking last night?' Hume got to the point: 'Do you think I can lead the party from Europe?'

Fitt practically choked on his gin and tonic. 'I told him no, you can't,' he recalled later. Who would look after the small but important

3

group of SDLP MPs at Westminster? Hume took Fitt further into his confidence. He was thinking of giving up his Westminster seat. He would retain his Northern Ireland seat in the European Parliament and lead the party from there. Fitt was appalled. In his view, Hume's place at Westminster was 'the key seat, much more important than Europe'. If there was ever to be a change in the constitution of Northern Ireland, it would be made on the floor of the House of Commons and the SDLP leader would have to be there to see it through.

Hume continued. He would make way in his native city for Mark Durkan, his chief fixer, an articulate Derryman and one-time chairman of the SDLP but little known outside the party. Durkan could be leader of the parliamentary party, while Hume maintained overall leadership. Fitt warned him that the party would not stand for this high-handed transfer of power; he was deceiving himself if he imagined that he could influence a British government 'through a big megaphone' by passing resolutions in the European Parliament in Strasbourg.

The two parted company, Hume apparently still set on his course of action, Fitt shaking his head in disbelief. Fitt's anecdote may have grown in the telling, and disillusion with his old party may have influenced his judgement, but his version of events as recounted to me is supported by others who had Hume's confidence. And though Hume himself told me he had 'no recollection' of this conversation, it echoes Hume's comments at other times both to myself and to others.

With only a few months to go before a Westminster general election, the omens were not good for any kind of radical rethink. Elections for a so-called Peace Forum in Northern Ireland in May 1996 had polarized opinion. Sinn Fein, the political wing of the IRA, emerged stronger. Hume's moderate party of reform was weakened, to the point where his Foyle seat looked vulnerable. If Hume stood down, his constituency – and his credibility – could be captured by Sinn Fein's articulate chairman, Mitchel McLaughlin.

John Hume is no quitter. He has a profound sense of duty. It was clear from his wrath at the newspaper reports of his imminent Westminster demise that he was preparing to do the opposite: to stand again, and continue his long struggle. As friends and family gathered for his sixtieth birthday on 18 January, Hume made a statement about his future. Ending months of speculation, he announced he would stand again for his Foyle seat at Westminster in the general election. He promised to keep up his work there 'and in other forums' until there was a negotiated settlement for Northern Ireland.

The news was greeted with elation by Jonathan Stephenson, chairman of the SDLP. Hume's strengthened commitment and dedication to the search for a lasting peace was, he said, 'a priceless gift' to the people of Northern Ireland.

In all the years Hume has campaigned for peaceful reform in 'John Bull's other island', he has refused to accept defeat. Like Brian Keenan, the Belfast-born teacher taken hostage in Beirut, he believes that 'while there is vision, there is hope'. Hume has a vision, fashioned both in the heat of street battles and in the quiet of his contemplative nature. He quotes approvingly the Irish poet John Boyle O'Reilly: 'A dreamer lives for ever / And a toiler dies in a day.'[1] His is a vision of New Ireland, in which the fundamentally different mind-sets – the Unionist, committed to a permanent place within the UK, and the Nationalist, committed to closer integration (if not physical unity) with the Irish Republic – can reach agreement on how to live together.

Hume looks to the United States of America and to Europe for role-models. The European Union, he argues, is engaged in a level of co-operation so intense that it has blurred the traditional bounds of sovereignty and notions of territorial integrity. Similarly, the political system of the USA commands the loyalty of its citizens despite the diversity of their ethnic make-up and experience. 'It cannot be said too often, it works,' he argues. For his part, he is willing to keep on saying it until the message strikes home. In the 'Quote Unquote' column of the *Independent*, he was quoted as saying: 'Political leadership is like being a teacher. It's about changing the language of others. I say it, and I go on saying it until I hear the man in the pub saying my words back to me.'[2]

And not just the man in the pub. This pedagogic style, which derives naturally from his training and experience as a teacher of French and History, is sometimes disparagingly referred to as

'Humespeak'. Yet it has had a profound impact on the way in which governments, political parties and terrorists alike address the Northern Ireland problem. His chief opponent, David Trimble, leader of the Ulster Unionist Party, agrees that Hume's 'great achievement is to have given northern nationalism a new form of language: a new Ireland, an agreed Ireland. The rhetoric is significantly different to the old Nationalist Party.'[3] Michael, Lord Ancram, Minister for Political Affairs in the Conservative administration, concedes: 'John Hume's major contribution has been to make possible levels of dialogue which previously had been regarded as impossible.'[4] Most critically, he was able to persuade a sympathetic Secretary of State for Northern Ireland, Peter Brooke, to adopt his formula of words about Britain's role in Ulster, enshrined in international agreement between London and Dublin, that Britain has 'no selfish strategic or economic interest in Northern Ireland'. This statement was the cornerstone of his approaches to the IRA, through the Sinn Fein leadership, during the 1980s for which he was reviled (not least within some sections of his own party), but which brought the first genuine hope of a permanent end to the violence.

The culmination of Hume's long search for peace was the Joint Declaration of British and Irish governments in December 1993. This document, signed by Prime Minister John Major and the Taoiseach, Albert Reynolds, seeks 'peace, stability and reconciliation established by agreement among all the people who inhabit the island'. It addresses the fears both of Hume's almost entirely Catholic and predominantly Nationalist community and of the Unionists, by accepting that it is for the people of Ireland alone, and by agreement, 'to exercise their right to self-determination on the basis of consent, freely and concurrently given, north and south, to bring about a united Ireland, if they so wish'. In other words, a united Ireland is the goal, but it can come about *only* with the express consent of both communities.

This consensual concept is a far cry from the politics of partition and boycott that the young John Hume inherited in his native city. Derry's sectarian divisions both shaped his outlook, and determined him to do something to improve the lot of his fellow-citizens. 'How many times have you seen me saying "Irish Unity"?' he asks. 'I am talking about an agreed Ireland. Gerry Adams doesn't talk about unity. We are now in a post-nationalist, post-nation-state world. That should make it easier for us to accommodate our differences, particularly in the context of the New Europe, where we can all retain our basic identities while living together with respect for one another,' he told me.

'The time has come to leave the past behind us and build a new future. It's very easy to call up the past to justify the present. But all that does is continue the paralysis of the situation. There is a common saying in Ireland that goes to the heart of the problem: the trouble with the English is that they never remember and the trouble with the Irish is that they never forget.

'I regard the European Union as the greatest example of conflict resolution in the history of the world. Study it, because therein lies the answer. The principles that emerge are clear. Difference is not a threat. All conflict is about seeing difference as a threat. But difference is natural. It is an accident of birth, whether it is religion, nationality or ethnicity. The answer to difference is to respect it, to create institutions which respect the differences and give victory to no one. We must work the common ground together, particularly in economics. As I put it, spill the sweat and not the blood, and that begins the real healing process. It breaks down the barriers of mistrust and eventually the healing takes place. If we apply the same principle to Ireland, and create institutions which respect differences with victory for no side, in a generation or two a New Ireland will evolve based on agreement and respect for diversity.'

Ulster is obsessed with flags and signs. They are a potent symbol of identity. Protestants fly the Union Jack and paint the kerbstones in their streets red, white and blue. Until relatively recently, it was an offence to fly the Irish red, white and green tricolor. It now blows freely in the breeze in Nationalist communities. John Hume's father, Sam, once told him, 'You can't eat a flag,' and that simple truth made a big impression on the growing boy. It is a key to Hume's pragmatic outlook, which has made a powerful contribution to rebuilding the economy of his native city and the neglected north-west of Ireland.

Derry and its hinterland in the 1960s, when Hume was cutting his political teeth, was an area in economic decline. The direct rail line to Dublin was closed. Sea links to England and Scotland were gradually severed, the docks went into decline and road communications with the rest of Ireland were poor. Ministry of Defence bases were shut down. Manufacturing industry shrank, and even the shirt industry, for which the city was famous and which kept so many women in work when their menfolk were idle, began to contract in the face of cheap competition from the Far East. Male unemployment was high, even for Northern Ireland, and there was a sense that the north-west was a forgotten region, ignored by the Unionist government at Stormont – not least because Derry had a Catholic majority and was among the least integrated parts of the Union.

Hume's long battle in the mid-1960s to gain university status for the city's Magee College may have failed (Ulster's new university was situated at Coleraine, in staunchly Protestant country), but the civic and political impetus generated by that struggle brought the problems of the region – and of Northern Ireland itself – to wider public attention. It was the beginning of a revolution in Derry's fortunes, which would have been thought inconceivable at the height of the Troubles. Today, seen from the Foyle waterfront, the modern city of Derry is virtually unrecognizable. The old walled city remains intact, substantially rebuilt after the bombs and arson attacks of the IRA, but it is now surrounded by new shopping centres and housing estates. In the suburbs, the electronics industry thrives and the new university is teaching almost 3,000 students. A new road bridge, partly built with European Union finance (and known locally as the John Hume Bridge), connects the city to Eglinton airport.

Plainly, not all of this economic regeneration can be attributed to Hume, though it is a common enough experience to hear even a Protestant farmer (on the plane into Derry airport) say: 'John Hume brought us prosperity.' A similar sea-change has taken place in the Irish Republic. Yet Hume's far-sightedness in realizing that political change – reform of the Unionist-dominated 'Orange State' – must precede economic change unquestionably played a key role in this regeneration. Hume was also the first Northern Ireland politician to realize the potential of public investment from the European Union, and private investment from the United States, where so many of Derry's sons and daughters were forced to emigrate.

Hume has been on countless business-gathering visits to the USA. On one such, in February 1993, he told American entrepreneurs: 'Forty-two million Americans described themselves in the last census as Irish in roots, many of them from the North. Since Irish business people have made such an enormous contribution to America it is not too much to ask them that they return the compliment. But I stress we are not looking for charity. We are offering a place in the biggest single market in the world – Europe.'[5] His audience that night was a group of business people, bankers, financiers and the media attending a function organized by Derry-Boston Ventures, a transatlantic body set up to exploit the 'special business relationship' built up by Hume over the years. The Unionists recognize his achievements in this field, if grudgingly, and pay him the compliment of copying his initiative. Hume has even co-operated with his greatest foe, the Rev. Ian Paisley of the hard-line Democratic Unionist Party, in the constant search for investment.

The long hoped-for 'peace dividend' has begun to bear fruit. Tourists are returning. The first cruise liner to visit the province in forty years tied at up the new deep-water docks downstream of Derry in 1995. Investment in the city in the five years to the end of 1996 totalled £450 million, and it has continued to gather pace despite the collapse of the IRA ceasefire. In April 1996, the US firm Seagate Technology announced plans to invest a further £50 million in an expansion that is increasing its workforce from 770 to 1,150. Stream International, the American IT firm, is setting up a Call Centre to service its UK operations. Fruit of the Loom has a big factory there, and Du Pont, which has kept faith with the city since 1959, is expanding its research and development capability. American executives praise the quality of the local workforce and its ability to be trained in modern technology, rather than John Hume, for siting their plants in Derry. An understandable political reticence could also be at work here.

Hume's relationship with the USA and Europe was initially a cultural one. He studied History and French at Maynooth, the Catholic seminary in County Kildare (giving rise to the Unionist taunt

9

that he is 'a spoiled priest'), and spent his summer vacations in France. In fact, he visited France before he set foot in England, and he remains a fluent French-speaker, much in demand on French television. Hume is one of the few genuinely Francophone members of the European Parliament elected in the UK, and one of an even more select band who can make the Parliament work to his and his country's best advantage.

Hume's concern with history stems in great measure from the Derry he knew during the Second World War and the immediate post-war years when he was growing up. The city had a substantial Catholic majority and a ruling Protestant (Unionist) minority, which ran the show through an intricate system of gerrymandering. It has been so since County Londonderry, against the wishes of much of its population, was included in the six-county province of Northern Ireland – Ulster to its Unionist rulers – at the time of Ireland's partition in 1921. The Protestants kept the best jobs, schools and housing. The Catholics lived outside the city walls, chiefly in the Bogside, a terraced slum overlooked by the ramparts of 'the maiden city', so known because her defences had never been penetrated.

Until the education reforms of the wartime coalition government at Westminster, enacted reluctantly by Stormont in 1946, working-class Catholics like John Hume were forced to make a living as best they could as unskilled labourers, or emigrate. It had been so for generations. Hume wrote his MA thesis on the economic and social structure of Derry in the mid-nineteenth century, noting in detail the tide of humanity flowing westwards to the ports of the then American colonies.

This connection with Northern Ireland was made much of in November 1995, when President Clinton became the first US president to visit the province. He received a rapturous reception in Derry, where he publicly heaped praise on Hume for his unrelenting search for peace. Clinton is only one of thirteen US presidents reputed to have ancestral links with Ulster. The Great Seal of the USA is the work of a poor County Londonderry orphan, Charles Thomson, who emigrated to America in 1782 and rose to become Secretary of Congress. His Latin motto, *E pluribus unum* (Out of many, one), is a favourite of Hume's and he regularly seeks to apply it to Northern

Ireland. Thomson also wrote the first draft of the Declaration of Independence.

Hume's diplomatic connection with the United States grew out of his initial role in the Ulster civil rights movement, which from 1968 disputed the Protestant Unionist ascendancy in much the same way that Martin Luther King challenged the white majority in the USA. They sang the same songs, staged the same marches and sit-downs, and attracted the attention of liberal America. In June 1969, Senator Edward Kennedy telegraphed the civil rights leader of Northern Ireland, promising they were not alone, and their cause was just. Later that year, Hume paid his first visit to Boston, Massachusetts, to preach his message of non-violent reform. To Irish Americans steeped in the politics of partition, it was a new message which initially fell on stony ground. Hume persisted, and growing confidence directed him to Washington where he made contacts on Capitol Hill.

Three years later, after Bloody Sunday, 30 January 1972, when British paratroopers shot and killed thirteen unarmed civilians in Derry, Ted Kennedy took a direct hand in events. 'I called him that fall and asked if he could meet me,' he recorded. 'Shortly afterwards, we had dinner together and I heard of his hopes and dreams for his people in Ireland.'[6] They met at the Irish embassy in Bonn, and there followed a long connection with the Kennedy clan and its associated political machine that substantially bolstered Hume's international standing – sometimes to the dismay of the British government and often to the fury of the Ulster Unionists.

Hume learned to work the American system, building up a formid-able range of contacts: Ted Kennedy, Tip O'Neill, the Speaker of Congress, whose family originated a few miles from Derry; Governor Hugh Carey of New York; and Senator Daniel Moynihan of New York State. These four became known as the 'Big Four' and, irreverently, as the 'Four Horsemen of the Apocalypse'. They consulted regularly with Hume, and initiated an annual St Patrick's Day statement on current developments in Northern Ireland. Hume exploited these senior figures to wean Irish Americans away from unthinking support for the IRA in favour of the moderate policies he himself preached. His greatest coup was President Carter's speech in August

1977, perceived as supporting the need for an 'Irish dimension' in any solution to the Northern Ireland problem, which (with varying degrees of enthusiasm) has guided American policy towards Ulster ever since. Central to that policy was American investment in the economy north and south of the border, strong enough to diminish the impulse towards violence. From the Four Horsemen came Friends of Ireland, which Hume rated as 'a very influential body of Senators and Congressmen' that always kept in touch with him. This body set up the International Fund for Ireland, which brought investment and jobs.

Hume's achievement over almost three decades of sedulous diplomacy in the USA has been threefold: winning over political and Irish American opinion to his policies of reform; easing successive US governments away from a blanket approval of British policy towards Ulster; and persuading American business to invest in the province. It must be asked now, however, if his influence in the USA is on the wane. Ted Kennedy remains in place and the Kennedy connection is still strong, particularly with Jean Kennedy Smith, US ambassador to the Irish Republic. Hume's visits to the USA are as regular as ever. Indeed, a senior figure in the SDLP noted drily: 'It is no longer St Patrick's *Day* [in the USA]. It is a fortnight.'[7] Hume's influence in a Republican-dominated Congress, however, may be shrinking, and his ability to exert pressure on the policy direction of the second Clinton administration – so evident when Gerry Adams was seeking a US visa, and in the run-up to the President's visit to Ireland a year before the presidential elections – is clearly faltering. While the ceasefire was still holding, Hume was able to write: 'Bill Clinton put peace in Ireland uppermost on his agenda.'[8] After the resumption of IRA bombings, and the attempted murder of a Unionist politician and his RUC plainclothes bodyguards in the children's intensive-care section of a Belfast hospital on 20 December 1996, the mood began to change. Congressman Joe Kennedy, visiting John Hume in Derry, said: 'I do believe that if we saw a long-term return to violence, if we began to see the IRA bombs again and counter-bombing by loyalist forces ... I think at a certain point President Clinton and the attention of the US will simply go elsewhere where they feel they can actually make a difference in bringing peace to a community.'[9]

On the ground in Ulster, there is a deep ambivalence about the future. Opinion poll after opinion poll supports Hume's search for peace, while offering ambiguous advice on what direction it should take. Unionist politicians, their position secured by the direct-action victory at Drumcree in July 1996, and by the Labour–Conservative bipartisan policy of keeping Sinn Fein out of all-party talks until there is an 'unequivocal' IRA ceasefire, can afford to take a hard line. David Trimble urged John Major: 'It is time for the government to come out of denial: to acknowledge the painful truth that John Hume's version of the peace process was a sham. Sinn Fein/IRA has not changed its spots; there is no way it can be accommodated consistent with democratic principles.'[10]

Where has all the optimism gone? Little more than a year ago, John Hume was confidently expected to win the Nobel Peace Prize. Within weeks of the IRA ceasefire, he was being talked of for the £622,000 honour by the European Socialists, the largest group in the European Parliament. Glenys Kinnock, wife of the former Labour leader Neil, was the driving force behind the move to have Hume's long record of peacemaking recognized internationally. Hume's response was a characteristic blend of humility and an eye for the headline that would advance his cause. 'The only prize I want is peace,' he declared.

Like the peace process itself, the Nobel tragi-comedy was an instructive lesson in how things connected with Northern Ireland can go wrong. Hume's nomination was controversial from the beginning. Nineteen ninety-five marked the centenary of Nobel's will, in which the major part of his estate was set aside in a fund to reward individual progress in the sciences, literature and 'fraternity among nations'; so the contenders were bound to be scrutinized with great care. (Alfred Nobel was a Swedish chemist who patented dynamite.) *The Times* led the way, pointing out in a leader on 30 September 1994 that even before the prize for *that* year had been awarded, 'paeans of praise' were already being sung in support of prospective candidates for 1995. It welcomed Hume's modest and rational response to Mrs Kinnock's 'egregious initiative', adding that the SDLP was right to be wary of the 'political jackpot'. An award to any individual, or to any permutation of the dramatis personae in the search for peace in Northern Ireland, would be an act of unalloyed folly, the paper argued, suggesting to naive observers that the problems of the province had been solved.

John Prescott, then the deputy Labour leader, stirred the pot vigorously a month later with a declaration on BBC1's *Question Time* that stunned the studio audience. He backed Hume's claims to the Peace Prize and added for good measure the names of John Major, Albert Reynolds, the Taoiseach, and Gerry Adams, president of Sinn Fein, who at that stage was still banned from entering Britain. 'It's all about peace,' Prescott said blithely. 'I would not exclude anyone who had made a contribution to peace.'

Hume's nomination by his fellow-MEPs commended his 'courage, vision and fortitude' in initiating the peace process with Gerry Adams, but looking back on previous Irish winners of the prize could hardly have filled Hume with hope. The first was Sean MacBride, lawyer, diplomat, human rights activist, former Chief of Staff of the IRA, and one time Foreign Minister in Dublin, who led an extraordinary life that brought him both the Nobel and the Lenin peace prizes. He was also the author of the much-disputed MacBride Principles, adopted in several states in the USA, that were designed to prevent American investment in firms which discriminated against Catholics in Northern Ireland. Hume had always taken a more relaxed view, arguing that depriving Protestants of jobs would not alleviate the lot of jobless Catholics. MacBride won the Nobel Prize in 1974, three years before he made a clandestine, and ultimately futile, bid to bring about an agreement between Loyalist paramilitaries and the IRA.

In the same year as MacBride's peace bid, 1977, two Belfast women, Betty Williams, aged thirty-four, and Mairead Corrigan, twenty-two, whose grief united them in despair at the violence in Ulster and prompted them to form the Women's Peace Movement, were awarded the prize. In fact, the prize was for the preceding year, 1976, because their nominations arrived after the 1 February deadline. The peace movement grew spontaneously out of the reaction to the death in a Belfast street of three small children, crushed by a runaway car driven by a man who had been shot by soldiers.

For a few, heady months, the 'Peace People' marshalled immense demonstrations against the violence. Hume gave the initiative his full support. However, the prize money, plus a further £176,000 collected by Norwegian newspapers, created friction among the 'Peace People'. Williams and Corrigan decided to keep the Nobel cash, and the movement tore itself apart over the ensuing three years. The two prizewinners fell out, and Betty Williams now lives in Florida. Anne Maguire, Mairead Corrigan's sister and the mother of the three children who died, committed suicide with a carving knife in 1980 as the peace organization went into a tailspin.

Against this unpromising historical background, Hume kept a low profile about the Prize. Others were not so reticent. Gerry Adams appeared on CNN's Larry King show by satellite with Ken Maginnis, the Ulster Unionist Party's spokesman on security, in October 1994. Presenter King manufactured a confrontation over the issue, asking Maginnis if Hume deserved the prize. Maginnis huffed: 'I'd like to think if there is peace, that the Nobel Prize goes to the person who played the biggest part in achieving that.' King shot back: 'And he did?' Maginnis: 'But maybe the people of Northern Ireland, the 90 per cent who reject violence, deserve the Nobel Peace Prize.' King pressed on, demanding to know if they both agreed. Adams accepted: 'Well, I certainly agree.' King exulted: 'This will be historic!' Maginnis added mournfully: 'I don't think we should be talking about prizes.'[11]

Indeed, it was too soon. A number of Irish MPs swiftly nominated the Taoiseach, Albert Reynolds. This made it harder for the five-member committee of Norway's great and good to award the prize to Hume. When several participants in a conflict are involved, the Nobel Committee almost invariably elects for balance: Yitzhak Rabin, Yasser Arafat and Shimon Peres in 1994: F. W. de Klerk and Nelson Mandela in 1993: Anwar Sadat and Menachem Begin in 1976; and, embarrassingly, in 1973 Henry Kissinger and Le Duc Tho, the Vietnamese 'peace' negotiator who turned down the honour. Hume and Reynolds – two-thirds of what the Unionists regarded as a pan-nationalist troika – had been proposed, but where was the balancing nomination, either from Britain or the Northern Ireland majority?

Friday 13 December was the date set for the announcement, at eleven in the morning. Hume was billeted in a Dublin hotel, besieged by camera crews who thought he had won. An injudicious report on Swedish television the previous night had tipped him as the winner, along with Albert Reynolds and John Major. The story had been picked up from Norway's leading national newspaper, *Aftenposten*, and was alleged to have come from background briefings from the supposedly watertight Nobel Committee. This was the first time that the Prime Minister's name had appeared in the frame. It had been widely assumed that he had not been nominated. Yet the tip was taken seriously, because the previous year the television station had correctly predicted the Middle Eastern winners. John Major, attending the Conservative Party conference in Blackpool, was said to be 'irritated' by the rumours, which detracted from the impact of his leader's speech that morning. However, the reports encouraged feverish media speculation that Hume had won.

In the event, the million-dollar prize eluded Ulster's would-be peacemakers. It went to an obscure British scientist, Joseph Rotblat, who had worked on the development of the first atomic bomb, and then spent the rest of his life campaigning against nuclear weapons. Rotblat, aged eighty-six and born in Poland, was president of the Pugwash Group of anti-nuclear scientists.

Hume was naturally disappointed. He has received many other peace awards in the USA and Europe – they line the hall of his County Donegal home – but the Nobel would have crowned his career as peacemaker. His biographer at the time, George Drower, recalled Hume's comment that the only reward he wished after his years of struggle was peace. 'That having now been achieved, he deserves to win the Nobel Peace Prize for his great acts of Christian leadership.'[12]

The biographer was premature, but so was Hume. His long haul was unquestionably Christian leadership; it is not yet peace. Hume shared Drower's misapprehension that the armed struggle, the long war, however it is characterized, was over. Hume wrote: 'The IRA have laid down their arms', and, 'By abandoning violence, the IRA have shown that they are serious about their political objectives.'[13] They had neither laid down their arms nor abandoned violence. According to Northern Ireland Office ministers, who relied on 'intelligence sources', the IRA continued to recruit and train, to run dummy missions, and to gather materiel for a resumption of hostilities. It was discovered that the lorry used in February 1996 for the Canary Wharf bomb had been bought by the Provos three months previously, when hopes for Sinn Fein involvement in multi-party talks were still high. Huge amounts of bomb-making equipment were found in London in September that year, in a safe house acquired by the IRA only two months after the beginning of the ceasefire in 1994.

There are conflicting theories about the long-term aims of militant Republicanism. In the late 1970s, a report drawn up by Brigadier General Glover, General Officer Commanding British forces in the province, claimed that the Provisionals had 500 full-time 'volunteers' with thousands more supporters willing to hide a gunman on the run or to store a weapon. It added: 'The Provisional leadership is deeply committed to a long campaign of attrition . . . Even if "Peace" is restored, the motivation for politically inspired violence will remain. Arms will be readily available and there will be many who are able and willing to use them.'[14]

Many, if not most, Unionists would share this traditionalist military analysis. A more sophisticated assessment draws on the change of thinking evident from the late 1970s, when Gerry Adams rose to prominence in Sinn Fein. His strategy document, *A Scenario for Peace*, argued that armed struggle alone could not succeed in driving the British out of Ireland. A serious political force was also needed – notoriously described as taking power 'with a ballot box in one hand and the Armalite in the other'. Sinn Fein's much higher electoral profile after the IRA hunger strikes of 1981 brought Republicanism into direct political competition with Hume's party, particularly in working-class districts.

Hume believed he could capitalize on this slow shift in thinking, away from violence to politics, and his success in brokering the longest ceasefire in twenty-five years of the Troubles signifies there was merit in his judgement. However, Ronan Bennett, a writer on Irish affairs, reported a conversation he had had with Gerry Adams a month before the ceasefire was called. 'The Army,' Adams said, 'are proving flexible. We've been working with Dublin and Hume, and it's really now just a question of tying up the loose ends.' A ceasefire was on. How long would it last, Bennett asked; three months? Six months? If 'the Brits' sat on their hands, Adams warned, it would be hard to maintain a ceasefire for that length of time. He believed that if the British failed to respond seriously, the IRA 'could get back to war'. The surprising thing about the Canary Wharf bomb was not that it exploded, but that it took so long in coming, concluded Bennett.[15]

In the months after the ceasefire, Hume constantly urged the British government to allow Sinn Fein into all-party talks without pre-conditions, that is without prior decommissioning of their arms. Without 'inclusive' negotiations, there was a risk of the ceasefire breaking down, he argued. To that extent, Hume clearly shared the more sceptical analysis that the ceasefire was tactical rather than a permanent turning away from violence.

A high-ranking Conservative politician closely involved in the peace process told me confidentially:

> We said to him [Hume]: We want to know this is for real. We were never convinced it was for real. We formed a working assumption. You could get into contact, but you do nothing that was irreversible. When the Canary Wharf bomb exploded, he said to me: 'I was shattered. I really believed it was over.' He thought he had done it, and all he had done was open a window.
>
> The idea that he can deliver is flawed. He opened up windows for people to find their own answers. He is the one who makes them move out, makes them address the wider issues and become political in the strict sense of the word, and that has been an extraordinarily important role to play. But he is not the great architect of the solution. His strength has been to open contacts. His weakness has been the view that he had a formula. I don't think he has a formula, or one that would be adopted by both sides at the same time. That is not to diminish his role. The most important thing was to move nationalism from the really hostile phase of 1969, and move British governments at least into dialogue looking for solutions, accepting there may be middle ways. Without him, that would not have happened.

Predictably, Hume's Unionist critics take a less generous line. The veteran Irish politician Conor Cruise O'Brien once mischievously asked whether Hume was the IRA's dupe or their accomplice. David Trimble, leader of the mainstream Ulster Unionists argues:

> Probably neither. But from the outset, there were serious flaws in his approach, which was to coax the IRA into a political path, because they did not need to continue the violence when they could achieve their objective – a new arrangement that goes significantly towards a united Ireland – by political means. This is probably what John Hume honestly believes. He is wrong, because Unionists will not agree to a new political dispensation that moves them significantly towards a united Ireland. It is simply not going to happen. I don't think John Hume realizes that.[16]

Early in 1997, the Unionists discreetly urged John Major to put the peace process on hold until after the general election. Unionist sympathizers on the Tory back-benches stepped up the pressure, arguing that 'the present peace process will fade away into nothing in a relatively short space of time'. Hume demanded an immediate general election, claiming that peace in Northern Ireland had become a hostage to parliamentary arithmetic as the Conservatives lost their majority in the Commons. It was a depressingly familiar picture of inertia at Westminster and bombs at home.

TWO

DERRY BOY

BY THE WATERSIDE of Lough Swilly in County Donegal, on the wildly beautiful Inishowen peninsula, lies a modest, single-storey stone building, approached from the Derry–Buncrana highway by a redundant bridge of massive, squared-off blocks of granite. It once took the road over a railway to Fahan pier. The trains and the motor boats have long since gone, but the bridge and the old station (now the Lough Swilly Yacht Club) remain, a century-old testament to the handiwork of a stonemason named Hume.

This was Willie Hume, great-grandfather of the Derry boy who was later to play such a critical part in the search for peace in Ulster. Willie emigrated to Donegal from the Scottish lowlands during Queen Victoria's reign. Some time in the mid-nineteenth century, he arrived in the village of Burt, a scattered hamlet by the lough, overlooked by the famous Grianan of Aileach, an iron age circular fort where the High Kings of Ulster once ruled. The whole area is steeped in Irish history. Ulster was the last province to hold out against the invading English commanders of Queen Elizabeth I, but after forty years, its resistance broke. In 1607 came the 'flight of the earls', when Ulster's chieftains fled by sea from Lough Swilly to exile on the continent.

The new king, James I, decided to subdue the province once and for all by colonizing Ulster with loyal English and Scots settlers, almost exclusively Protestant in religion. These new 'plantations' were often established by England's wealthy trades guilds. The ancient monastic settlement of Derry, a few miles away on the river Foyle, was given to the rich men of London to colonize, and they renamed it Londonderry in their own honour. They built a fortified city, which still stands, and laid the foundations of a Protestant ascendancy that lasted virtually unchallenged for almost four centuries until John Hume's generation cut away its legitimacy.

Had great-grandfather Hume, a Presbyterian, remained true to the religious tradition to which so many of his migrant fellow-countrymen held fast, there would probably have been no story to tell. But he married a Roman Catholic and, according to custom, his children were brought up in the faith. This unusual mixed marriage was to yield exceptional descendants: Irish, with a powerful dash of Scots individuality and dourness. They were discernibly different from those around them. As Hume's first biographer, Barry White, observed: 'In the Humes of today, there are some of the Scottish traits of taciturnity, single-mindedness and a lack of emotion which distinguish them from their contemporaries.'[1]

Such was the family into which John Hume was born on 18 January 1937, in the bedroom of his grandparents' terrace house, number 20 Lower Nassau Street, Rosemount, then on the northern fringe of Londonderry. The house still exists, smartly pebbledashed today. The short street shelves steeply towards what was then open country, and is now cluttered with factories and modern housing.

John's father, Sam, aged forty-seven, had married Annie Doherty, then aged thirty-two, the previous year. She was born in a famous row of houses in the Bogside, in an area known since the Troubles of the 1960s as Free Derry Corner. Two of John Hume's aunts still live there. Annie's father was a docker in the flourishing port of Derry. Like many, if not most, local couples, Sam and Annie were forced by the city's chronic housing shortage to occupy a single room in their parents' home.

Many years later, John Hume recalled his parents with affection: 'My father was a very special man. His formal education ended at primary school – I remember him telling me that he left school when he was twelve – yet he was a great reader, especially of westerns and detective stories. He had exquisite copperplate handwriting.' One of young John's earliest memories is of sitting alongside his father at the wooden table where the family ate their meals, watching as he wrote letters to government departments for local people with unemployment, housing and other problems. 'From my earliest years,

I was very conscious of the human effects of the serious social and economic problems of our city.'

His mother Annie was 'very intelligent, but totally uneducated, as she had not had the chance to go to school'. She could write only her own name, yet like many of her generation in Derry she was the dominant influence in the family. Many local women worked in the factories by day, and at home at night. John's mother was an outworker for the shirtmaking industry, a 'patent turner', a preparer of shirt collars. Her eldest son was her secretary, sitting up late at night, counting the collars, tying them up and writing down the numbers.[2]

John's birth compelled his parents to move out of their single room, initially to share with an old republican friend in the Brandywell district and then to the first home of their own: 10 Glenbrook Terrace. This is a redbrick row in a neighbourhood known as the Glen, only a few hundred yards from his birthplace, but if anything closer to the green fields and beckoning hills of Donegal. By now, with the founding of the Free State and the partition of Ireland, these hills were over the border in the Irish Republic. It was a porous frontier, particularly for Derry's Catholics who felt a strong emotional pull to their country, from which they had been excluded by the Protestant Unionist majority's threat of armed struggle against the British government. But it was a border all the same, just a couple of miles from the fast-flowing brook where young Johnny played in the summertime, building dams to create a place to swim.

He had Protestant playmates then. The Glen was a mixed area, though with a majority of Catholics, like Derry as a whole. 'There was a great sense of neighbourhood,' Hume recalls. 'The district where we lived was Catholic, but up beside us were Glasgow Street and Terrace and Argyle Street and they were mostly Protestant. But working men met together at the street corner and had discussions and would go to the two pubs. There was a sort of working-class friendship that didn't exist anywhere else. There was a sense of community.'[3] They played each other's games, and John even became an accomplished cricketer. Today, after the sectarian divide brought about by the Troubles, the Glen is almost exclusively Catholic.

In those inter-war years of economic depression, Sam Hume was exceptional in that he held down a white-collar civil service job, of the kind usually reserved for Protestants. He was a clerk in the British government's Ministry of Food. At the outbreak of the Second World War, he had the important job of issuing food and clothing ration books. Some attribute this position to his military background and his relative worldliness. Sam Hume had been beyond his native Derry. Unemployment drove him to Glasgow in 1902 at the age of twelve, where he lived at his sister's home and worked in the local shipyards. When the Great War began in 1914, he joined the Royal Irish Rifles and saw action in the trenches in France. After the war was over, he returned to Ireland and served in the fledgling Free State's army, but eventually returned to the North.

Londonderry in wartime was a boom town. The strategically-situated deep-water anchorage of Lough Foyle made it the largest entrepôt for Atlantic convoys, with as many as 150 warships riding at anchor there and hundreds of merchantmen at any one time. It boasted two airbases and was also a big troop centre, accommodating up to 4,000 officers and men from Britain, the USA, Canada and other parts of the Commonwealth. The Americans made it their main communications base in Europe. Professor J. W. Blake, the official Northern Ireland war historian, wrote that Londonderry 'held the key to victory in the Atlantic ... [it] became our most westerly base for repair, the working up and the refuelling of destroyers, corvettes and frigates.'[4]

Attracted by the high wartime wages for shipyard workers, Sam Hume quit the civil service and returned to his old trade as a riveter, working in the Harland and Wolff repair yards along the Foyle. He certainly needed the money, as the Humes, like virtually every other Catholic family, had many children. There were four boys, John, Harry, Patrick and Jim, the youngest born just before the war ended; and three girls, Annie, Sally (twin to Patrick) and Agnes. Cramming them into a tiny two-bedroomed terrace house was difficult. Sam and the boys slept in one bedroom, Anne and the girls in the other. Downstairs, the family shared a kitchen and a sitting room. There was no bathroom, and the toilet was outside in a walled yard, along with the ashpit emptied once a month by a man with a horse and cart.

Though it was remote from the fighting, Derry had to endure

the blackout common to the whole of the UK. Streetlamps were extinguished for the duration, and householders were obliged to fit heavy curtains to their windows. It was an offence even to light a cigarette in the street. The city was attacked only once, by a lone Luftwaffe bomber in April 1941, but fifteen people died, and for months afterwards some inhabitants slept in the countryside or took the 'Blitz Train' to the seaside town of Buncrana in the Republic.

Young Johnny Hume (he remains known by the diminutive to close friends) walked the unlit streets of Derry to St Eugene's Boys' School. Close by was St Eugene's Catholic cathedral, built on a hill facing the summit of old Derry city, and clearly intended to rival St Columb's, Ireland's first Protestant cathedral, built in 1633. St Columb's, named after the great Irish saint of the sixth century who is credited with founding Derry, dominates the walled city. St Eugene's, a gothic masterpiece with a 236-foot-high spire, is a commanding presence over the Bogside and other Catholic neighbourhoods – and their people. For the last three decades, the cathedral has itself been overlooked by ugly fortifications of Rosemount RUC station. Hume was an altar-boy at St Eugene's from the age of eight, and often served Bishop Neil Farren his bacon and eggs breakfast in the bishop's residence hard by.

Hume's stern Catholic education was balanced at home by an atmosphere of generosity of spirit that continues to affect him. With the end of the war came the end of ship-repair work, and Sam Hume was laid off. He tried to get back his old job in the Ministry of Food, but he was now in his late fifties, and they had no use for him. He was never to find another job. If the government had no use for him, local people did. Sam, whose copperplate handwriting was widely admired, was much in demand to write this letter or fill out that form. His payment was usually a packet of cigarettes. His eldest son would sit at one end of the kitchen table doing his homework, but taking it all in. 'I used to sit, and all I heard was other people's problems. Unemployment problems. Poverty. Housing. And my father wrote letters for them all.'[5]

The 'common sense community' of the Glen was never anti-Protestant, in Hume's memory, 'But we were against the injustices being perpetrated by the politicians.' Politics was never discussed within the family. In those days, politics in Derry was rooted in partition, which was still a recent memory. 'It was felt, quite simply, that the border would not last, that eventually it would have to go. Nationalist politics was always emotional; elections were about flag-waving.' Hume's father was 'oriented towards socialism', but there was no effective Labour Party in the city.

Young John's earliest political memory, which he frequently quotes, is of going to an election meeting at the top of Glenbrook Terrace. It was a Nationalist Party meeting, 'and they were all waving flags and stirring up emotions for a united Ireland and the end of partition'. When Sam Hume saw his son was affected, he put his hand gently on his shoulder and said, 'Son, don't get involved in that stuff', and John asked, 'Why not, Da?' His father replied: 'Because you can't eat a flag.'

'That was my first lesson in politics and it has stayed with me to this day,' he wrote later. 'Politics is the right to existence – the right to life – bread on your table and a roof over your head. It doesn't matter what flag you wrap around you when you stand in the dole queue, or are forced to emigrate to another country to earn a living. A flag should symbolise the unity of the whole community. It should never be used as a party political or sectional emblem.'[6]

St Eugene's primary was typical of its times: bare, gas-lit and severe. Writing was done on slates. Class sizes were enormous by today's standards: forty was the norm and they were sometimes larger. One teacher would take the entire class for all subjects, except music. The wartime atmosphere was spartan, and over everything brooded the influence of Catholicism.

Neil McLaughlin, a classmate of Hume's and a fellow-altar-boy, recalls:

The main thing was, the spiritual dimension of life was always put in front of you. Prayers were part of the daily routine. We were marched down to sacraments from school. There was a children's Mass at 10 a.m. and we all went to it.

In comparison with today, the Catholic community was more close knit, and more in obedience to the church. The authority of the church was more respected, not like nowadays when people do their own thing. It was rare to have an unmarried mother with children. Broken families were unusual. Within the class, there was never any indiscipline. The cane was there, and it was used. It was part of the culture of the school.[7]

The teachers were chiefly local men, trained at Catholic education colleges in England.

McLaughlin remembers that Hume was 'very able ... he was at the top of the class, not always, but in most things'. Young Johnny was also prominent in extra-curricular activities, whether it was joining the boys' gangs who chased each other across the nearby allotments or in his school under-twelves football team run by Father Desmond Mullan. He was a 'useful' right-half, who also showed early ability in organizing and managing. Hume still shows pride in his captaincy of the Glen Stars team when they won the Father Brown Shield two years in succession. Fr Mullan described him as 'always older than his years – serious but not humourless, and self-assured without being cocky. The boys looked up to him as a natural leader and, although he mixed well with the others who were from the same background, he was not quite one of them. He was extraordinary.'[8]

There is little mention of the political dimension of Catholicism in previous biographies, but there can be no doubt that it played a critical role in the shaping of the young Hume. Eamonn McCann, a near-contemporary of Hume from the Bogside and later his revolutionary left-wing opponent in Derry's politics, is clear on this point:

We, the Catholics, were the majority in our city. But it was controlled by the Unionists because of partition. That was something you learned on your mother's knee.

The Catholic church dominated every single aspect of people's lives. All the great men we were taught about at school were overwhelmingly from the church – Cardinal Mindszenty of Hungary, Archbishop Stepinac of Croatia, persecuted by the Communists. The suffering we were undergoing was part of the age-old persecution of the church by evil regimes down the years, including Luther and the Reformation. It was the survival of the church down to this day that proved it was right. What we were going through was not just the price you paid for being Catholic in Northern Ireland, but part of the condition of being a Catholic and therefore ennobling in its own way. I was taught about the massacres of priests and nuns in the Spanish civil war when I was only seven. These two things came together: the suffering of the Catholic church world-wide and the suffering of the Irish people under British domination.[9]

Labouring at his lessons by gaslight, and swapping the popular comics of the day, Johnny Hume was unaware that he was about to be lifted out of the poverty and obscurity of the Catholic community by education reforms forced on the Unionist-dominated government at Stormont by pressure from London. In Britain, the wartime consensus between the political parties produced the 1944 Education Act which introduced compulsory state-funded secondary education for all. It was a huge educational and social breakthrough for working-class children, and initially the Unionists were reluctant to introduce parallel legislation in Northern Ireland because it would boost Catholic schools. It was two years before they followed suit.

Terence O'Neill, a future prime minister of Northern Ireland, made his debut at Stormont as the Education Bill was completing its passage. In his maiden speech, he appealed to fellow-MPs not to 'alienate the mother country' or allow the legislation to be 'wrecked on the rocks of clerical controversy'. The reforms were carried into law in 1947, and O'Neill later observed that they had 'a dramatic effect on the rising generation. An effect which many people of my generation were quite unable to comprehend when it hit them in the late sixties and early seventies.'[10]

Hume was one of the first beneficiaries of this revolution in education. One winter morning, while still aged only ten, he sat what became known as the 11-plus examination to assess whether he should go on to St Columb's, the city's prestigious Catholic grammar school. 'We were in a large class,' he recalls. 'I remember the teacher telling me to go home and tell my mother I had passed. She said "What does that mean?" I said, "It means I am going to the college." She replied: "We can't afford that."'[11] At that time, the fees for St Columb's were £7 a year; too much for an unemployed man with six other mouths to feed. It had not yet dawned on working-class mothers like Annie Hume that the state would now pay to educate its brightest children. Two other boys – one of them Neil McLaughlin – passed the same day.

'It was public education that transformed our community,' says Hume. 'The Unionists tried to postpone it for that very reason.' Nevertheless, going up to 'the grammar' was a cultural shock for the boy from the Glen. Until the intake of 1948, St Columb's had been exclusively for those who could afford it: the sons of well-to-do local farmers, professional people and businessmen. Around one in five were boarders, often from rural Tyrone or from Donegal over the border. Many were destined to become priests – the school called itself a 'junior seminary'. Those who did not go into the church would form the backbone of the Catholic middle class. The new generation of working-class boys was not universally well received. Eamonn McCann, who followed the same route a few years later, was asked on his first day in school by one of the teacher-priests: 'Where are you from? Who is your father.' When he replied he was from the Bogside, Fr Regan said: 'Oh, yes, that's where they wash once a month.'[12]

Hume was initially placed in a class for under-age pupils, but performed so well that he progressed right through the school a year younger than his classmates. St Columb's was a strongly academic, traditional school. Boys were set long hours of homework, which at first he found difficult; not because he could not master what had been set, but because he was still doing a newspaper round to supplement the family income and because it was hard to study in a small house full of noisy siblings. He was once caught by one of the 'professors' (as the school's teachers were known) out delivering papers at night. He stuffed the papers up his jacket to avoid detection. Years later, the teacher, Jack 'Rusty' Gallagher, told him he had spotted his guilty move, but wisely ignored it. He also said that Hume and his fellow-pupil, the Nobel literature laureate Seamus Heaney, were 'the two most intelligent people I ever taught'.

Discipline at school was stern. About half the teachers were priests, some of whom (it appeared to the boys) took a particular delight in physical punishment. Use of the strap was common, and not just by priests 'seeking to encourage respect for your betters'. Hume was once thrashed by prefects for an offence he did not commit – stealing the strap – and was freed from blame only after an inquiry by the Dean. Unlike English public schools, physical recreation did not play a large part in the curriculum. The school had no gymnasium and only two rough football pitches.

Academically, St Columb's had a good record. Sometimes its Catholic ethos took precedence over textbooks. 'History lessons did not always rigidly follow the curriculum laid down by the Northern Ireland Ministry of Education,' McCann insists. One slightly eccentric teacher 'was at pains to discredit English propaganda, such as that which suggested that Charles Stuart Parnell and Mrs Kitty O'Shea had been anything more than good friends'.[13] He would order pupils to strike out references to 'our Queen' and British Rule in their textbooks.

Primarily St Columb's strove to turn out the whole Catholic man, educated, but faithful to his church. The school's motto was *Quaerite Primum Regnum Dei* (Seek first the Kingdom of God), and 'modern' influences such as newspapers, comic books, books that had not been taken from the carefully vetted library and radios were forbidden on college premises. 'In so far as it could be organised and enforced, nothing alien was allowed to penetrate the defensive walls of the school grounds, nothing which might disrupt the educative process designed, in the words of Archbishop John Charles McQuaid, "so to train the child entrusted to us that supernatural habits may become more firmly and more deeply rooted in its soul".'[14]

Most days, the young Hume went to his grandmother's in the Bogside for his lunch. 'In those days, you lived in a community. You knew everybody in the neighbourhood. You walked up to school together, and made your own games in the street. You went to mass together on Sunday,' he recalls.[15] 'There was a great sense of community. That gave great stability, even though there was heavy unemployment. Crime was virtually non-existent. There was a sense of order, and of respect for one another.'

Being a junior seminary, St Columb's also sought out some of its best pupils for the priesthood. 'They picked the brightest to be altar-boys. I had been an altar-server throughout my school days. I was very close to the church. One of the things that the school strongly encouraged its pupils to do was to consider the priesthood.' His schoolmate Neil McLaughlin remembers that a 'significant number' of the boys went on to study for the priesthood. Some boys 'naturally aspired' to the cloth, but there were also social pressures: 'For parents, having a priest in the family in those days would bring respectability.'[16] For those whose did not have a family business to go back to, the church was as attractive an option as teaching or becoming a bank clerk. For Hume, so used to mixing with priests at school and on the sports field, it was a natural choice. Sam Hume, less religious than his wife at this time, asked him directly: 'Are you sure you know what you're doing?' He replied: 'Yes.'

So instead of Queen's University, Belfast, where his more worldly classmates were about to learn their social radicalism, Hume aimed for a place at St Patrick's College, Maynooth, the leading Catholic seminary in the Irish Republic. He sailed through his Advanced Level General Certificate of Education, winning a university scholarship (one of only ten that year in Derry city), and then went on to take his Bishop's examination. This involved a difficult Latin examination and an oral examination by the bishop himself.

Maynooth wanted, and got, the best. Paradoxically, it was a British foundation, set up in 1795 to counter the spread of revolutionary ideas from the continent by ensuring that Irish priests were trained in conservative Ireland rather than France, where the mob had over-thrown the monarchy only a few years earlier. If it was intended as a sop to Roman Catholics, still voteless and their church heavily discriminated against, Maynooth was a signal political mistake on the part of the British government. Instead of burying nationalist feelings behind high seminary walls, St Patrick's nurtured and encouraged the growth of constitutional nationalism.

John Hume arrived there in 1954, a dark, wavy-haired boy of seventeen. This was his first excursion away from the bosom of a big family and a lively community, and the cultural shock was great. Though the wind of change was beginning to blow through the Catholic church, Maynooth in the 1950s was more like a monastery than a college. Originally recognized as a pontifical university by the authorities in Rome in 1895, offering degrees in philosophy and canon law, it became a 'recognized college' of the new National

University of Ireland in 1910. From that date it could offer regular Bachelor and Masters degrees, but not until after the Second Vatican Council did the college begin admitting lay students.

Professor Liam Ryan, a Maynooth contemporary of Hume who still teaches there, remembers that the regime was in those days 'pretty spartan':

> It was a very closed college. We got up at six in the morning, and went to bed at ten o'clock at night. No newspapers were allowed. No sweets, chocolate, confectionery or anything like that. Outside visits were extremely rare, one or two days a year. Looking back, it was really the old-fashioned method that churches and armies used, of isolation and indoctrination.[17]

There was no radio (television was not yet available), and alcohol was banned.

The day's regimen was spelled out in Latin, beginning with *E lectulo surgitur* – getting up, washed and dressed, in silence – at 6 a.m. Morning prayers, meditation and the first mass – *Meditation et Missa Jentaculum* – followed from 6.30 to 7.45. Breakfast was taken at 7.45, and only afterwards could the students speak, in their brief free period, *Tempus Recreandi*. After half an hour's study, lectures (*Schola*) continued until 12.30, when there was a meagre lunch of a cup of tea and slice of bread. There was then a further half-hour period of recreation before lectures resumed. 'Dinner' was taken at 3 p.m., followed by another hour and a quarter break, then two hours of silent study and a spiritual lecture at 7 p.m. and a five-minute *Examen conscientiae particulare*. Supper was served at 7.45, and the students then had an hour's free time before *Oratio Vesperina* (night prayers). At 10.15, *Omnes in lectulo sunt, et lumina extinguuntur* – all in bed, and lights out. The daily routine never varied, except on Sundays when there were more religious services.

There was some surprising leniency: the students could kick a football around during their break, and everyone was allowed to smoke, though not inside the buildings. There was also undue strictness. A notice on the library door forbade the removal of books on pain of excommunication. 'If you were caught speaking after night prayer until after breakfast the next morning, you could be expelled,' said Professor Ryan. 'And no student was allowed to enter another student's room,' presumably a caution against homosexuality as well as a means of keeping discipline. Hume fell foul of this rule in his final year, in wholly innocent circumstances. He was by this time sharing a room, as students in their third year were permitted to do, and he was caught talking with a visitor by the Dean. Protesting his innocence, Hume was reprimanded by a college disciplinary committee, and sentenced to be deprived of the 'tonsure' – the small ritual shaving of part of the scalp, and the first of the holy orders that would eventually end in ordination after seven years at St Patrick's.

Some of the social barriers began to come down during the later stages of Hume's time at Maynooth. First *The Tablet*, a Catholic journal, appeared and then, in the aftermath of the Soviet invasion of Hungary in 1956, newspapers: the *Irish Independent* and the *Irish Press*. The process of change was accelerated by Thomas O'Fiaich, a brilliant graduate of the class of 1940 who returned from Louvain University in 1953 to teach history, Hume's joint honours subject. Traditionally, the only way to ask a question of a lecturer was to write it out and send it to him. O'Fiaich, later a Cardinal, encouraged students to talk to him as he walked around the austere quadrangles of Maynooth, even going as far as inviting them to his room for a cup of tea and a chat. He was also mad about sport, keener even than Hume who was still 'very slim' and played inside-left at soccer.

Under O'Fiaich's tutelage, Hume made very good academic progress. At the close of his first year, he won first-class grades in History and French, and second in English. He had before him two more years combining religious observance with studying for an academic degree, before moving on to four years of Divinity required for ordination. However, despite his unquestioned faith, he was beginning to have doubts about his fitness for the priesthood. This process of disillusion with his religious calling may owe something to the prolonged glimpses of the outside world he experienced during the summers he spent in France while studying the language. Officially, according to a souvenir publication celebrating Maynooth's bicentenary in 1995, Hume 'felt suffocated by the rigidity of the system in pre-Vatican II Maynooth'.[18]

His biographer Barry White records the doubts Hume was having about his vocation. 'He was still a retiring, self-conscious boy in his own eyes, and he soon began to feel he was not at home in the clerical atmosphere. It was difficult to describe and he never talked it out properly, either with staff or students, but he knew instinctively that this life was still not for him.'[19] If the church was bound up with so much bureaucracy and so many rules, he was unsure if he could be part of it. His contemporary, Professor Ryan, agrees that Hume was 'shy and retired', though he took part in the regular class debates that were a feature of life at St Patrick's. 'The emphasis was always on compliance,' says Ryan. 'The greatest crime you could commit in the eyes of the senior don, Montague, was "singularity". He gave a terrible hard time to anybody who deviated in his view from the image of "the sound man".'

Hume chafed at this closed society. 'After two and a half years, I decided it was not the life for me,' he told me. Even now, more than forty years later, he does not like to delve deeply into the subject. In his own book, *A New Ireland*, Hume passes over the experience as quickly as possible. 'On leaving school, I studied for three years to be a priest, but eventually decided to give it up.'[20] Yet he was not alone in his doubts. Only 55 per cent of Hume's class stayed the course, and this was not very unusual at Maynooth. There were many reasons: the authoritarian system, the rules, the lack of money (not a problem in Hume's case; he even saved from his student grant to help out at home), and the difficulty of sustaining a lifetime vocation determined in one's teens. And of course there was celibacy. 'That was the most common reason,' said a student in Hume's year. 'That, linked to the simple lack of commitment to give your life to the church. What seemed attractive at seventeen began to fade at twenty-one.'

Sam Hume, sitting at home in Glenbrook Terrace, regretted the young man's decision, but understood. He argued: 'It takes a good man to enter the priesthood – and an even better one to leave it.' Hume left Maynooth at the end of the academic year in June 1957, and before he could return in September to sit his BA exams he was taken ill with severe stomach pains. 'I spent the summer in hospital and missed my finals,' he said.

This was a minor disaster. He was twenty, educated but unqualified, and back at home in a city where unemployment was still widespread in the Catholic community. Moreover, if not a 'failed priest', he was a Maynooth student who had lost his vocation. Fortunately, he was taken on as a temporary full-time teacher at the Christian Brothers' Technical School in Derry, teaching French. This post brought a valuable wage into the Hume household, the first for many years. Hume sat his finals the following year, and graduated with a 'good' second-class honours BA. He was then able to look for a permanent post, and landed a job at St Colman's, a new secondary school in nearby Strabane, a strongly Nationalist border town in County Tyrone with a very high rate of unemployment. Here he faced the formidable task of imparting a foreign language to boys who had failed the 11-plus intelligence test and were mostly destined for manual jobs, if they were fortunate.

THREE

THE TOWN I LOVE SO WELL

JOHN HUME RETURNED to his native city to find it on the brink of radical change. For three centuries, Derry had been ruled by Unionists whose victory over the Catholic forces of James II in 1689 still informed the thinking of the Protestant majority in Northern Ireland. The Catholics of Derry, however, drew their inspiration from a much earlier religious source, St Columba, the founding saint, whose monastic oak grove gave the settlement its name in A.D. 546. The saint is remembered in street names, in wells and in the old Longtower church on the founding spot. 'Derry,' Hume is fond of saying, 'is the mother of us all.' At the slightest pretext, he breaks into the Phil Coulter anthem, 'The Town I Love So Well' (in the right company, in fluent Irish).

To be born in Derry, and reared in the city, has 'a unique effect' on its citizens, according to Professor Sean Breslin, a contemporary of Hume's. 'They cling to it with more than the usual *pietas.*' Even its many exiles both love and loathe the ugly, beautiful, shameless sprawl of housing and factory and church on both sides of the river Foyle. It has the feel of a genuine Irish city, quite unlike Belfast, which the casual visitor could easily mistake for Glasgow or Leeds.

The 'simple and strong' faith of Derry's Catholic majority has given them their sense of community, Hume argues. 'It has been a strong factor in moulding their endless patience in the face of adversity.'[1] That endless tolerance was on the verge of giving way, as the new generation of educated, working-class Catholics began to emerge from the universities and colleges. They did not have the patience of their fathers and grandfathers, nor did they share their preoccupation with the border above all other political topics. The bread-and-butter issues of housing, jobs and the gerrymandering by which the Unionists maintained their ascendancy in Derry now came to the fore, and the new Catholic graduates were ready to take them up.

First, however, Hume had to earn his living. He was determined to be radical in his teaching of French, drawing on his experience at Maynooth. 'Until that time, languages were taught by grammatical methods, especially Latin and Greek,' he explained later.[2] 'I decided to teach French as a spoken language before moving to the grammar. Talking about simple things: the classroom itself, and everything in the room. You do that for a few days, and then talk about the home, the kitchen and the bedroom. You make the language come alive for them, and give it meaning.' His pupils, written off as failures by the 11-plus, responded magnificently. Thirteen of his seventeen boys entered for the Junior Certificate examinations passed with distinction.

His novel but successful teaching methods came to the notice of the school inspectors, and the French consul in Belfast. The Northern Ireland education authorities circulated his scripts throughout the province as a model of their kind, and he was invited to France. 'I spent a month in the summer of 1960 in St Malo and Brittany, where my teacher was a French novelist.'

While teaching at St Colman's, Hume was also hard at work on his MA thesis, entitled *Social and Economic Aspects of the Growth of Derry, 1825–50*. Encouraged by his post-graduate tutor, Thomas O'Fiaich, he researched the economic history of his home city, reading local newspapers of the period but also investigating shipping and trade records to establish how and why Derry had become the place it is today. A typescript copy of his thesis still exists (in woeful shape, with pages missing) in Derry public library. Hume attributed the rise of the city to its natural geographical situation as a deep-water port on the Atlantic trade route. Exports handled between 1826 and 1853 had risen almost six times, to 234,000 tons.

He noted grimly: 'The principal export in this foreign trade was human beings. Emigrants formed the main cargo on the North American bond ships, as Derry was one of the principal emigration ports in this country. The only other article usually on board was pig iron, imported from Glasgow, carried as ballast and sold by agents on the other side of the Atlantic.'³ The human tide flowing across the Atlantic fluctuated in size, from fewer than 2,000 a year to almost 10,000 but it was constant. People, chiefly Catholics, were Ireland's major export to the New World.

Hume was the first lay post-graduate to win a second degree at Maynooth. The visiting professors awarded him a second-class MA rather than the first he and his tutor had hoped for. However, his academic efforts found a wider audience. The American writer Leon Uris later used Hume's thesis as source material for his bestselling novel about Ireland, *Trinity*.

Investigating his city's past social woes, while living with its present inadequacies and discrimination, naturally turned the young teacher towards doing something about the problems he saw around him. He was not an agitator of the socialist school, like some of his old St Columb's classmates who had gone to Queen's University. His social concern derived from a less ideological standpoint, from the mutual self-help practised by his father, who was always ready to help write a letter for a friend or give advice around the kitchen table. It also stemmed from the strong pastoral tradition of the Catholic church, particularly in Northern Ireland where its members felt (with justice) that they were second-class citizens, always last in the queue for jobs and houses.

In Derry, it was a vicious circle. Catholics could not persuade the Unionist-dominated City Corporation to build public housing for them. Nor had they the money to build their own, even if they could get planning permission. The banks were not interested in lending to the unemployed and the badly-off, who had no collateral. There was only the pawnshop and the loan-shark. These were basic, practical issues, far distant from the strident anti-partitionism of the Nationalist Party, which commanded most Catholic votes. Hume saw homes, jobs and income as more important – because more immediate – than the ultimate dream of abolishing the border between North and South. He was already feeling his way to a pragmatic, social democratic view of the world that he could communicate to others.

Its beginnings were modest. In 1958, he met Paddy Doherty, a

Catholic Bogsider who had refused to take 'No' for an answer to his request for council housing, and had built his own home. Hume and 'Paddy Bogside' formed the nucleus of a group of like-minded Derrymen who agreed that something had to be done to alleviate the plight of the city's majority, ill-served by the flagwaving politics of the Nationalist Party. Hume looked for new departures. 'Part of my philosophy in those days was that in our community, the Catholic community, politics was the politics of complaint, which was natural, complaining about injustice. But we were the first generation to get educated. My view was: what are we complaining about? Our heads and hands are as good as theirs. So let's organize. I had a conversation with Paddy Doherty, in the garden of the house he built. I talked to him about why didn't we organize our people to do our own things? We decided to set up our local development committee. We started to get people talking. Then I read an article by a US officer serving at Prestwick in Scotland about the Credit Union, founded in Nova Scotia. I got the literature on it and we called a meeting in the Rossville Hall. Father Anthony Mulvey helped us get a crowd.'

About seventy people turned up to this public meeting in 1960. 'I told them what the Credit Union was. I remember the reaction was not very positive,' says Hume. At the inaugural meeting, only four others turned up: two fellow-teachers, Doherty, and Father Mulvey. They emptied their pockets onto the table. Their combined capital amounted to seven pounds and ten shillings (£7.50), and with that they established the non-profit-making Derry Credit Union, the first of its kind in Northern Ireland. It now has 18,000 account holders, often several in a family, and assets of £23 million. The Bogside branch has smart offices in the heart of the community, and the write-off rate for bad debts is less than 1 per cent because the Bog-siders know it is 'their bank'.

Hume, at the tender age of twenty-three, was its first (unpaid) treasurer. He takes some satisfaction from this classic form of mutual self-help. 'If I had done nothing else in my life, if I was asked what have I done that I have been proud of, I would say the Credit Union. It was an enormous boost for local people. It created self-help and self-confidence.' In the ensuing years, he tramped the province as a missionary for the Credit Union, taking the message even into the heart of Protestant East Belfast, though here it fell on stony ground.

He was also learning the rudiments of the political trade. 'I was not a good speaker in those days,' he admits. 'I remember my first speeches, through sheer nervousness, running out of words. That's where I learned to speak in public. That has been central to my whole approach. I keep repeating the same language. That is deliberate. It is the old teacher in me. If you are genuinely trying to lead people and persuade people, you have to keep telling them. Not everybody hears or reads a speech. Or even thinks about it. But in public life, if you want to change things you must keep repeating yourself.'

Hume cast around for ways in which to repeat the success of the Credit Union in harnessing the natural talents of his people, and alighted inevitably on the issue of housing. But first he had more personal business. With some friends, he had set up the grandly-titled DDC – the Derry Dancing Club, to hire a hall where people of his age could provide their own entertainment. It was not long before he met Patricia Hone, at a Legion of Mary dance. She was the youngest of a family of six living on the Waterside bank of the Foyle, and her father was a staunch republican who worked as a house repairer. Like her future husband, Pat was a success story of the 11-plus generation. After grammar school, she trained as a teacher at St Mary's College, Belfast.

They had a nine-month courtship and married in 1960. White observed:

> Hume had to marry a Derry girl, and from every point of view it was a perfect match. Clever, perceptive, diplomatic, self-sufficient, good-humoured and unflappable, she was to bring up a family of five in turbulent conditions, smoothing feathers that John, with his occasionally blunt manner, had ruffled, and generally making life as agreeable as possible for a man who had so little time to spare for domestic details.[4]

They lived at first in a tiny terrace house on the Waterside, but soon moved to a bungalow on Beechwood Avenue, between the Bogside and the Creggan housing estate.

Armed with his MA, Hume was able to get a post at his old school,

St Columb's, teaching French and History. Relieved of the nuisance of commuting daily to Strabane, he could throw himself more energetically into community affairs. Michael Canavan, a fellow-director of the Credit Union, recalls: 'Once people had seen the strength of the productive idea and involvement in self-help, they thought it could be extended to other activities. It opened people's eyes. It made them feel that by joining together for a common purpose they could make things happen.'[5]

The progressive Fr Mulvey was determined to tackle Derry's chronic housing problem. In 1965, he set up a Housing Association and asked Hume to be the first chairman. 'We set up office and invited people with housing problems to come along. It was only open at night, and it was all voluntary work again.' They carried out a detailed investigation of Derry's housing problem and decided there were three types of homeless: those who could afford to buy, but didn't realize it; those who were paying high 'Rachman' rents, and could afford to save up a deposit to buy if only they paid normal rents; and those who would only ever be able to rent, and might have to have their rent paid from public funds. The first group they advised on home ownership. The second they helped by buying up large houses, dividing them into flats, charging high rents and then giving the couple back half their rent after two years to use as a house purchase deposit. In the first year, they housed one hundred families. And when they tried to build public housing, they learned the limits to self-help in Unionist-dominated Derry.

John Hume first came to serious public attention – that is, nationally, in Ireland – in the late spring of 1964. Soon after appearing in a television discussion programme, *Target Derry*, to speak on local issues, he was asked by the BBC to write the script for a documentary about his native city. This was a defining point in his career. Hume teamed up with a fellow-teacher and amateur cameraman Terry McDonald, a Protestant clergyman, the Rev. Brian Hannon, curate of All Saints' church at Clooney and a trade unionist active in the General Post Office. Hume wrote the words, and Hannon narrated them, imparting an unusual ecumenical flavour to the film. They finished the film in a month, at a cost of £50.

Entitled *A City Solitary*, it was screened on BBC television in the first week of May 1964 to accompany the coverage of the city's first arts festival. It was also shown to a festival audience in Derry Guild-hall. By coincidence, Michael Viney, a Dublin-based senior features writer for the *Irish Times*, was then engaged in writing a week-long series of reports from the province under the general heading 'Journey North'. He arrived in Derry just as the city was talking about the film, and was given a private screening in the attic 'cinema' of Terry McDonald, with Hume present.

Viney found the film 'remarkable' in several respects. 'First, that it was made by amateurs to a most accomplished standard. Second, that these amateurs are Roman Catholic laymen *and* a Church of Ireland clergyman. Third, that it carries a message of co-operative goodwill to the city of Londonderry.'

A City Solitary traced the development of Derry from the eight-eenth century, when the first crowds of (Catholic) emigrants were carried from the port's quays in great wooden sailing ships. This was familiar territory for Hume, having formed the basis for his thesis. 'Today,' said the narrator, 'the flood continues, and for the same basic reason – dissatisfaction with their lot at home and with their almost total lack of opportunity.' This sombre opening gave way to a straightforward historical account, recording the arrival of John Wesley and the foundation of Methodist groups and the rise of the Protestant merchant class within the city walls. Without the city arose the 'cabin suburbs' of the native Irish Catholics, and on another side what was at first called Wapping after the dock area of London, and is now named the Fountain, to house the lower-class Protestants. 'The divisions of modern Derry had been laid.'

Hume and his fellow-film-makers sketched the fortunes of the two main religious and occupational streams that make up the modern city, arguing that the contrast in living conditions between the Protestant merchants of Victorian times and those of the Catholic labourers they (often reluctantly) employed 'explain, in part, the depth and strength of modern Derry's religious divisions'. In a poig-nant passage, the camera focused on the face of a man who had been unemployed most of his life while the narrator described 'an idleness drawing the strength from the city, shrouding it in hopelessness . . . The effect on the soul of the city is immeasurable.'

As the camera tacked away from the slums to the two-deck bridge over the Foyle that links the two parts of the city, the film ended on an optimistic note. It called for unity of 'the great streams of Derry's population . . . The independence and seriousness of the Derry Protestant, allied to the discipline and the resourcefulness of the Catholic will build the bridge for Derry's future.' In a remarkable gesture of conciliation towards Unionist sensibilities, the script suggested that 'the symbol of the bridge could be the future full acceptance of the term "Londonderry", for in it is summed up the two great traditions of the city'.

The *Irish Times*'s man applauded the film's idealism, and called for it to be shown on RTE (Irish state television). He wondered aloud if what he had been watching was less a history of two great traditions than of the exploitation of one class by another. 'If I were a jobless Derry Catholic,' wrote Viney, 'I would wonder if *A City Solitary* was not asking me to stay the industrious underdog and be glad of it.'

However, he was forced to admit that the effects of the film had been 'quite startling'. One declared Nationalist who saw it in the Guildhall stood at the end for the National Anthem for the first time in his life. Another, a businessman, told Hume the next day that he had written Londonderry at the top of a reference for an employee for the first time in his life. He had also changed his mind about supporting the Arts Festival and had sent off a cheque to the organizers. A middle-aged Catholic housewife living in a mixed street said: 'This is the first television thing about Derry I have been able to discuss with my neighbours.' A young Protestant dramatist was excited about the festival's impact. It was a piece of history. 'These people have just the same interests in plays and painting and music, but they've never spoken to each other before. Now look at them. Don't underestimate the importance of what is happening.'[6]

Viney found his journey to the North one of the most depressing experiences of his life. His gloomy verdict was that:

The common people of the North certainly are oppressed and exploited – but not by force of arms or imperialist domination. They are oppressed by armchair, atrophied attitudes to life and politics which they themselves are tricked into sustaining: on the one hand by a Unionist Party whose public attachment to power and privilege is often mediaeval in its cynicism; on the other by a corps of Nationalists who, with a few exceptions, encourage slogans as a substitute for thought. Both sides have exploited the religious division – not always and not necessarily viciously but often simply to keep their seats in Stormont with the least intellectual efforts.'

He found a confusion of intellectual loyalties among the new generation of middle-class, educated Catholics, between the idea of a united Ireland and solving the more immediate crisis of social and economic injustice. 'Many will decide that humanitarian considerations demand action which uses the existing constitutional framework and postpones ambitions for change in the status quo.'[7]

Viney's praise for *A City Solitary* did indeed prompt RTE to show it in the Republic, where it triggered such interest that the *Irish Times* commissioned Hume to write a keynote article on the changing nature of Catholic opinion. Hume was quick to respond to the challenge. His two articles, entitled 'The Northern Catholic', appeared in consecutive issues only ten days later. Even more than *A City Solitary*, they represent his political first-fruits.

Hume accepted that 'great political frustration' existed among Northern Catholics. The crux of the matter for the younger generation was the continued existence, particularly in the Catholic community, of great social problems of housing, unemployment and emigration. It was the struggle for priority in their minds between such problems, and the idea of a united Ireland, that had led to frustration and a large number of 'political wanderers'.

'It may be that the present generation of younger Catholics in the North are more materialistic than their fathers,' he wrote, 'but there is little doubt that their thinking is principally geared towards the solution of social and economic problems. This has led to a deep questioning of traditional Nationalist attitudes.' The principal blame for the situation must lie at the door of the Unionist government at Stormont, but the Nationalist Party also shared responsibility. 'Good government depends as much on the opposition as the party in power. Weak opposition leads to corrupt government. Nationalists in opposition have been in no way constructive.' In forty years of opposition, the Nationalists had spoken loudly about their rights, but little about their duties. They had not produced a single constructive contribution to the social or economic development of Northern Ireland which was, after all a part of the united Ireland that was their goal.

'Leadership has been the comfortable leadership of flags and slogans,' Hume wrote. 'Easy no doubt but irresponsible.' Nationalists had not encouraged Catholics to develop their resources and make a positive contribution in terms of community service. Unemployment and emigration remained heavy, but the Nationalists could only repeat that the removal of discrimination would be a panacea. 'It is this lack of positive contribution and the apparent lack of interest in the general welfare of Northern Ireland that has led many Protestants to believe that the Northern Catholic is politically irresponsible and immature and unfit to rule.'

These were sharp words indeed coming from within the Catholic community, but there was more to come. Hume wrote: 'Bigotry and a fixation about religious divisions are the first thing that strike any visitor to the North. The Nationalist line of the past forty years has made its contribution to this situation. Catholics of all shades of political thought are expected to band together under the unreconstructive banner of Nationalism. This dangerous equation of Nationalism and Catholicism has simply contributed to the postponent of the emergence of normal politics in the area and has made the task of the Unionist Ascendancy simpler.

'Worse, it has poisoned the Catholic social climate to the extent that it has become extremely difficult for a Catholic to express publicly any point of view which does not coincide with the narrow Nationalist line. Disagreement with, or criticism of, the Nationalist approach – or lack of it – inevitably bring down on one's head a torrent of abuse. "Obsequious", "Crawling", "Castle Catholic", "West Briton" are samples of the terms used. The result has been that many Catholics have been unwilling to speak their minds for fear of discrimination.'

Hume accused the Nationalist press of being chiefly responsible for this situation, and pointed out that when this 'climatic censorship' was added to a similar phenomenon on the Unionist side, it quickly became apparent how little freedom of thought or expression existed in Northern Ireland, and the tremendous obstacles that lay in the way of the emergence of a third force.

'The greatest contribution therefore that the Catholic in Northern Ireland can make to a liberalising of the political atmosphere would be the removal of the equation between Nationalists and Catholics,' Hume insisted. 'Apart from being factual, it ought also to be made fashionable that the Catholic Church does not impose upon its members any one form of political belief.' He accepted that in recent times, some church leaders had become conscious of the dangers of too close a political identity, but he urged Catholics to go further. Another step towards easing community tensions and removing 'what bigotry exists among Catholics' would be to recognize that the Protestant tradition in the North was as strong and as legitimate as their own.

This, practically a heresy in the Catholic community, was only a 'first step' towards better relations. 'We must be prepared to accept this, and to realise the fact that if a man wishes Northern Ireland to remain part of the United Kingdom it does not necessarily make him a bigot or a discriminator.'

Hume's Derry readers must have drawn breath before moving on to his equally radical proposals for a rethinking of attitudes towards the constitutional question. By their stance on the constitution, the Nationalists had not only given the Unionist Party valuable ammunition during the volatile times of an election, he argued; they had also alienated the sympathies of liberal Protestants while denying themselves a role in the development of Northern Ireland. In Hume's polite language, their attitude was also vague. On the one hand, they took their seats – and their salaries – at the 'unrecognized' Stormont Parliament; yet they refused to be present at a function in Derry City held to bestow civic honour on an industrialist who had given substantial employment to their fellow-Catholics.

Hume's strategy was as direct as it was unorthodox: 'The position should be immediately clarified by an acceptance of the constitutional position. There is nothing inconsistent with such acceptance and a belief that a thirty-two county republic is best for Ireland.' In fact, if Catholics seriously pursued a policy of non-recognition, the only logical policy was that of Sinn Fein. 'If one wishes to create a United Ireland by constitutional means, then one must accept the constitutional position. Such a change would remove what has been a great stumbling block to the development of normal politics in the North. Catholics could then throw themselves fully into the solution of Northern problems without the fear of recrimination. Such an attitude, too, admits the realistic fact that a United Ireland, if it is to come, and if violence, rightly, is to be discounted, must come about by evolution, i.e. by the will of the Northern majority.'

Here, in the starkest possible way, Hume set out the principle of change by consent and evolution that was to become both his guiding philosophy and his political trademark for the next thirty years. His explanation was equally direct: 'It is clear that this is the only way in which a truly United Ireland (with the Northern Protestants integrated) can be achieved. Who can conceive of a prosperous North attached to either London or Dublin without the Northern Protestant? If the whole Northern community gets seriously to work on its problems, the Unionists' bogeys about Catholics and a Republic will, through better understanding, disappear.'

At this point he is, of course, talking more than four years before the Troubles broke out in his native city with such disastrous and bloody results. His naïvety may be excused as the idealism of a twenty-seven-year-old schoolteacher and budding businessman who is exasperated by the recalcitrant Nationalism that frustrates his social ambitions and those of the new Catholic community he wants to build. He did allow himself a wry note: 'It will, of course, take a long time.'

For now, however, there were practical considerations. 'On the party political front, the need for a complete revitalisation of the Nationalist Party has long been felt. The necessity for a fully-organised democratic party which can freely attract and draw upon the talents of the nationally-minded community is obvious.'[8] Hume hoped that the new Nationalist Political Front, an *ad hoc* body of pragmatic political reformers, would create such an organization. Evidently, he believed that the Nationalist Party itself was beyond reform.

In his second article on the following day, in reality the conclusion of his first, Hume was more generous to some Nationalist MPs – in particular to Eddie McAteer, the Derry MP he was later to displace – noting that they had shown some awareness of the short-comings of their approach and that the voters were slow to accept any change of image: 'Nationalist politicians are prisoners of an image built up over forty years.' He argued that the need for action on the non-political front was greater, given the existing political impasse.

'There exists in the North at this moment a greater wealth of talent – young business men, professional men and graduates – than ever before and there is a growing desire among them to get together, to pool these talents and to tackle community problems.' Such cross-community work could water down the deep prejudice that lay at the root of discrimination. At the same time, he was clear that 'the considerable heart-searching and sincere self-examination going on among Catholics in the North at the moment does not absolve the Unionist Party from certain obligations if they are sincere about their concern for the future of the North.'

Hume warned: 'To date, none of their leaders has shown any response to repeated statements of Catholic willingness to get together. Unionists must realise if they turn their backs on the present goodwill there can only be a considerable hardening of Catholic opinion, only this time it will be supported by liberal Protestants who will have lost faith in Glengall Street [the Belfast HQ of the Unionist Party].' In terms of tougher Catholic attitudes, he was absolutely correct. On the prospect of liberal support, he proved only partly right, and not for long enough.

Hume then laid down some tests for Unionist co-operation: first, they must accept that discrimination, whether religious or political, was unjust and had to be removed – in the first place by inviting Catholics to take seats on bodies where they did not have them; second, they must accept that Nationalism in Ireland was 'an acceptable political belief' which people were entitled to express in public without prejudicing their right to seek any post; and third, they should realize that the vast majority of Catholics were responsible people, anxious for better relations and for a better Northern Ireland in which to live and rear their children.

He concluded: 'It is only perhaps when many of the above suggestions are in operation throughout the Northern Community that religion will begin to make its exit from politics and that socially it will no longer be necessary to forewarn about the presence of those who "dig with the other foot".' Then he added: 'In the waiting, the fear is that frustration may force one to leave the North. It is little wonder that many do.'

Hume was maturing rapidly, both in his chosen profession and in the wider world. After a shaky start, he had shone in debates at Maynooth, and now he brought his speaking skills to the Columcille Debating Society in Derry, then an all-male Catholic battleground of ideas and opinions. (Here, one of his chief opponents was Eamonn McCann.)

An issue to test his burgeoning and debating skills lay just over the horizon. After the wartime boom years, Derry was becoming mired in economic recession. Shirtmaking, a staple industry of the city employing more than 7,000 women who were often a family's sole breadwinner, was losing trade to cheap Far Eastern products. Derry's passenger sea-links to Liverpool and Glasgow were cut in 1964. The railway line south to Omagh and the Irish Republic followed them into oblivion. Stormont, oblivious to the claims of Northern Ireland's second city, concentrated economic growth in the east of the province. The Unionist administration built a new city – Craigavon, provocatively named after the first Northern prime minister who called Stormont 'a Protestant parliament for a Protestant people' – in the Protestant heartland between Lurgan and Portadown.

The issue now was education. Northern Ireland needed a new university. Queen's, Belfast, was bursting at the seams, and demand for higher education was expected to double by the 1970s. Derry had a ready alternative: Magee College, in the heart of the city. Magee opened its doors to students in 1865, originally to prepare candidates for the Presbyterian church. It was a logical choice for the second university. For once, Protestant and Catholics concurred. The Londonderry Corporation published a manifesto in 1963, arguing that Derry was well placed geographically to support a new seat of higher education, the establishment of which would 'help restore the equilibrium of Northern Ireland, educationally, economically and culturally'.

Fired by this unique example of collaboration across the religious divide, and conscious of the new spirit of ecumenism abroad, Eddie McAteer, the Nationalist MP, approached Stormont's new premier, Captain Terence O'Neill, who took over that year from the long-serving Lord Brookeborough. O'Neill had promised to 'transform the face of Ulster', but he too was a captive of hard-line Unionists and swiftly rejected McAteer's proposal for 'Orange and Green' talks. Instead, the government appointed an English academic, John Lockwood, to inquire into the whole question of a second university.

Hume, back at his *alma mater*, St Columb's, teaching French and History, was apprehensive about the prospects of success. Leaks from the Lockwood Inquiry suggested that Derry was yet again to be disappointed. Hume had joined a group of concerned Derry citizens, Protestant and Catholic, who were determined to keep the issue alive, and in January 1965 they alerted people to their fears in a statement: 'There is a growing feeling in Derry, even among Unionist supporters, that government policy seems directed towards the isolation of the north-west in general and Derry in particular. It is now generally felt that the acid test as to the truth of this assertion will lie with the government's shortly expected decision on the question of the second university.'

An inter-denominational 'University for Derry' committee representing the Catholic, Church of Ireland, Presbyterian and Methodist churches was established, with Hume, still only twenty-six, as its chairman. In February 1965, he led a delegation to the Stormont premier to press the city's claims. According to a contemporary: 'Hume was cogent and incisive, O'Neill sympathetic but silent.' Hume urged him to take the opportunity to do something that would not only earn his undiluted applause in Derry but also help build reconciliation in Northern Ireland.

Hume recalled later: 'We did not know of course that even as he listened to our appeal, the decision against Derry had already been taken, and his government was on the point of launching a White

Paper accepting the Lockwood Committee report and its recommendation that the second university should be located in the small Unionist town of Coleraine, thirty miles from Derry.' Two days before the Lockwood Report was published, 1,500 Derry people filled the city's historic Guildhall to overflowing and demanded a university. Hume made the final speech, a rallying cry for the two traditions of the city to unite for the good of their city. His speech 'perfectly caught the mood of the meeting, and brought the crowd to its feet in recognition of this new idea, so powerfully expressed by someone who was unmistakably a Derry man and yet could not be slotted into any of the existing pigeonholes'.[9]

The Derry protest was ignored, and its people were understandably outraged. Hume organized (but did not take part in) an unprecedented protest motorcade to the Stormont parliamentary buildings on 18 February, attended by 25,000 people. Shops, offices and businesses in the city were closed for the day, and the roads to Belfast were crammed with cars. O'Neill, who only a month earlier had taken the first tentative step towards his 'new Ulster' by welcoming the Irish Prime Minister Sean Lemass to this same spot, was unmoved. He not only imposed the party whip on Unionist MPs to get the Lockwood Report through his parliament, but made the issue a vote of confidence in his government. Even some Unionist MPs complained that the decision was being thrust upon them. It was carried by a vote of twenty-seven to nineteen, with Edward Jones, Unionist MP for the City of Londonderry, dutifully voting for the government.

The second university was a political watershed. Hume noted that the 'isolation of the West' was to be continued under the so-called reformist O'Neill just as rigidly as under any of his predecessors. 'He lost all credibility in Derry as a crusading premier, and reinforced among the Catholic community all over the North the conviction that the Unionist leopard could not change its spots.'[10] For Eddie McAteer, the outcome was devastating. He blamed himself for keeping quiet over O'Neill's rejection of 'Orange and Green' talks, observing bitterly that his 'charitable silence' had enabled the Unionist premier to build up and retain an undeserved reputation for liberalism. McAteer's traditionalist Nationalism suffered equally. Dublin even 'forgot' to invite the northern Nationalist Party, technically representative of half a million partitioned Irishmen, to the Republic's presidential inauguration that year.

Friends said the failure of the university campaign was 'traumatic' for Hume as well, but unlike McAteer he took the political struggle to a larger arena. By now, he had come to the notice of Westminster's recently founded Campaign for Democracy in Ulster (CDU), an all-party coalition of MPs substantially dominated by Labour MPs on the centre-left of the party. The natural sense of injustice felt by Labour MPs over Ulster was compounded by the fact that Harold Wilson's Labour government had a majority of only three, and twelve Ulster Unionist MPs sat and voted with the Tory opposition. They could, and did, vote against Wilson's mildly socialist reforms in Britain but, by a long-standing parliamentary convention, MPs in London could not raise issues relating to Northern Ireland.

The CDU invited Hume to travel to London and speak on the university issue. The public meeting was held at Fulham Town Hall on a Friday night, 30 June 1965. Paul Rose, MP for Manchester Blackley, a barrister and founder-member of the CDU, remembers Hume as 'a very clued-up academic, who knew what he was talking about. Until then, I didn't know him. I thought his role was pivotal. He represented very much the new generation of educated Catholics, who were not going to be kicked around any more, yet who was consistently moderate in his stance.'[11]

Hume made a strong impression on his London audience, and ensured that his speech also had an impact at home (the *Derry Journal* gave him a whole page). Hume outlined the economic and political background of the Lockwood scandal to the Fulham meeting, pointing out that none of the members of the inquiry committee was a Catholic. He asserted: 'Not a single academic criterion is to be found in the report for the choice of Coleraine.'[12] He disclosed that a well-known Unionist MP, Dr Robert Nixon, had exposed outright government interference in the location of the university, and these moves had been supported by 'bigoted and influential Unionists from Derry itself'.

So, insisted Hume, 'the plan stands clear. The minority in Northern Ireland resides mainly in the western counties of Derry, Tyrone and Fermanagh. To develop these areas is to develop areas opposed to the government and to lose the few Unionist seats held there. The plan is therefore to develop the strongly-Unionist Belfast–Coleraine–Portadown triangle and to cause a migration from West to East "Ulster", redistributing and scattering the minority so that the Unionist Party will not only maintain but strengthen its position. The British taxpayer is paying for these schemes. The new university will cost £20 million. The new city over £200 million. Yet it would appear that the British Treasury doles out this size of capital without attempting to scrutinise in any detail the uses to which it is put.

'The tragedy is that this plan comes at a time when the "Northern Ireland" problem shows more hopeful signs of internal solution than ever before. It is my belief that the problem can only be fully solved by the people there themselves and only then when the mental border that divides the community has been largely eradicated, when bigotry and intolerance have been driven from our shores.'

Great strides, he added, had already been made in community relations. 'There has been a great growth in liberal feeling, but, unfortunately, it is my fear that by the time this upsurge in tolerance and right thinking reaches the corridors of power in Northern Ireland, it will be too late for places like Derry and irreparable damage will already have been done.'

It was for this reason, he told his audience, that he had looked beyond Northern Ireland for assistance. The Unionist administration 'must be taught that they could not run away' from Derry and west Ulster, and that if they seriously wanted to create a modern community they must treat all citizens with dignity and equality. He appealed to MPs and citizens alike to use their influence with the government to halt O'Neill's 'sinister plan'. In so doing, they would be making a swift and lasting contribution not only to the Northern Ireland problem, 'but towards the creation of a solution that can be applied to the many problems of community division throughout the world'.

His speech is worth quoting at length for the strands of his thinking it illuminates. First, at this time Hume is still talking of 'an internal solution' (though Paul Rose MP found him remarkably knowledgeable about what was going on in Dublin government circles), whereas he would later insist that an internal – i.e. Northern Irish – solution was impossible, and that London and Dublin must be involved. Second, and this perhaps for his metropolitan audience, he claims 'great strides' have been made in inter-communal relations, when the burden of his political remarks points to the opposite. Third, he warns, but not in apocalyptic terms, that change may come too late. And fourth, he exhibits a communitarian vision of conflict resolution that he believes could prove to be a world-wide model.

Hume's emerging philosophy set him apart from the Nationalists, although they had tried to woo this interesting new political talent. He had talks with McAteer's organization in Derry, but dismissed the Nationalist Party as coterie politics: a small group of people without a genuine mass membership. 'I felt even then that to have an effective voice in politics in the North, to be capable of effective political action, the minority needed a party with an effective organisation.'

His criticism was well grounded, but not wholly fair. The Catholic Registration Association worked ceaselessly to keep track of voters, publishing an annual register. In Derry in 1965, Catholics outnumbered Others by two to one: 20,075 to 10,666 on the Stormont register. On the Derry Corporation, however, because of gerrymanding, the eight Catholic councillors represented 2,500 voters each, whereas the twelve non-Catholic councillors who made up the majority represented fewer than 900 voters each. In vain did the Catholics' chief registration agent, Joseph Campbell, rail: 'Against this perennial injustice, this association can only renew its immemorial protest and let the figures speak for themselves.' McAteer warned impotently that if the Unionists did not meet Nationalist efforts to improve community relations, they would take the issue of discrimination to Westminster 'or even the United Nations'.

Despite his distance from old-fashioned Nationalism, Hume was moving ineluctably into politics proper. At a meeting organized by Derry Chambers of Commerce in October 1965, he harried Edward Heath, Conservative Leader of the Opposition, on economic development for north-west Ulster, and later that month delivered an address to the New Ireland Society in Belfast on the theme 'The West's Asleep'. He rejected the thesis that the west of Ireland was soporific and complained: 'We feel instead we are being suffocated.'

A general election for Stormont loomed in 1965, and Hume came under pressure to stand against the Nationalist Party. McAteer was known to be nursing hopes that he could step down for business and family reasons. The *Derry Journal* reported on 5 November that 'speculation is growing that the 28-year-old school teacher' would stand. A group of local people had approached him. It was understood that Hume was 'undecided about his course of action'. The Nationalists might have been willing to embrace him, but they were not going to be beaten by him. McAteer was drafted, Tammany Hall-style, to run again. Hume wisely left the field to him, saying in a statement: 'I have been approached by an independent group with a view to contesting the seat. I have given the matter a lot of thought, but I am not anxious to enter active politics, and I have decided not to let my name go forward.'

Some of his backers were upset, and urged him to reconsider. It was even said that he 'lacked guts'; but he had nerve enough to refuse these fresh blandishments. McAteer easily beat an independent Labour candidate, trade unionist Seamus Quinn. On election night, the victorious Nationalist MP was carried shoulder-high down Derry's Shipquay Street while crowds sang Republican anthems, 'The Soldier's Song' and 'Kevin Barry'. Milk bottles were thrown and police baton-charged the crowd, an ominous foretaste of things to come.

After the election, Derry subsided into its customary torpor. The authorities announced that the city had the highest tuberculosis rate in the UK because of overcrowding. The Bishop of Derry, Dr Farren, detected some gain from the university campaign – a new unity between Catholics and other denominations which made it possible to work together – but nothing came of it.

In May 1966, John Hume made his first formal foray into politics, not as a candidate but as election agent for his friend Claud Wilton, a Protestant solicitor, a political novice who was standing for the vacant North Ward of the Derry Corporation. 'I was a Liberal with a big L,' he said later. The party leader, Jeremy Thorpe, sent Wilton a letter of support. Hume's name has occasionally been linked with the Liberal Party, but there is no evidence of interest beyond anecdote.

The campaign was run on a 'fair play, no discrimination' platform. 'We had outdoor, soapbox meetings on street corners,' Wilton recalls. 'Then maybe we'd adjourn to the pub afterwards for a bit of a yarn. Hume spoke very well. He wanted a new society, everybody getting a fair crack of the whip.'[13] The message clearly struck home in some quarters. Wilton was beaten by the Official Unionist by only 400 votes out of 4,000 and demanded a recount, which was refused. Accusations that the city was 'a municipal Rhodesia' fell on deaf ears.

Hume consoled himself with another dabble in film-making, this time a 16mm programme in Derry's Gransha Mental Hospital entitled *Open Door*. The medical authorities praised it as 'a magnificent job' that would help rid people of old-fashioned ideas about mental illness. Hume was also honoured that summer by the World Credit Union, which made him president of the Credit Union League of Ireland.

Behind the scenes in Derry, and beneath the ice at Westminster, pressure for change grew stronger. Captain O'Neill met Harold Wilson for talks, at which it was pointed out that the British financial subvention to the province was running at almost £48 million a year, yet Nationalist moves at Stormont to reform the corrupt boundaries of the city were consistently voted down by the Unionists. Derry's Unionist mayor, Albert Anderson, arrogantly proclaimed that company votes and plural votes (which favoured the Protestants) were 'something to be relished. Those who pay the piper are entitled to call the tune. One man one vote is not the law, and is not a basic principle in local government elections.' He dismissed as 'artificial agitation' a citizens' protest against gerrymandering.

McAteer warned that 'things are rapidly rushing towards a showdown', and wrote an anxious letter to Alice Bacon, Minister responsible for NI affairs at the Home Office. Gerry Fitt, newly elected Republican Labour MP for West Belfast in the 1966 Westminster Parliament, began testing the parliamentary convention that Ulster should not be debated, and in January 1967 he brought over a group of MPs to Derry to see the unemployment, bad housing and political corruption for themselves. As factory closures accelerated, Hume followed suit, inviting his new admirer Paul Rose and two other Labour MPs Stan Orme (later a Northern Ireland Minister) and Maurice Miller.

Prompted by this trip, *The Times*, still regarded in those days as 'the house journal of the British establishment', investigated Nationalist claims of discrimination and found them convincing. Its report, and the impressions gained by the MPs, triggered a motion in the House of Commons, signed by seventy-three Labour MPs, calling on the government to ensure that British funds to Stormont should be conditional upon an end to discrimination. Hume sent a telegram to Harold Wilson urging action, but Economic Affairs Minister Peter Shore observed complacently: 'When London gets a chill, Northern Ireland gets the flu and Derry gets pneumonia. It's that sort of relationship.' Home Secretary Roy Jenkins saw McAteer for twenty-five minutes, but then told Parliament there would be no interference in the administration of Northern Ireland.

On the ground, street protest in Derry was growing. Young Republican activists fought evictions of Catholics and, in spite of a ban on Republican Clubs by Home Affairs Minister William Craig, the demonstrations continued. Jobless former workers at the Monarch Electric factory organized a march to the Guildhall to protest at the failure of the government to bring industry to Derry. 'The age of street protest had arrived,' said the then editor of the *Derry Journal*, Frank Curran. Noisy public protest also punctuated meetings of the City Corporation. McAteer again warned Stormont on 7 March 1968 that the Unionist administration was 'pressing the spring to a dangerous point. It behoves us as people of common sense to do our best to avert what might very well be a permanent catastrophe to community relations.'

He was too late. As the Nationalist Party belatedly tried to regain the initiative by adopting a policy of 'non-violent disobedience' to Stormont, the young bloods were already out on the streets of Derry, testing the will of the Royal Ulster Constabulary (RUC). Eamonn McCann proclaimed: 'People can take power in the city into their own hands, if they really want it.' The newly-formed Derry Housing Action Committee blocked a city-centre street with the caravan of a homeless family, and eleven protesters were arrested. Gerry Fitt, whose acute political antennae sensed that the Nationalists were losing control, promised to set up a branch of the Republican Socialist Party in Derry, warning that if constitutional methods could not produce justice and democracy, 'I am quite prepared to go outside constitutional methods.'

Hume watched the growth of militancy with mounting apprehension, but from the sidelines. To the astonishment of some, in 1967 he gave up schoolteaching to go into business with his fellow-campaigner from the university battle and joint founder of the Credit Union, Michael Canavan, a local bookmaker and publican. Canavan had worked with Hume on efforts to attract industry to north-west Ireland, and the two decided to start their own business. 'We looked for something that could be started up locally, and would have a high mark-up when it was processed,' recalls Canavan. 'We decided that smoked salmon offered the best opportunity for that. We both knew that the Foyle was a very good salmon river, but all the fish were boxed and sent off to England for processing.'[14]

Canavan had already taken a lease on a spacious, disused bakery building in the centre of Derry with an eye to a business opportunity, 'and this seemed like a good one'. They started up in 1966, knowing nothing of salmon smoking. They hired a man from Dublin to show them how to do it, bought ovens in Scotland and set to work. Hume gave three months' notice to St Columb's and joined the firm, Atlantic Harvest, full-time in 1967 as managing director. 'He rapidly learned the basics of the business,' said Canavan. 'He was a very good businessman, and he worked at it himself, giving a hand in all the operations.' They had a staff of two, a local man and a young woman in the office. From small local orders, they progressed to supplying Jewish fish shops in London through Hume's contacts. He also drove to Southampton to sell Foyle smoked salmon to the purchasing manager of Cunard Shipping, who ordered substantial quantities and put it on the menu of cruise liners including the QE2.

Politics was never quite off the menu. Canavan and Hume both became convinced by their experiences in the university campaign and the Credit Union that in Canavan's words:

A stronger form of protest on the political front would be needed really to change things. Radical political changes would be needed as well. There were a number of indications that 1968 was going to be a crisis year. We were heavily committed with the various enterprises we were involved in, but we were very acutely aware that the younger, radical elements were already operating.

FOUR

CIVIL RIGHTS,
UNCIVIL TIMES

THE ORIGINS OF THE NORTHERN IRELAND civil rights movement lay not in the spontaneous, violent street protests of Derry, but in the patient, dedicated research and propaganda work of a small group of middle-class professionals. Its founders were a husband-and-wife team, Dr Conn and Patricia McLuskey, who took up the housing grievances of a group of young Catholic housewives in Dungannon, County Tyrone. In May 1963, the women petitioned Unionist-dominated Dungannon Urban District Council, complaining that their pleas to be rehoused were repeatedly ignored despite living in overcrowded, insanitary conditions while Protestants, often from outside the town, were given council houses. When picketing of council meetings also failed, they formed the Homeless Citizens' League with Mrs McCluskey in the chair. Their aim was to shame the council into ending its discriminatory housing practices. When persuasion failed, they tried the concept – novel for Northern Ireland – of 'direct action', squatting prefabricated houses due for demolition.

Housing was not just a social issue. As elsewhere in the province, it had deep political roots. Dungannon's population was almost evenly split between Catholics and Protestants, but if the Unionists were to maintain their political hegemony on the council, the allocation of council housing had to be carefully managed to secure 'guaranteed votes and automatic re-election'.[1] Of 194 houses built by the council since the Second World War for letting, all had gone to Protestants.

The Homeless Citizens' League scored some successes, occasionally compelling the council to house Catholics and embarrassing the

59

Stormont administration. It also galvanized articulate, middle-class opinion in a way that decades of traditional Nationalist politicking had failed to do. Instead of abstentionism, there was now engagement. There were also stirrings of a political consciousness, and a sense that Catholics in Northern Ireland had something in common with black people in the USA, whose civil rights movement was capturing the imagination of the world. One woman picketing the council said: 'They talk about Alabama. Why don't they talk about Dungannon? Dozens of houses and not a Catholic to be found amongst them. It's a cut and dried case of religious discrimination.'

Having wrung some concessions from Stormont, the McLuskeys found themselves deluged with letters of support. They realized that there was 'a tremendous yearning among the Catholic people for oganisation and leadership', and resolved on the spot to set up a group of educated people 'who would articulate the frustrations of the minority'.[2]

The outcome was the Campaign for Social Justice (CSJ), composed of thirteen Catholic professional people, launched at a press conference at the impeccably bourgeois Wellington Park Hotel, Belfast, in January 1964. Its stated aims were to oppose Stormont's policies of 'apartheid and discrimination', principally by collecting and disseminating 'to as many socially-minded people as possible' accurate facts about unjust treatment of the minority, particularly in the fields of jobs and housing. The border question did not figure on its reformist agenda, and from its outset the CSJ had no truck with Nationalist politicians. Its members consciously modelled themselves on the 'democrats and liberals' of the British National Council for Civil Liberties, though it was interesting that their key objective was 'social justice', a phrase powerfully redolent of Pope Pius XI's encyclical *Quadragesimo Anno* of 1921.[3]

Given the shameless nature of Derry politics, it could not be long before the CSJ turned its sharply analytical eye on events there. In February 1965, the campaign published a hard-hitting pamphlet, *Londonderry: One Man, No Vote*. This opened with an economic critique of Stormont's determined attempts 'to further weaken and depopulate' the three counties west of the river Bann by closing down railways, concentrating industrial development in the relatively prosperous east and rejecting Derry as the site for a new university.

The document pointed out that to 'neutralize' the Stormont seat of Londonderry, which had a majority of Catholic voters and therefore returned a Nationalist MP, the Unionists had sliced the constituency into two. One of the new constituencies, named Foyle, took in most of the city on the west bank of the river for which it was named. The other, absurdly named City, took in the Waterside area and then plunged eight miles into the countryside to garner sufficient Protestant farming votes to ensure a comfortable Unionist majority.

It was in local government, however, that injustice was at its greatest, remarked the CSJ. 'In local elections in Britain, all adults over twenty-one have a vote. In Northern Ireland, only a householder and his wife can vote. In addition, limited companies are allocated six votes each. Catholics are denied houses and therefore lose voting strength. This is Conservative (i.e. Unionist) policy.'[4]

The total population of Derry, according to official government census figures, was 53,744. Of these, 36,049 were Catholics, and 17,695 were Protestants. In other words, Catholics were in a two-to-one majority. Yet the local government franchise was so gerrymandered that the Unionists enjoyed a permanent 12–8 majority over the Nationalists on the city council. This outrage was accomplished by adjusting the boundaries so that most Catholic voters were to be found in the populous South Ward, which returned only eight councillors, while two very much smaller wards, each with a Protestant majority, returned twelve councillors. The Unionist minority not only gerrymandered the city: its Unionist mayor was ex-officio a salaried member of the Senate at Stormont, Northern Ireland's Upper House.

The pain was even more sharply felt among Catholics because so many of them were homeless, or housed in substandard accommodation, deliberately to perpetuate the Unionist hold on power. The council would not build or grant permission for houses for Catholics, except in the South Ward ghetto – where all appropriate land had been used up. Nor would the council extend the city boundaries. All council housing was allocated by one man: the Unionist mayor. 'The housing committee does not function', the CSJ noted bleakly. Small wonder that there were more than 2,000 Catholic families on the housing waiting list while there were 'practically no Protestants unhoused'. It was a powder keg waiting to explode.

October 5, 1968, changed the course of Irish (and British) history. On that day, the armed forces of the Unionist ascendancy were seen in action, in public, in front of the television cameras, batoning, water-cannoning and finally crushing a peaceful civil rights march in Hume's native city. At the end of that day the journalistic cliché was well aired: nothing would ever be the same again. Nor has it been. From the Nationalist, or Catholic, perspective, things are better, though at a terrible cost in human lives.

The origins of the march are today the subject of much dispute and historical rewriting, as is the role of Hume in the events of the day. It is clear from Eamonn McCann's account[5] that the débâcle was a mixture of conspiracy and error. Three months earlier, a hastily organized, and partly fictional, James Connolly Commemoration Committee had tried to organize a march into the city centre of Derry to commemorate the centenary of the great Irish labour figure. The aim of the organizers was 'to ensure a head-on clash with the authorities', but predictably the march was banned by the RUC.

There was no protest on that occasion, but, emboldened by the first partially successful civil rights march in Dungannon on 24 August, the young activists of Derry decided to try again. They invited leaders of the recently established Northern Ireland Civil Rights Association to come to the city and discuss the idea, and met in a room above the Grandstand Bar. It was 'immediately clear' to the Derry activists that the five-member Belfast delegation did not understand the political geography of the city. They approved a highly provocative route that would take the marchers from Duke Street, outside the railway station, across the Craigavon Bridge, through the city walls hallowed to Protestant memory and into the Diamond in the commercial heart of the walled city. McCann said later: 'We knew there was no chance whatsoever of this route being accepted by the RUC, and therefore the march would be banned. The Belfast people were quite unaware of this quirk of local life. They calmly agreed to it in the name of NICRA. We had stitched them into it.'[6]

It is difficult to believe that, in so small a political society as Northern Ireland, the Belfast NICRA officials could have been so naïve. Certainly, civil rights moderates in Derry itself were not taken in, and were anxious. The march, fixed for 5 October in the mistaken belief that the local football club was playing away that Saturday, was mobilized by a ramshackle Ad Hoc Committee, composed chiefly of young socialists, republicans and housing activists. The preparations were almost comical. The organizers used a duplicator owned by the Derry Canine Club to turn out leaflets and by night plastered the city with crude fly-posters demanding 'Working Class Unite and Fight!'

Hume was approached to endorse the march, but refused. He was asked to be one of the two men to sign a document notifying the police of the route of the march – which would also have made him legally responsible for it – and declined. He supported the general idea of the march, but did not like the organizers, correctly surmising that some were on the far-left. He wanted an organization that was specific to civil rights, and would attract all sections of the community. According to the then editor of the *Derry Journal*: 'He decided to go as an individual, but to take no part in the organisation.'[7]

Before anyone could take a firm and final decision, William Craig, Stormont's Minister of Home Affairs, stepped in on 3 October and banned the march. Derry police chiefs told him they 'apprehended danger' if the march was allowed to go ahead. The Protestant Apprentice Boys of Derry, who are neither apprentices nor boys but part of the quasi-military structure of Unionism, had conveniently discovered they were due to have a march over the same route on the same day and at the same time. Craig, who thought the civil rights movement was only a flimsy cover for a republican plot to subvert the Northern Ireland government, needed no further prompting. He closed the centre of Derry to all bands and parades that day.

These developments came at a time of personal crisis for Hume. Months before, his attempts to win government approval for a large housing development in the city for homeless Catholics had been rejected, despite a detailed and well-argued case. Hume despaired of reforms from the 'liberal' Terence O'Neill and his reactionary

Unionist Party. 'When we were turned down,' he recalled, 'that is when I realised that civil rights was the way forward. It also coincided with the US civil rights movement. I was very conscious of that. Martin Luther King is one of my great heroes. The first thing you see on the wall of my Donegal home are his words "I Have a Dream", and John F. Kennedy's "One Man Can Make a Difference, and Every Man Should Try".[8] Craig's ban, he says, 'was the biggest mistake they ever made. I might not have become a politician and brought them down. When it was banned, I then marched.' His attitude nevertheless remained ambivalent: 'I didn't agree, but agreed with their right to do it.'

When the ban was announced, the annual policy-making conference of the ruling Labour Party was in session in Blackpool. Labour MPs who championed civil rights were incensed. Paul Rose MP, chairman of the Campaign for Democracy in Ulster, protested to the Home Secretary, James Callaghan. NICRA sent a telegram to Prime Minister Harold Wilson, asking him to intervene urgently, and warning: 'Situation inflammatory. People will not continue to suffer the indignity of second-class citizenship.' Still the government did not intervene, mindful, unquestionably, of the old English fear of getting involved in Ulster.

However, the impasse at Westminster was about to be broken. Gerry Fitt, Republican Labour MP for West Belfast, was attending the Blackpool conference. He hastily put together a small delegation of observers from the Parliamentary Labour Party. 'To the Unionists, Derry was such a symbol. This was the place to have a confrontation about what was happening,' said Fitt. 'I persuaded them that this was going to be a turning point in the civil rights movement. I also knew we were going to get thumped.'[9]

Three MPs, husband-and-wife team Russell and Ann Kerr and John Ryan, all members of the left-wing Tribune Group, agreed to travel to the province with Fitt. Their move alarmed Harold Wilson. The *Irish Times* reported that their presence 'is an embarrassment for the government. It would be happier if they did not go, especially if there is a risk of violence. This attitude may marginally increase the interest in one or two of them going.'[10]

Predictions based on numbers attending the Dungannon march

put the likely turnout at 5,000. In the event (and despite many reports to the contrary), the figure was probably one-tenth of that. The marchers assembled outside the old LMS railway station on the east bank of the river Foyle, a handsome Italianate granite building now a local radio station, in mid-afternoon. They were four to five hundred strong, milling around in the road – 'not very well organized' in the view of one of the leaders. Some had undoubtedly been put off by the fear of a conflict with the heavily-armed RUC, and others had gone to follow the fortunes of their football teams. Catholic Derry was not yet ready for an uprising.

The police saw things differently. They were determined to impose the ban. When the ragged ranks of the demonstrators moved off, the police quickly drew up a cordon across Duke Street (in those days a much narrower thoroughfare, with stepped ginnels leading off it) to prevent access to Craigavon bridge. With the Westminster MPs, Stormont members Eddie McAteer and Austin Currie, Ivan Cooper and Dublin politicians at their head, the marchers moved only a few hundred yards before the massed ranks of truncheon-wielding RUC men blocked their path. As the marchers came head-on, the police attacked. Fitt went down first, his head streaming with blood.

The organizers appealed for calm, but marchers trying to retreat down Duke Street found a second police cordon. A placard was thrown from within the marchers' ranks, and the RUC charged. Fergus Pyle of the *Irish Times* observed 'a brutal and sickening display of what can only be called concerted violence' as officers punched, batoned and pursued the marchers, ripping up the civil rights banners as they went. Groups of policemen chased individuals, clubbing them to the ground. When the street was 'pretty near clear', the RUC brought up armoured water-cannon wagons, and indiscriminately sprayed the streets with dirty water. Shoppers, some of them Prot-estant, were caught up in this final assault, which signalled the end of the attempt to take civil rights peaceably to the streets of Derry.

Where was John Hume in all of this? By his own account, he was there. He does not figure in the two most detailed contemporary accounts, in the *Derry Journal* and the *Irish Times*. Eamonn McCann recalls asking himself whether Hume is 'on the march, or is he observing the march? He had one foot on the pavement, and one foot on the road. He was there, at least.' His first biographer, Barry White, wrote that Hume was 'among the crowd, an ordinary citizen'. When police at the head of the column moved in to disperse marchers, he tried to escape back down the street 'but like the rest, found himself trapped by another line of police to the rear'. Eventually, he found an escape route up the steps at the foot of Duke Street.' George Drower, his second biographer, records it differently: 'Hume had been on the march, but had not been one of its leaders. When the police attacked, he had been fortunate to discover an escape route *down* some steps' (my italics). This seems most unlikely. Steps down from Duke Street would lead into the river. Gerry (now Lord) Fitt even claims that Hume 'did not turn up on the day'. Clutching the blood-stained shirt he wore on the day of the march, Fitt told me in his House of Lords office: 'John Hume admitted to me he wasn't there on the day. But ten years later he said he was there, standing on a bridge watching it all. As years went by he wanted to rewrite the whole thing. But he definitely was not there.'

Fitt's position at the head of the march would almost certainly have prevented him from seeing Hume in a less prominent role, whether as observer as McCann recalls or as a marcher as Hume and his previous biographers insist. Fitt's recollection must also be read in the context of the split that later developed between the only two leaders the SDLP has had. It does, however, shed some light on the bitterness of feeling that Irish politics has traditionally generated.

Whatever he did that day, and the balance of evidence is strongly in his favour for he returned home soaked by water-cannon, the events had made a permanent impression on John Hume. The hatred he saw on the faces of RUC officers and the violence with which they laid about them could not have done otherwise. Hume said later that a bonfire of resentment had been built for years, and 'the batons were the spark'.

The bonfire went up in Derry that weekend. As news of the Duke Street police riot spread through the staunchly Nationalist Bogside and Creggan enclaves, sporadic fighting broke out. Police cars were stoned, some petrol-bombs were thrown, shop windows were smashed, and a 'flimsy, token barricade' went up in Rossville Street which links the Bogside with the commercial area. By early Sunday morning, seventy-six riot casualties had been taken to Altnagelvin Hospital, the city's main hospital on the Waterside. Twenty more were to follow that day. Of the ninety-six injured, only six were policemen. Later on Sunday, helmeted, battle-wielding police repulsed a crowd of about 800 angry people – they were not yet all tagged with the label of Nationalists or Catholics, but they undoubtedly were – trying to break into the walled city. The protesters regrouped and fought running battles late into the night. Petrol-bombs reappeared, and more shop windows were smashed. The streets were littered with stones.

The reaction of the Northern Ireland government was customarily robust. Home Affairs Minister Craig refused to hold an inquiry. Without a trace of irony, he rejected charges of brutality and praised the RUC for 'the efficient and discreet manner' in which they had 'prevented a situation that could have had fearful consequences'. He added that the activities of the civil rights movement indicated that it was a Republican body, and events in Derry had proved that. Genuine supporters of civil rights movements were 'extremely ill-advised' to associate 'as they were doing' with the IRA 'or Communism'. In view of his warnings, Craig looked to leaders of opinion to take a responsible stand.

Mixed in with his crazy rhetoric about IRA communists seeking to attack NATO facilities at Derry, Craig had touched on a serious point. The gathering orgy of Nationalist violence was almost as disturbing to Hume as the RUC riot. McCann and his political associates had quickly seized their opportunity. They called a meeting in the City Hotel, proposing a second march the following Saturday that would mobilize 10,000 people. Moderate opinion, which included Hume, was agitated. 'After the police attack, there was a huge mood across the city, which was very dangerous for us. Left uncontrolled, it would have led to widespread violence,' Hume said.[11] Against that background, Hume worked through his contacts in organizations in the city to wrest the initiative back from the hot-heads, who by their own admission had set out to make the police over-react.

The hard-left radicals discovered that another meeting had been called in the City Hall a day after theirs. A decade later, McCann was still saying: 'It was not, and still is not, clear who had organized it.' In fact, it was Hume. 'I organized the meeting to discuss further moves, and I proposed setting up a broad-based committee – the Citizens' Action Committee – whose objectives were civil rights for everyone. But also, knowing the mood, it had to be non-violent. That was central to its philosophy. If we were going to protest, it had to be highly organized.'

The difference between the radicals' meeting and the one convened by Hume the following day, 9 October, could not have been more stark. By McCann's own admission 'about fifteen' turned up to the left activists' gathering, while Hume's discreetly organized meeting attracted around 120 people, in the main business and professional men, clergy, trade unionists and political leaders. The *Derry Journal* neatly summed up their motives: 'Unless the growing spirit of the [protest] movement could be harnessed coherently, mob rule would replace unionist minority rule. Clear leadership was essential, and quickly.'

McCann initially took the chair at Hume's gathering, but when it became clear that his own group was to be subsumed into a more 'respectable' protest organization, he quit, denouncing the Derry Citizens' Action Committee (CAC) as 'middle-aged, middle-class and middle of the road. It could give the kiss of death to the developing radical movement in Derry.' Hume was still only thirty-one, and some of the young radicals stayed with the CAC, so it could scarcely be dismissed as middle-aged, though it was certainly more middle-class and more middle of the road than the Ad Hoc Committee that had organized the 5 October challenge to the authority of Stormont.

Ivan Cooper, the best-known Protestant supporter of the Labour Party in the city, was elected chairman, and Hume was chosen as his deputy. Michael Canavan, Hume's business partner, became secretary. This was Hume's formal launch into politics. His insistence that the CAC would follow his non-violent philosophy carried the day. Canavan remembers: 'We wanted action, because we could see that the Credit Union movement and the housing movement had only got us a certain distance. Political changes were necessary as well. We wanted action that would involve a large number of people, but there was no question of anything other than peaceful action.'[12] It would also be a pragmatic organization, concentrating not on the border question or socialism but on civil rights objectives such as jobs, housing, and one-man one-vote. 'We separated for the first time the whole question of national issues from nationalism,' said Canavan.

Their first task was to calm a seething city. Hume and his colleagues did this by calling off the second march arranged for the following Saturday, and promising a 'programme of action' on civil rights to be put before the people of Derry at a public meeting within ten days. In the meantime, the committee 'earnestly appealed' for restraint, and offered the confident view that its broadly-based composition presented 'a strong hope for real change in our city'. The new leaders of the protest movement promised: 'We guarantee a programme of positive action to achieve a united city where all men are equal.'

Derry began returning to normality. A march proposed by the hard-left and a token, one-hour general strike in the city were called off. Nevertheless incidents continued – police were lured to a social club where petrol-bombs were thrown. After Hume's appeal for restraint, the city had its first calm night for a week. Students at Queen's University, Belfast, who were rapidly becoming engaged in the civil rights struggle, also unanimously adopted a policy of non-violence.

Within an extraordinarily short space of time, Hume's strategy had shown itself acceptable to the people of Derry and radical students alike. They saw that years of discrimination and suffering could not suddenly be reversed by violence. Catholic Derry was essentially a church-going, deeply conservative society, disapproving of extremes of behaviour. Recognizing that the 9 October founding of the CAC was '*the* key moment for Hume', McCann is remarkably generous to his old rival: 'John Hume has never challenged the people of the Bogside and Creggan about their core beliefs. He has never caused intellectual pain. He has always been reassuring. He has always been safe to follow. In that sense he is a conservative leader: safe and reassuring. People needed that at that time.'[13] The Citizens' Action

Committee's strength was that its mood perfectly matched that of the Catholic masses, and Hume was its personification: reasonable, respectable, righteous, solid, non-violent and determined. The average Bogsider wanted to do *something* about 5 October, McCann added:

> He could go out and march behind Hume, confident that he would not be led into violence, in no way nervous about the political ideas of the men at the front of the procession and certain that he was, by his presence, making a contribution to the struggle. The CAC did not challenge the consciousness of the Catholic masses. It updated the expression of it, injected life into it, and made it relevant to a changed situation.[14]

The Action Committee had been so called on the insistence of Canavan, who believed that deeds were needed as well as words. One immediate challenge presented itself: to reclaim the centre of the city where Catholics were a majority. The CAC called a sit-in in Guildhall Square. In doing so, the Committee had its first casualty. Major Campbell Austin, a Protestant and ex-Unionist, resigned in protest at what he saw as civil disobedience. Hume insisted that it would be a peaceful demonstration. 'Anyone who causes trouble will be regarded by the Committee as an enemy of the civil rights movement,' he said. And so it turned out. Some 5,000 people turned up for a peaceful protest that culminated in the singing of the civil rights anthem 'We Shall Overcome', led by Hume.

Emboldened by this success, the CAC decided to take up other unfinished business: to retrace the steps of the banned march of 5 October, but this time to walk the whole route. How could it be done without repeating the violence? The CAC decided that all fifteen of its members would march on 2 November, in a token affirmation of the right of Catholics to march in their own city. Walking three abreast, with Hume, Canavan and Cooper in the front row, the silent march from the railway station, down Duke Street, across Craigavon bridge and into the walled city was a propaganda coup. Two hundred stewards, largely recruited from Derry's boxing clubs, patrolled the route which was lined by several thousand spectators. Supporters followed, making their way on footpaths to the Diamond, the heart of the city. There, an eleven-year-old boy read out the UN Declaration of Human Rights, and there was more singing of 'We Shall Overcome'. By now, they were beginning to learn the words. The CAC said in a statement: 'The citizens have once again proved that a public demonstration does not lead to violence in our city.' It promised further opportunities to march in the coming weeks.

After the march, leading figures in the burgeoning civil rights movement repaired to the City Hotel, which was rapidly becoming the nerve centre of civil rights activity, to mull over the political situation with pints of Harp lager. Ivan Cooper, the chairman, moved around the various groups laughing and joking, 'while John Hume moved silently around the foyer with a serious countenance and a real nose for the presence of reporters,' Dr Raymond McLean, an emerging figure in the movement recorded later. 'John was a better drinker than any of us, was less jovial in his manner, and had always appeared to be working and worried. He had a better understanding than any of us of the necessity to break down the paper wall which then existed between our movement and the general public, both in England and the south of Ireland.'[15]

The CAC's tactics enraged hard-line Loyalists, who made abortive attempts to attack the march. More significantly the softly-softly strategy began to unsettle the ruling Unionist clique in the city. Cracks appeared in its hitherto smooth façade. One Unionist councillor, who had several business votes, admitted publicly that 'one-man, one-vote' was inevitable. On 4 November, Terence O'Neill met Harold Wilson in London, who told him in no uncertain terms that reform must come. The very next day, Londonderry Corporation agreed to reform its housing allocation system, permitting a Catholic influence for the first time.

Disquiet was not confined to Unionist ranks, however. The veteran Nationalist MP for Derry, Eddie McAteer was 'personally uneasy' about the pace and direction of the civil rights movement, which by its very nature played down the importance of the border and partition, hitherto the lifeblood of northern Nationalism. 'It was this subtle difference of emphasis that marked the division between the young men – epitomized by Hume – and the old generation of nationalists under McAteer,' judged *Derry Journal* editor Frank Curran.

There followed the biggest challenge to the government's crack-down on civil rights. The CAC proposed a mass march on the original banned route for 16 November, and Home Affairs Minister William Craig promptly banned it, adding for good measure that 'such force as is necessary' would be used to uphold the prohibition. Conflict appeared inevitable. The Bishop of Derry and Raphoe, Dr Charles Tyndall, contacted Hume to offer support and help. He offered to open St Columb's, the Church of Ireland cathedral, for an all-night peace vigil, but was anxious not be isolated. Hume persuaded the Catholic Bishop of Derry, Dr Farren, to make a similar gesture at St Eugene's, and in an act of ecumenism unprecedented in the city, both cathedrals threw open their doors for mixed prayers from 10 p.m. until 6 a.m. on the day of the march. Hume attended both services.

The day began with a bright blue sky. The huge crowd, 'almost frightening in its calmness, with a spiritual presence which was recog-nisable', gathered once again at the Waterside station. There were unconfirmed rumours of 'men from Tyrone' with guns among the front ranks. Women by the roadside blessed themselves. Tension rose as some 15,000 demonstrators crossed Craigavon bridge and met police barricades drawn up across the other side. Police halted the march there, but four pre-selected leaders vaulted the barriers. Stewards held the rest of the marchers back, and Hume appealed for calm. 'We have broken the ban,' he argued. 'This was an effort by Mr Craig to show the people of Derry to be divided and incapable of peaceful protest. We intend to throw that back in his teeth.'

However, at this point, Loyalists from the nearby Fountain area began stoning the marchers, who defied the stones and bottles and swept through police ranks, directed by Hume standing on a traffic bollard, into the walled city to regroup in the Diamond. Police wisely withdrew, and a euphoric crowd heard Hume say: 'We are within the walls and we will stay here.' He excoriated Craig for banning the march, pointing out that it had been non-violent – on the part of the marchers, at any rate. 'I am not a law-breaker by nature, but

I am proud to stand here with 15,000 Derry people who have broken a law which is in disrepute. I invite Mr Craig to arrest the lot of us,' he added, to roars of applause.

The following week, local magistrates adjourned charges against civil rights activists arising from the 5 October march. Following scuffles with police outside the court house, rumours of fresh disturbances brought 4,000 dockers marching inside the walled city in protest. Hume met them and welcomed their spontaneous demonstration, telling police who gathered nearby to leave. 'We can control our own people,' he said. 'We can keep the peace ourselves.' He promised continued firm leadership from the CAC. But the dockers set everyone else marching, and for days there were impromptu parades in the city. Factory workers, shop owners, nurses, the unemployed and even business people exuberantly defied Craig's ban.

Another ecstatic meeting in the Guildhall voted overwhelmingly to re-elect the Action Committee, which immediately called for a end to spontaneous marches, not least on the grounds that Hume had policed at least ten such gatherings and was 'dead on his feet'. Hume told the meeting that Derry's legacy was that it had always been divided by class, creed and politics. Community relations had been much talked about, but the people really attacking this cancer were those in the civil rights movement. 'I am proud that in this movement so far we have shown no hatred to any man, even those who differ violently. Rather do I pity them at times ... Let the message go out tonight that when we have got our civil rights there will be no revenge. We who have suffered so long from social injustices will not perpetrate them on anyone else.' Another speaker said: 'I have watched John Hume going through hell.'

The dam broke. Six days after the march, on 22 November, O'Neill delivered the reforms demanded by Wilson. He scrapped the corrupt Londonderry Corporation, putting in its place an appointed Development Commission. A fairer system of council house allocation was set in train. An ombudsman to investigate citizens' grievances was established. Universal adult franchise in local government was finally conceded, and sections of the detested Special Powers Act which allowed arbitrary arrest and detention would be repealed.

Though O'Neill was later to call this a 'small, timid reform package', it was a remarkable breakthrough for a movement still only six weeks old. He admitted in his autobiography that the civil rights movement had won reforms that would otherwise have taken years to wring from a reluctant government.

Derry folk responded to their leaders, and paused. The Catholic majority had not got everything it was seeking. The unelected Development Commission, for instance, was no substitute for a democratically elected council which they would undoubtedly dominate. The Citizens' Action Committee gave the reform package a cautious welcome, and appealed for continued restraint. Instead of calling further demonstrations, it launched a petition calling for implementation of the UN Universal Declaration of Human Rights in Northern Ireland, attracting support from almost half the city's people.

On 9 December, O'Neill addressed the 'nation' – that is, the people of Northern Ireland – saying that the province was 'at the crossroads'. He admitted that British public and parliamentary opinion had been 'deeply disturbed by the events in Londonderry', but he asked for a swift end to the growing civil disorder throughout Ulster. The Prime Minister warned: 'We are on the brink of chaos.' He reassured the civil rights movement that its voice had been heard, and he meant business with his reforms. He appealed for their help in promoting calm, 'before blood is shed'. Two days later, he summarily dismissed Craig, his turbulent Home Affairs Minister, whose tactics had been so counter-productive.

In fact, largely at Hume's prompting, Derry was relatively quiet. There had been a narrow squeak in Armagh, where, watched by Hume, the RUC prevented a violent Loyalist onslaught on a civil rights march, but as the observer noted: 'The majority of the people in the Bogside, and in the Catholic community in Northern Ireland generally, felt that the trouble was over.'[16] John Hume urged a truce so that the reforms could be given a chance to work.

In one quarter, however, his appeal fell on deaf ears, with catastrophic results. People's Democracy (PD), an ad hoc radical group based in Queen's University, Belfast, possessed a firmly militant leadership that despised 'Green Tories' (traditional Nationalists) almost as much as it did 'Orange Tories' (Unionists of every stripe), and decided to defy the truce with a 'long march' from Belfast to Derry. The march, consciously modelled on the Selma–Alabama black protest in the American South, was called just before Christmas. Hume condemned the organizers for playing into the hands of the Unionists, who could accuse the civil rights movement of being disruptive.

The march went ahead on 1 January 1969. On their seventy-three mile trek through the Ulster countryside, the eighty marchers were constantly harried and attacked by Loyalists until a final ambush at Burntollet bridge just outside Derry. There, watched impassively by the RUC, the marchers were attacked on 5 January by hundreds of club-waving Unionists. There were many casualties, and when the bloodstained marchers arrived in the Guildhall square to tell their story, the patience of the young Bogsiders snapped. They clashed with the RUC, rioting into the early hours. When they were finally driven back into their enclaves, the police pursued them and staged a riot of their own. Shouting and singing, many of them drunk, they batoned any 'Fenian bastard' they could lay their hands on, and did considerable damage to property.

Lord Cameron, a Scottish judge who later headed an official inquiry into disturbances in Ulster, concluded that the police 'were guilty of misconduct which involved assault and battery, malicious damage to property in streets in the predominantly-Catholic Bogside area'. Young men began arming themselves with makeshift weapons, and barricaded entrances to the Bogside. A rebel radio station began transmitting appeals to join vigilante patrols. The inspired slogan 'You Are Now Entering Free Derry' appeared on a street corner.

Hume and his moderate colleagues were appalled, and appealed yet again for restraint. Hume addressed a crowd estimated at 10,000, and then led a silent protest march to the police barracks, asking the crowd to behave as though they were in a funeral procession. 'Observe complete silence, and bow your heads as an expression of shame for police misconduct,' he urged. RUC officers dismissed their catalogue of police misbehaviour out of hand.

Hume had already had first-hand experience of what the police could do. In one dangerous street confrontation on 4 January while the PD march was nearing Derry, he asked police to withdraw a water-cannon he believed was only inciting conflict. A policeman said: 'If you take another step forward, I'll beat your fucking head in.' He was then hit by a stone thrown by a policeman, but refused to be provoked and asked the crowd not to retaliate. Inwardly, he decided then that the police 'wished to destroy the peaceful nature of the civil rights movement and bring the Catholic people to the limits of their endurance'.[17]

In the Bogside, there was wild talk of 'getting out the guns' – though they had none at this time – and Hume's authority was under strain as never before. According to the Cameron Report, this was a deliberate move by People's Democracy radicals. The PD march divided the civil rights movement, and weakened the Derry Citizens' Action Committee. The Cameron inquiry felt that the PD leaders intended to weaken moderate reforming forces. 'We think that their object was to create tension, so that in the process a more radical programme could be realized.'[18]

Extremist elements in People's Democracy and Hume's moderate Derry group were clearly competing for support among the Catholic population. Hume and his Citizens' Action colleagues allowed the situation to cool for a few days – the RUC avoided the Bogside – and then 'descended on the area with a series of brilliantly-timed speeches' that convinced the vigilantes to dismantle the barricades. At this stage they could not have defended them anyway in the face of a concerted attack from the RUC.

Hume reflected on ten days of trouble and sought to reassert his non-violent philosophy. Speaking out on 13 January, after more Catholic violence in Newry, he argued: 'It would seem there are irresponsible elements who do not understand the purpose in the reason behind non-violent protest. It is not the purpose of civil rights marches to attack the police or Paisleyites, however much they may be provoked by either. It is the purpose of civil rights marchers to get civil rights. These can only be attained by attracting publicity to the injustices and getting public sympathy on our side. This sympathy is more easily won if we are seen to be marching for a just cause and accepting provocation, injury and damage to our homes, without retaliation. If, however, we loot, burn and attack, we lose all sympathy.' He added that the civil rights movement was not an attack on the Northern Ireland state, only on its abuses.

This reaffirmation of his belief that no worthwhile change can be won by physical force, came at a critical time. The ruling Unionist Party was splitting apart on either side of the fault line of reform. O'Neill set up the Cameron Commission of Inquiry on 15 January, and barely a week later his brilliant, ambitious, young deputy, Brian Faulkner, resigned, followed shortly afterwards by the Health Minister, William Morgan. Rebel Unionist MPs held a secret conclave in Portadown the following weekend, and on hearing of the hostile gathering, O'Neill took his courage in both hands and called a snap general election for the Stormont Parliament.

Polling day was set for 24 February, and though the election was called to shore up the failing premiership of Captain O'Neill, it bitterly divided his party. More importantly for John Hume, it presented an unexpected political opportunity to put his principles into practice. He had just turned thirty-two, and had turned down various suggestions to stand for Stormont or Westminster. He had rejected two approaches to stand as a candidate in UK parliamentary by-elections. He spurned a proposal from the New Democratic Party, a short-lived centrist group, to fight Armagh and similarly refused to stand as a unity candidate in Mid-Ulster – handing the seat over to PD activist Bernadette Devlin.

It was on his own home ground that he had to make a stand. There had been speculation that he might stand as a Liberal, and Barry White insists that Labour also tried to recruit him but was deterred by his Nationalism. In the event, Hume decided to stand as an Independent, but on a clear platform that a social democratic party should be formed to give voice to people of his persuasion. He discussed the idea with Dr Raymond McLean, who supported him fully. Hume rang the press to announce his candidature. 'We were now entering a new phase,' he wrote later.[19]

Just how new became clear only subsequently. 'I decided I wanted to found a Social Democratic Party,' he disclosed. 'In my election manifesto I said I was standing as an Independent, against Labour and against the Nationalist Party to seek a mandate to found a party on social democratic principles.'[20] The idea had long been maturing in his mind. After his first articles were published in the *Irish Times* several years previously, Sean Lemass, Prime Minister in the Republic, had despatched one of his political lieutenants, Senator Owen Ryan, to find out more about this young man. The senator advised Hume that while people sought their ultimate objectives, they still had to work on day-to-day issues. 'And what you also have to have is an organized political party, with members and branches.'

The advice was not lost on Hume. Naturally, the Nationalists were alarmed. Their party was essentially an ad hoc organization, resuscitated at each election. Eddie McAteer was reluctant to stand again, but his traditionalist backers, who were unhappy with Hume's apparent lack of passion about the border issue, bullied him into allowing his name to go forward.

Hume felt, correctly, that the times were moving with him, rather than McAteer. He made his position clear in a statement of four principles.

- I will work for the formation of a new political movement based on social democratic principles, with open membership, and an elected executive to allow the people full involvement in the process of decision-making.
- The movement must provide what has been seriously lacking at Stormont, namely a strong and energetic opposition to Conservatism, and pursuing radical social and economic policies.
- The movement must be completely non-sectarian and must root out a fundamental evil in our society, sectarian division.
- The movement must be committed to the ideal that the future of Northern Ireland should be decided by its people, and no constitutional changes accepted except by the consent of its people.

These principles ring down the years. At the time, Hume claimed to be reluctant to stand against McAteer, though this sounds rather less than convincing set against his ambitious, ground-breaking manifesto. He justified himself in later years: 'I felt that a more aggressive political attitude and movement was vital. I had the feeling that the movement on the streets had attained its immediate objectives, and must be consolidated by political advance. I did not share the fear and forecast of many that my decision would cause a deep split amongst the Catholic people. Any divisions would be temporary.' Significantly, he recognized his main support would be the Catholic vote, whatever his anti-sectarianism.

He was confident, even a little cock-sure: 'I was certain change was in the air and that if I did not enter the field somebody else would.' At the same time he admitted he was 'more idealistic than realistic' in his hopes of breaking the sectarian mould of politics. 'I felt at that time that the Protestant people, or at least a considerable proportion of them, were ready for dialogue and negotiation. I still believe that an accommodation could have been arrived at but for the outbreak of violence and the emergence of the IRA.'[21]

It was an entertaining election. The Hume camp took over the Rossville Hall in the Bogside. Michael Canavan was election director. Dr McLean, responsible for recruiting poll-booth agents, recalled that the atmosphere was 'electric and jovial'. Hume had a large band of willing workers, and his supporters believed the result was a fore-gone conclusion. Apart from McAteer, Hume was opposed by Eamonn McCann standing as official Labour candidate with some Republican support. McCann's campaign was somewhat marred by the disappearance of his election agent together with the £150 deposit.

With something approaching civil war in the anti-Unionist camp, it was inevitably a hard-fought campaign; Nationalists were furious with the Hume camp's doorstep slogan, 'Let's face it, Eddie's past it'. On polling day it was plain that the wind was indeed blowing Hume's way. He sailed home, taking 8,920 votes to 5,267 for McAteer and 1,993 for McCann, who lost his deposit. Citizens' Action chairman Ivan Cooper also took a seat from the Nationalists, powering home in Mid-Derry with almost three times their vote. Another like-minded Independent, Paddy O'Hanlon, was returned in Armagh. Hume was satisfied with the outcome. 'That is a fair start,' he said. 'We will take it from there.'

For Terence O'Neill, the poll was merely disaster delayed. He retained his own seat in the face of a ferocious attack from the Rev. Ian Paisley, but of the thirty-nine Unionists returned, ten were elected on an anti-reform ticket, with two others undecided. The Nationalists still had six seats, with two going to Republican Labour and two to the NILP. Among these were Paddy Devlin, a former Republican wartime internee, elected in the Falls division of Belfast, and Gerry Fitt, bloodied on the 5 October march in Derry, who retained his Dock seat in Belfast. Both were swiftly to become prominent in the struggle to find a new political identity in Northern Ireland.

They began working together at Stormont almost immediately. On 20 March, the sitting was suspended when opposition members staged a sit-down protest in the chamber during a debate on the new Public Order Bill. This was the long-promised measure designed to legitimize peaceful demonstrations. It was much too draconian for the Opposition, who tabled forty amendments and kept the House sitting until three in the morning. The next day, the dominant Unionists used a parliamentary ruse to close the debate while Hume was still speaking, forcing the issue to a vote in their favour. The new member for Foyle took the tactics of the street to the floor of the House. He and seven others sat down and sang 'We Shall Overcome'. After a half-hour suspension, they still refused to take their seats and when they left one at a time they were suspended for a week.

The work of building a new party continued apace in Derry, giving shape to Hume's vision. Immediately after his celebration night, supporters decided to establish an independent organization, even if this was something of a contradiction in terms. Dr McLean was elected chairman. The organization set up branches and advice centres in Hume's Foyle constituency. It produced a periodical, *Independent Forum*, and arranged meetings with speakers to recruit new members. It was a promising start, though far from the organization that Senator Ryan had urged.

In any case, events on the ground (and in the underground) in Derry soon began to shape developments much more than the antics at Stormont. A series of bombings in the province, which seriously disrupted water and electricity supplies, was attributed to the IRA. They were later discovered to be the work of the Loyalist Ulster Volunteer Force (UVF). The annual Easter commemoration in

Derry to honour the heroes of the 1916 Rising in Dublin attracted 5,000 people, a reminder of the growing strength of Republican sentiment. Hume watched with mounting concern.

Then, local civil rights activists announced a march to Derry over the infamous Burntollet bridge for 19 April. Hume and the senior people in the Citizens' Action Committee went out to Burntollet to assess the situation. Loyalist men and youths, carrying large sticks, recognized him and shouted, 'There's Hume the bastard, let's get him.' They chased the car up a hill. When Hume stopped to complain to police about the menacing crowd, they almost caught him. He got in the car when they were only ten yards away, while the driver, Dr Raymond McLean, cursed him for waiting. 'Privately, I reflected that in addition to John's political ability, I was now assured of his physical courage also,' he recorded later.[22]

On the day it was scheduled, the government banned the civil rights march, on the grounds that it would meet 'bloody and violent opposition' from Loyalists. Home Affairs Minister Robert Porter said there was a possibility of firearms being used against the marchers. Once this news was related back to Derry, trouble was inevitable. A large Catholic crowd gathered in Guildhall Square. When they came under fire from stone-throwing militants, the RUC charged the civil rights supporters. Teenage Bogsiders ignored Hume's appeals to disperse, and staged sit-down protests. Police action against them turned from scuffles into running fights involving stone-throwing and petrol-bombs.

The RUC set off in hot pursuit of the rioters. Some escaped through a terrace house in William Street and over the back wall. RUC officers smashed down the door. Cheated of their real quarry, they beat up Sammy Devenney, a popular taxi-driver who lived there. He had no interest in politics and belonged to no political organization. The beating was so savage that there was blood on the floor, on the chairs, on the walls and even on the ceiling. When he died after two heart attacks in July, Sammy Devenney became the first 'Catholic martyr' of the Troubles. Also that night, a policeman fired two shots, the first salvo of what was to become a long war.

Overnight, eighty-nine policemen and seventy-nine civilians were treated at Alatnagelvin Hospital for injuries sustained during the first battle for the Bogside. Hume realized that the community was on the brink of an abrupt slide into total violence. The next morning, Sunday 20 April, police gathered in force at the entrance to the Bogside, clearly intending an invasion. Hume decided that the only safe course was evacuation of men, women and children. They were ferried up to the heights of the Creggan, a Catholic housing estate high above the Bogside. Most walked. Some had to be carried.

Hume then turned his attention to the menacing presence of the RUC, persuading priests and the Churches Industrial Council to join him in a direct appeal to Home Affairs Minister Porter to withdraw the police. At 2 p.m. he also gave a direct ultimatum to local police commanders: 'The residents intend to return at 5 this afternoon, and if the police are not out of the area by then we will not be responsible for the consequences.' Ten minutes before the ultimatum expired, Porter gave the order for the police to withdraw. Hume, together with church and civil leaders, had given an undertaking to preserve the peace if the RUC retreated.

In his report, Lord Cameron agreed that there had been 'an acute risk of very grave violence that day'. It was only averted by the constructive actions of responsible citizens.

> It may be invidious to name a single individual, but Mr Hume's work in Londonderry since October has been so outstanding that it seems appropriate to name him. On 20 April, he realised there was a strong chance of further rioting ... It was a very dangerous situation, since members of the police reserve force with their riot equipment took up their position in the Bogside at about 10 a.m. Mr Hume then succeeded in persuading the residents to evacuate the Bogside area at 3 p.m. and assemble at the Creggan that afternoon for a meeting. This was an astonishing achievement, which reduced the risk of violence against the police, and gave the Bogside residents a more constructive project.[23]

Rarely has an official government report heaped such praise on an individual.

Hume led the Bogsiders back to their homes, only just controlling the surge of people that threatened to turn into a mob. Angry Catholics confronted the police at the entrance to the walled city, and Hume climbed on to the shoulders of Father Anthony Mulvey to beg them to go back to their homes. He would get them justice, he promised. They dispersed, and Derry breathed again.

But something had changed, deep down. In truth, the election that sustained O'Neill in office and brought civil rights MPs into Stormont had altered nothing of significance in Northern Ireland. The Unionist government was still reluctant to introduce one-man, one-vote in local elections. The RUC had allowed itself to be seen as the armed wing of the Unionist Party, which would invariably side with the Loyalists against Catholics. In the Bogside, McCann noted that after the April conflict, 'the talk was of the next time and there were some who said that we ought to be prepared. No one doubted that there would be a next time.'[24]

O'Neill soon caved in to his critics, resigning on 28 April to be replaced by Major James Chichester-Clark. The latter's first announcement on 6 May was an amnesty for all offences connected with demonstrations since 5 October, including charges against Hume. He promised to be 'fair' and follow O'Neill's policy of extending the local government franchise. He also pledged to end the gerrymandering. Hume and his civil rights colleagues urged their supporters to give him time, but in the Bogside and elsewhere, McCann reported, 'the rioting classes were not impressed'. The unemployed youth of such areas had been used as marching fodder; energetic and instinctively aggressive, they could be counted on to turn out for street protests. He argued: 'It was their energy and aggression which had powered the civil rights campaign through its first frenetic months. In the end, it was they – not the RUC – who frightened organisations like the Citizens' Action Committee off the streets. The CAC died in Derry after 19 April.'

Not quite. The CAC lingered on for a few more months. In June, it met the new prime minister to argue that the RUC should be excluded from the general amnesty, but he rejected the plea. The civil rights movement was at a crossroads. An academic expert on the subject, Bob Purdie of Ruskin College, Oxford, argues that the movement finally failed because it created hopes which could not be fulfilled on one side – the Catholics' – and fears that could not be assuaged on the other – the Unionists'. In particular, the Derry Citizens' Action Committee 'overestimated the time-span during which it could keep control over what was, essentially, a communal upsurge of Catholics' in the city.[25]

Unhappily, the moderate forces gathered around Hume could not offer an alternative means of expression, and as a Stormont MP, Hume was no longer vice-chairman of the CAC. By ending demonstrations, the moderates took away from the youth any channel for expression other than a riot. 'The rage and frustration which lay just beneath the surface of life in the Bogside could no longer be contained within the thin shell of the CAC's timid respectability. The "hooligans" had taken over, and the stage was set for a decisive clash between them and the forces of the state.'[26]

FIVE

VIOLENCE BEGETS POLITICS

ALL THE ELEMENTS of a summer of discontent and violence were falling neatly into place. The new Prime Minister, Major James Chichester-Clark, was regarded by moderate Nationalists as 'basically a decent man as Unionists go', but not up to the job of reconciling the social and political forces unleashed in Derry. With the approach of the traditional marching season in Northern Ireland, tensions began to rise, particularly in Belfast. In the unseasonably warm weather of late spring, there were nightly clashes between Catholics and Protestants. Catholic families were driven from their homes by intimidation.

By midsummer, the rioting had become serious. Hume and his fellow-MPs feared that two flashpoints – the Protestant demonstrations on 12 July which remember the victory of King William III over the Catholic James II at the Battle of the Boyne in 1690, and on 12 August, to commemorate the relief of the Protestant Derry from the long siege of 1689 – would plunge the province into chaos.

Amid the sectarian tensions of 1969, the Unionist festivities were seen as provocative. Youths clashed with police and 'Twelfth' marchers returning to Derry from Limavady; this was the first time they had attacked rather than retaliated. There were running battles in the streets, and shops were looted. Hume and the CAC condemned the hooliganism, which was also censured from the pulpit of St Eugene's cathedral as having nothing to do with civil rights or religion. The tension was heightened by the death on 16 July of Sammy Devenney. More than 20,000 local people attended his funeral. Aged forty-two, Devenney left a widow and young family.

Hume realized that if the authorities did not call off the 12 August march by the Protestant Apprentice Boys, the city – and probably the whole province – would slide into civil war. He was in the paradoxical position of asking the government to ban a march, having only nine months earlier led a mass movement of his own people on to the streets to defy a marching ban. His anxieties were privately shared by the Wilson government in London, which sent 150 troops to Derry on 'stand-by' duty. Home Secretary James Callaghan was worried that the RUC would not be able to contain the violence. Their total strength was only 3,000 but they had to control 5,000 square miles of territory and 1.5 million people. In addition there were about 8,000 members of the exclusively Protestant Ulster Special Constabulary, the 'B-Specials', who were hated and feared by the Catholic community.

With other concerned opposition MPs, Hume appealed to the Stormont government to ban the march. He must have known that this was politically impossible for a Unionist administration trying to placate a confused and resentful Protestant majority. They rejected his plea, and Hume, undeterred, set off for London and Dublin to enlist support. He got a good hearing from Jack Lynch, the Irish Taoiseach, but no action. In London, Callaghan did not even listen, but sent his deputy, Lord Stonham, to a ten-minute briefing with Hume. The fact that this session turned into a three-hour lunch at the Athenaeum was scant consolation.

Indeed, the British government was preparing for the worst. Callaghan later admitted: 'We were debating whether we should intervene, but hoping and praying that we should not have to. The advice that came to me from all sides was on no account get sucked into the Irish bog.'[1] As the nightly violence spread from Derry to Belfast, the Home Secretary agreed with Defence Secretary Denis Healey to send in the soldiers if required. The Northern Ireland government asked for troops, in principle, on 3 August. Callaghan, after consulting with Wilson by telephone at his holiday home in the Scilly Isles, agreed. 'So simply was a momentous decision taken,' he recollected a few years later.

Having rejected warnings that to do so would be 'an error of unpardonable proportions', the RUC gave permission for the triumphalist Orange procession in Derry to go ahead. Hume acknowledged

... am and Annie Hume at the back of their terrace ... ome in Glenbrook, Londonderry, circa 1960.

The graduate: John Hume graduating BA in French and History from Maynooth College, 1958.

John Hume marries local Derry girl Pat Hone, 1960.

Pat Hume with their second son, and fourth child, born on Human Rights Day, 10 December 1968.

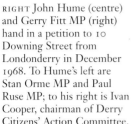

RIGHT John Hume (centre) and Gerry Fitt MP (right) hand in a petition to 10 Downing Street from Londonderry in December 1968. To Hume's left are Stan Orme MP and Paul Ruse MP; to his right is Ivan Cooper, chairman of Derry Citizens' Action Committee.

BELOW 'We shall overcome': Hume leads a sit-down civil rights protest in the streets of Londonderry, March 1969.

LEFT While Stormont MP for Foyle, Hume is restrained by police as he protests about the arrest of a protester in Waterloo Place, Londonderry, April 1969.

BELOW At an early civil rights demonstration on Craigavon Bridge in Derry, 1969.

RIGHT John Hume and Austin Currie, also a Stormont MP, cross through the barricade in Monaghan Street on their way to the start of the protest march in Newry.

BELOW John Hume and Austin Currie (to his left) at 'Free Derry Corner' in the Bogside, Londonderry, during the early days of the Troubles, 1970.

YOU
ARE NOW
ENTERING
FREE DERRY

that the Apprentice Boys had a right to march, but questioned their wisdom in insisting on doing so at such a sensitive time. 'It is on their shoulders and the government's that will rest the final responsibility if trouble does arise,' he said. Later, he remembered a conversation with a 'kind and decent' Orangeman. Hume asked why it was necessary to perpetuate these provocations. 'We have to show them who's master,' came the chilling reply.

This time, the Bogsiders were not going to be caught unawares. They set up their own Derry Citizens' Defence Association (DCDA), a self-defence group which had its origins among traditionalist republican (including IRA) elements. The DCDA fully intended to meet violence with violence. It had only a vague plan of campaign. It produced maps showing forty entrances to Catholic territory, and barricade materials were stockpiled at each. But the very fact that it had been formed was regarded by Frank Curran, editor of the *Derry Journal*, as 'a public affirmation of the community's will to resist at all costs'.[2] Hume, still preaching non-violence and urging restraint on the Catholic community, was deliberately excluded from the DCDA. His Citizens' Action Committee, in which so much moderate hope had been vested, met and agreed to nominate two people to the DCDA. The CAC ceased to exist.

On the afternoon of 12 August, Hume stood on the front line between the Apprentice Boys' march and the Catholic crowd, begging them not to attack. They had stopped listening to him. A volley of stones felled Ivan Cooper, standing alongside him, and the full fury of the Bogsiders then fell on the procession. The police and Loyalist supporters counter-attacked, but were met with a hail of petrol-bombs. The RUC responded with CS gas (tear gas), against which the rioters wore water-and-vinegar-soaked rags.

The battle for the Bogside went on for two days, with the Catholics gradually consolidating their hold. Hume was reduced to walking the streets of his community, seeking to limit the violence where he could. He succeeded in persuading a gang of youths not to fire-bomb the Rosemount RUC station, high above the Bogside near his home in Beechwood Avenue. For his pains, the police fired a CS cartridge at his chest as he went to parley with them.

Hume was carried away semi-conscious, but was quickly back on his feet to negotiate a truce on the use of tear gas. The police contemptuously dismissed the idea that Hume had 'saved' them, showing off a rack of sub-machine-guns and saying: 'We always had these.'[3] Hume's view at this time, amply borne out by events, was that the naïve violence espoused by hard-left elements exasperated by his pacifist line would not bring about the Marxist millennium to which they aspired, but a military revival of the IRA, which had been virtually inactive for a decade. In Belfast, Gerry Adams responded to a tape-recorded call for help from Derry by leaving a meeting at Stormont 'to make petrol bombs'.[4]

Jack Lynch, the Taoiseach, intervened with a televised address, in which he accused Stormont of losing control, warning that the Irish government could no longer stand by and see innocent people injured and perhaps worse. He proposed a UN peacekeeping force, followed by early negotiations on the constitutional position of the Six Counties – that is, on reunification. The Unionists were outraged, and even the cool-headed Callaghan observed: 'We had to consider the possibility that within the next twenty-four hours we might face both civil war in the North and an invasion from the South.' A rumour spread that Irish troops were on their way, though Lynch had in mind only the stationing of field hospitals just over the border in Donegal. Hume was again shut out from these developments, treated as a novice politician of only four months (which essentially he was) and as a puppet of the British establishment (which he certainly was not).

In Derry, the exhausted police began a tactical withdrawal from the Catholic heartlands. The dreaded B-Specials were then seen through the acrid CS smoke parading in the city centre, armed. Something akin to panic spread. Catholics feared a massacre. With the riots spreading to Belfast and elsewhere, partly as a diversionary Nationalist tactic to exhaust the RUC, Home Secretary Callaghan signalled 'Permission Granted' to Chichester-Clark's request for troops to be deployed immediately. Late in the afternoon of 14 August, 400 heavily-armed men of the 1st Battalion, the Prince of Wales Own Yorkshire Regiment, came marching over Craigavon bridge to restore the peace.

They were welcomed by the Bogsiders, because the violence

stopped immediately. Army officers agreed a form of peacekeeping role for the Derry Defence Committee. But the presence of the British Army, initially in Hume's city and then in Belfast and right across the province, exacerbated the already murderous possibility of conflict. Journalist Max Hastings, watching the developing anarchy, believed that any sense of Ulster as an entity disappeared that month: 'Every man spoke for himself and his own cause – Catholics and Catholic church leaders, Protestants, Paisley, the Orange Order, the police, the Falls Road, People's Democracy, John Hume and Ivan Cooper, the Bogside, the IRA, the Stormont – each man was his own voice and nothing more.' Talking to one man or one group meant nothing to any of the others. 'A state of spiritual anarchy had been created.'[5]

Amid this political fragmentation, the Stormont Parliament met in emergency session on the day the soldiers moved into position. The Unionists, their backs to the wall, mobilized their majority behind a motion defending the decision to let the fateful march go ahead and congratulating the police on their courage and discipline. Home Affairs Minister John Taylor also disclosed he was calling up another 11,000 B-Special reserves, presumably to crush the National-ist uprising. Hume was aghast at this aggression and warned: 'We are quite firm. We will not be moved.' With that, he and his six like-minded MP colleagues walked out.

The walk-out was less welcome to some members of the group than to others, and pointed to future political frictions. Paddy Devlin, the forthright Northern Ireland Labour Party MP for the Falls div-ision of Belfast, said he and Gerry Fitt, soon to be co-founders of the SDLP, wanted to stay on the opposition benches. 'Hume was the guy who pushed for it,' he said. 'We thought we were elected to represent the people, and we should stay in parliament. We were doing well.'[6]

Devlin judged Hume to be a deeply complex man, 'probably the most intellectually able among us,' whose mind could grasp the stra-tegic elements of an issue and express them in concise language. However, from the outset of their relationship, Devlin had doubts about Hume's motives and questioned the strength of his loyalty to the Stormont group. 'He had a tendency to identify the most powerful and influential people among those we encountered and go off into corner-huddles with these pace-setters and opinion formers,' Devlin observed later.[7] Editors of important newspapers and television programmes were those 'most regularly endowed' with special briefings, he added, which laid the groundwork for Hume's future reputation as both political visionary and a manipulator. Political envy apart, there is some validity in this charge. Hume never made any secret of his ability to find the man most likely to influence.

These misgivings, shared by Fitt, did not stop the group meeting virtually every day to plan tactics at Stormont. They watched developments at Westminster and in the Irish Parliament, and soon found that they could out-think Unionist ministers unused to being forced on the defensive by accurate, informed questioning on the floor of the House. And with 'Free Derry' firmly in the hands of the Defence Association, Hume increasingly turned his attention to being an MP. Nor had the prospect of a new political party been forgotten.

Hume returned to the Bogside, however, for James Callaghan's visit to Derry on 28 August. The Home Secretary was determined it would be a 'cocked-hat affair' to re-establish the authority of Her Majesty's Government. He toured the riot-stricken areas of Belfast, and over dinner with Chichester-Clark promised the Unionists that he had not come to accede to the Bogsiders' demand for the abolition of Stormont. However, he warned that the British government had 'contingency plans' should law and order break down completely and Stormont become incapable of functioning. The Unionists either misconstrued or simply failed to believe that veiled threat.

Callaghan did not know what to expect in 'Free Derry', where the Northern Ireland government's writ did not run. He was escorted through a barricade by Hume and Ivan Cooper, and was immediately overwhelmed by his reception. A Catholic woman knelt down before him and kissed his hand. They made their way through dense crowds at a run, negotiating more barricades, rubble and broken glass. Callaghan was becoming tired by the constant pushing and jostling when Hume spotted an old lady at her door. She invited the Home Secretary in, and her daughter-in-law, Mrs Kathleen Docherty, made them a cup of tea. Callaghan asked Hume to bring the Defence Association deputation he was due to meet to the house. There, in the tiny front room, he listened to their demands: disband the B-Specials, disarm the police and abolish Stormont. Callaghan rehearsed the government's position: no to abolition of Stormont, but yes to further internal reforms that would bring 'a sense of belonging' to everyone.

Then, flanked by Hume and Cooper, he addressed the crowds from Mrs Docherty's bedroom window. His impromptu speech echoed the Catholic community's sense of grievance over justice and equality. 'I will promise to do my best,' he said, and to loud cheers he pledged to come back. The visit made a remarkable impression on Bogsiders, going a long way towards restoring faith in the democratic process, though in Westminster rather than Unionist-dominated Stormont. And when, six weeks later, the Hunt Committee, set up to investigate policing in Northern Ireland, recommended abolition of the B-Specials and disarming of the RUC, there was euphoria. Free Derry was opened up to military police patrols, and the barricades came down. Callaghan's promised return visit in October brought reforms in legal administration, the allocation of housing and fair employment practices. The Home Secretary went back to the Bogside, asking Hume to find him a safe house in which he could repeat his *tête-à-tête* with the Defence Association. Hume took him to the home of an RAF corporal who was on leave, and the meeting with community leaders passed off without incident.

The calm of Derry was deceptive. Callaghan's reforms triggered Protestant riots in Belfast, which claimed the life of the first policeman to die in the Troubles. Constable Victor Arbuckle died, ironically, at the hand of a UVF gunman. By the end of 1969, thirteen people had died in disturbances, and eight bombs had been planted. Hume knew that the lull concealed terrifying developments below the surface. In Derry, disaffected hardliners simply did not believe that the Unionist-controlled 'statelet' could be reformed peacefully. Through the autumn, military preparations were going on in a terrace house in the Brandywell district, a neighbourhood where Hume had lived briefly as a baby. Republicans and their supporters were taught how to use sub-machine-guns and make bombs. They crossed over the border into Donegal for 'practice shoot-outs'.

The IRA was undergoing a transformation. Disorganized and without guns, it had been unable to 'defend' the minority Catholic enclaves of Belfast from vicious Loyalist attacks. The slogan 'IRA = I Ran Away' appeared on walls. But after the riots of August 1969, republicans worked frantically to raise money, get hold of weapons and build up the organization. 'In a remarkably short time,' claims Gerry Adams, 'a people's army took shape; closely-knit with the nationalist community, it was made up of the sons and daughters of ordinary people, its members indistinguishable to any outside observer from the rest of the community.'[8] In Nationalist areas, it was simply known as the 'Ra'.

Secret meetings in Belfast confirmed a growing division which split the Republican movement into two factions: the Marxist-orientated Officials, who stood accused of being too obsessed with revolutionary politics and of failing to protect Catholic families in their hour of need; and the Provisionals, who repudiated the official line and pledged support for the IRA's 'basic military role'. A statement from the self-styled IRA Provisional Army Council on 28 December 1969 confirmed the birth of 'the Provos', and the start of a murderous new phase in the Republican struggle.

Excluded by his political philosophy, Hume could only watch these frightening developments from the sidelines. He channelled his energies once more into finding a democratic way out. His independent organization in Derry could now boast 200 adherents. Throughout September, when his opponents were learning how to dismantle Sten guns, he was persuading and chivvying the disparate anti-Unionist forces in Stormont to form a loose coalition that could act as an official opposition. By the end of 1969, he had managed to persuade ten of the thirteen MPs to take Shadow portfolios. This gave the opposition some of the flavour of an alternative government, and encouraged MPs to develop expertise in their field. It was leadership from the top, nonetheless, and Hume still favoured the formation of a single party to bring together all the anti-Unionist elements.

In pursuit of this goal he brought those crucial to the enterprise together for weekend talks at Bunbeg, a quiet holiday resort on the Donegal coast where tourists rent boats to visit the isle of Inishfree. They formed a diverse group: Hume, the thirty-two-year-old teacher-turned-businessman, deep and determined; Paddy O'Hanlon, even younger, the civil rights activist from Newry; Ivan Cooper, the former shirt factory manager, a Protestant and natural soap-box orator who had been a Unionist and had flirted with Labour before becoming a civil rights Independent (these three had closely-matched constituency organizations and had been elected on the same wave of political advance earlier that year), and Austin Currie, the youngest MP ever to be elected to Stormont when he was returned as a Nationalist in East Tyrone in 1964, and who had blazed a progressive trail with the first direct action of the civil rights movement.

Aligned to these four, but most unlike them, were the much older and more politically experienced Belfast pair, Gerry Fitt and Paddy Devlin. Fitt, who started his working life as a soap-boy in a barber's shop, was a merchant seaman for more than a decade and had served in the Arctic convoys to the Soviet Union during the Second World War. Self-educated in the law and politics, he left the sea and won election to Belfast City Corporation in 1958 for the waterfront Dock ward, beating a Unionist to move effortlessly into Stormont four years later. He had his own party, Republican Labour, and he became the most controversial Irish Nationalist voice at Westminster when he beat another Unionist to win West Belfast in 1966. Fitt and Devlin brought the necessary political ballast and, even more import-antly, the Belfast working-class dimension to what would otherwise have been a middle-class, intellectual – even 'Green Tory' (as the Nationalist right is sometimes insultingly called) – grouping.

Hume was conscious of the suspicion with which the two Belfast men regarded him. Devlin had publicly rebuked him for trying to 'fix' a Stormont Senate seat for his old Derry friend, Claud Wilton, while Fitt, injured in the 5 October march a year earlier, had noted his rival's discretion in street protests. There were also ideological differences. Fitt and Devlin belonged to the traditional Labour left, while Hume had been caught 'thinking aloud' in *Die Welt*, the Ger-man newspaper: 'The programme of the Labour Party is too Socialist, even today.' He wanted a party 'more in the centre, representing moderate Socialism'.

Nevertheless, what they shared was greater than that which divided them. Devlin argued: 'With the overwhelming need for real, not sectarian, politics, the growing inevitability of our position was that we should form a new broad-based labour party with a portfolio of reforming policies based on the civil rights demands.'⁹ The core of six MPs made no secret of their alliance – it would have been impossible in the goldfish-bowl of Northern Ireland politics, anyway. Weekend gatherings, punctuated by some serious socializing, gradually minimized their differences. The appearance of a potential rival, the Alliance Party, formed in April 1970 to unite Catholics and Protestants of moderate outlook, also concentrated their minds. In July 1970, Hume and Currie stayed up the whole of one Sunday night to compose a formal constitution for the new party.

There was almost a last-minute failure. Devlin claims he was tipped off by a friendly Catholic lawyer that Hume had been at another weekend meeting in Donegal discussing the formation of a Catholic political party. Devlin saw Hume's activities as not only divisive but aimed at strangling the cross-community party at birth. 'There was likely to have been a bit of self-interest on Hume's part,' he suggested later. 'In such a Catholic party he would have been the undisputed leader, whereas Gerry Fitt, as the most experienced and senior politician among us, with a seat at Westminster, was the obvious leader of our intended party.'[10]

In this version of events, both Devlin and Austin Currie moved quickly to defuse the situation by issuing statements that they were forming a new party, with Gerry Fitt as its leader. 'That's how Gerry became leader,' insists Devlin. 'It was not because of his great strengths. It was because John Hume could not be trusted with it.'[11]

With hindsight, Devlin insists it was right to protect the momentum of 'their' initiative and forestall any alternative plan by Hume. They subsequently claimed that Hume had met the stillborn National Democratic Party and members of the Nationalist Party to persuade them to join his nascent group. Typically, Devlin, devoutly anticlerical in politics, discerned the hand of the Catholic church in general and the deeply conservative cardinals in particular in this plot. He thought the church, anxious at the fading fortunes of the old-style Nationalist Party but even more fearful of socialism, wanted a party that was safer and more predictable than the new Stormont coalition with its radical agenda.

This near-fatal turn of events must have alerted Hume to the endemic strains in his new party. Devlin and Fitt thought that Hume saw them as 'some sort of political plague' or 'revolutionaries from black Belfast', while they suspected him of being unduly influenced by the church, and too hostile to their Labour background. But once the six MPs had signed the Bunbeg document, things settled down. Devlin saw this as a retreat by Hume: 'He quickly realized that we had pre-empted him, abandoned his own moves and immersed himself in the ongoing situation.'

They still did not have a name for their party, however, and this gave rise to another interminable argument. The MPs, together with Senator Paddy Wilson (later murdered by Loyalists) held a meeting at Toomebridge, County Antrim, at the mouth of Lough Neagh, famous for its eel fishing. To evade the media, the room was booked in the name of eel-fishing enthusiasts. The party's name proved harder to catch than the fish. The younger MPs, Hume and Currie, conscious of the German model, favoured the simple title of 'Social Democratic Party'.

Fitt and Devlin held out for the word 'Labour' to be included. Quite apart from their own socialist principles, they felt this would be necessary to attract voters in the industrial heartland of Belfast where Nationalism was less important among the Catholic working class than social issues. Indeed, Labour should not only be in the title, it should be the first word. Hume capitulated for the sake of harmony, and carried on with the agenda. Suddenly, Devlin awoke to the dangers of being known as 'the LSD party'. The title was hurriedly changed to Social Democratic and Labour Party, and has survived so for nearly thirty years.

While the would-be comrades were arguing about their new party, politics in the wider world had undergone a convulsion. Harold Wilson took his Labour government to a snap general election in the hot summer of June 1970, believing that good local council results in May and a 3 per cent lead in the opinion polls were enough to return him with an enhanced majority. He could not have been more wrong. Instead, Tory leader Edward Heath was propelled into Downing Street with a clear overall majority of thirty seats.

Northern Ireland had not been an election issue among British voters, who were more concerned with the state of the economy. Ulster politicians, however, particularly Hume and his colleagues, who felt they 'could do business' with the disarmingly avuncular James Callaghan, were now faced with a new Home Secretary, Reginald Maudling, of whom they knew very little but from whom they feared plenty. Not for nothing is the Tory Party correctly titled 'The Conservative and Unionist Party'. Historically, the Tories always listened receptively to Unionism. Callaghan detected a 'sense of liberation' in Protestant areas, where the people felt they were back in the ascendancy and could expect entirely new treatment. Maudling, a languid figure with no obvious interest in Northern Ireland, formally signalled his support for Labour's reforms, but the outgoing Home Secretary described the election outcome as 'a disaster for Northern Ireland'. His initiatives were not followed up, and the break in continuity came at 'the very worst time' in the struggle to prevent the Provisional IRA from capturing the sympathy of the nationalist community.

The Westminster general election had caught Hume, like everybody else, by surprise. The SDLP was still in preparation. Hume's Independent organization entered into an election pact, with Eddie McAteer's fading Nationalist Party in Derry, acting as his agent and drawing up its manifesto on much the same lines as Hume's own Stormont platform of the previous year. It was also understood that the Nationalists would merge with Hume's party when it was established. Strangely, McAteer described this as 'Mr Hume's finest hour'.

These were political gains for Hume on his own territory, but they went down badly elsewhere. Hume's support for McAteer rather than his Stormont allies' choice of Claud Wilton, who as a Protestant could have drawn votes from across the sectarian divide and given the social democratic movement valuable encouragement, merely intensified suspicions about his real agenda. Some of his parliamentary allies would not speak to him for a time, delaying progress towards a unified opposition party. Nor did the election pact work. Instead of McAteer, Robin Chichester-Clark, brother of the Northern Ireland Prime Minister, was returned with a majority of more than 12,000. Worrying also for Hume was the respectable vote of more than 7,500 for Eamonn McCann who was standing as an Independent Labour candidate.

So far that summer in Derry, the streets had been reasonably quiet. There was an affray in the city on Easter Sunday when two Republican parades commemorating the 1916 Rising (one Provisional, one Official – the split was now final) took place. Hume ritually condemned this breach of the peace. Then, only six days after the Westminster election, Derry was again gripped by rioting when Bernadette Devlin, just re-elected as MP for Mid-Ulster, was stopped at a roadblock outside the city and taken to Armagh prison to serve a six-month gaol sentence imposed for her part in the Derry riots the previous August. Fighting went on for two days.

Rioters who had welcomed the troops to their streets ten months earlier as a bulwark against the B-Specials now pelted them with petrol-bombs, and the Army replied with CS gas. Hume's supporters negotiated a truce with the authorities, but it was daily becoming more plain that the talking war was degenerating into a shooting war. 'Few issues of the *Derry Journal* went to press without another statement from Mr Hume reiterating his belief in the efficacy of "peaceful methods",' noted Eamonn McCann. The violence – mainly stone-throwing by young hooligans – settled into a regular pattern, despite a new Criminal Justice Act that laid down six-month mandatory gaol sentences for disorderly behaviour. Hume and his colleagues at Stormont supported this measure as part of a deal with the Unionists for a law against incitement to religious hatred.

In the political dog days of August 1970, according to Barry White, Hume 'decided to strike'. While on a visit to Dublin, he inspired the *Irish Times* to run a front-page story that a new political party was being formed in the North, and only the choice of a leader was holding back the public launch. The publicity baton was immediately picked up by Hume's ally Austin Currie, who went on Irish radio to deny there was any trouble over who was to be leader. It would be Gerry Fitt. He then rang Hume and told him what he had done. Hume concurred, saying the issue had dragged on too long.

The next step was to find Fitt, and confer the crown. Eventually he was tracked down by means of the public telephone in a bar near his holiday cottage in north Antrim, and invited to the Radio Telefis Eireann studio in Belfast. There, live on radio, he accepted the leadership proffered by Hume and Currie. 'It must have been the first time in history that an acceptance of party leadership had been made in response to a radio interviewer's question,' records White. 'Privately, Fitt was less buoyant. "This won't last," he told another doubtful participant, Paddy Devlin, "but it would be unfair not to try it." '[12] For once, Fitt's political sagacity deserted him. The SDLP would last, and Hume with it, while Fitt wandered into the political wilderness.

Against an unpromising backdrop of intensifying Provisional bomb attacks on the security forces and 'economic targets', the introduction of rubber bullets and sectarian killings, the SDLP was unveiled at a press conference in Belfast's Grand Central Hotel on 21 August 1970. Fitt prefaced his introduction of the Bunbeg document with an alarming warning. There was 'a real possibility that there might be an extreme right-wing takeover' of the government of Northern Ireland, wiping out the civil rights gains of the last eighteen months. He predicted that Westminster would intervene, and would want to hear the voices of those opposed to Unionism. Fitt also forcibly asserted the SDLP's anti-sectarian nature. He emphasized the party's left-of-centre credentials, including the just and adequate distribution of wealth, support for trade unions and co-operatives, a minimum wage and equal pay for women and a measure of state ownership of industry. The SDLP's third aim, journalists noted, was: 'To promote co-operation, friendship and understanding between North and South with a view to the eventual reunification of Ireland through the consent of the majority of the people in the North and the South.' Fitt argued for the continuation of Stormont 'at the present time' as it was the only institution that could bring about the desired reforms. 'We do not believe that Ireland can be united by violence,' he said. That was also Hume's central credo. Hume played a low-key role in the briefing, simply offering the hope that both communities in Northern Ireland would examine the SDLP's aims and make up their own mind.

The SDLP got a fair reception from the press, but old hands at Stormont were not convinced. Ken Bloomfield, deputy secretary to the Cabinet, conceded that the party's leading figures were articulate, engaging, as ready with a song or a 'jar' as with a manifesto, and happy to stay up half the night chatting to a visiting MP or Congressman. But he also observed that the new party contained within itself from the beginning 'a dangerous tension': an uneasy alliance between Belfast left-wing populists, 'republican-tending cadres' of the border areas obsessed with Irish unity and 'philosopher-kings' (exemplified above all by John Hume), who dreamed grand conceptual dreams, but who were characterized by Fitt, in unbuttoned moments, as 'those f——ing schoolmasters'.[13]

For the day, there was enough to celebrate. The party started life in two rented first-floor rooms in College Square, North Belfast, with a £1,000 bank loan and immeasurable optimism. Advertisements in the *Belfast Telegraph* offered membership for 50p, and some Protestants did join. The SDLP adopted an open attitude to the media, which was second nature to its leaders in any event, and generated much friendly publicity. In the current security climate, they wisely assumed that their mail was being screened and their phones intercepted. Almost the SDLP's first act at Stormont was to refuse to deal with a new hardline Home Affairs Minister, John Taylor, who bitterly opposed the civil rights reforms. That momentous year ended with Hume's dream in place, but with the Provisionals' campaign moving into gear. In 1970, twenty-five people died in the Troubles, there were 213 shootings and 170 bombs were planted.

In the New Year, 1971, the violence claimed its first British Army victim. In February the Provisional IRA shot Gunner Robert Curtis. RUC officers got their guns back. In early March, Reginald Maudling (who had famously said 'What a bloody awful country!' after his first visit to Northern Ireland) addressed both Houses of Stormont in a portentous speech that left SDLP MPs fuming. Hume said the visit had raised hopes of some British initiative on the way, but the speech had done nothing to satisfy those hopes.

Days later, the cold-blooded murder of three off-duty Scottish soldiers lured from a Belfast pub precipitated a new crisis. Chichester-Clark flew to London to ask for more troops to combat the IRA and restore military and police rule to the 'no-go' areas in Derry and Belfast. He was given 1,000 additional soldiers, which was not enough, and resigned on 20 March because he could 'see no other way of bringing home to all concerned the realities of the present constitutional, political and security situation'. He was replaced by

Brian Faulkner, scion of the Ulster business community, who struck up an immediate rapport with Edward Heath. The British Prime Minister made it clear that he wanted London's policy to continue.

From Hume and the SDLP's point of view, Faulkner made a promising start. In his Cabinet, he included a non-Unionist minister for the first time: David Bleakley, a former Northern Ireland Labour Party MP, became Minister for Community Relations. Faulkner announced a reasonably successful arms amnesty. He promised to be scrupulously fair to everyone, under the law. In June, the month Stormont celebrated its fiftieth anniversary, Faulkner offered the opposition an olive branch. He proposed all-party involvement in parliamentary committees, including three new ones dealing with social, environmental and industrial matters. The SDLP cautiously welcomed the move, despite its initial view that Faulkner had been 'one of the chief architects of Northern Ireland's sick society'.

However, John Hume had been pursuing a more ambitious agenda of his own. On 1 June, the newspapers carried long reports of a statement he had made to his local SDLP executive. In it he called for the 1920 Government of Ireland Act to be scrapped in favour of a new system that would neutralize sectarianism and encourage all sections of society to participate at every level. He invited Heath to declare the new system as a principle, and seek all those with an interest to give their views. 'Only then,' he said, 'can we begin to create a united and prosperous community.'

Pursuing his argument, Hume said the logic of the British intervention – starting in the Bogside in 1969 – had never been faced, either by Northern Ireland politicians or by the British government. 'The arrival of British troops to maintain law and order, the forcing by the Westminster government of a reform programme on Stormont and the continuing presence of British watchdogs is the clearest possible public admission that the Unionist government are and were incapable of governing Northern Ireland in peace, justice and stability. Their intervention when allied to the continuing presence of a Unionist government has created a situation of permanent instability in Northern Ireland, and we have no less than three Prime Ministers in two years to prove it.' No one should under-estimate the serious dangers inherent in the situation, he concluded.'[14]

In one sense, Hume was picking up the theme of Chichester-Clark's resignation speech: security is a critical function of the state, and if the Northern Ireland state could not police itself, then it could not continue in its present form. Faulkner utterly rejected this analysis, arguing that Stormont as parliament and government must be maintained. 'Direct rule would undoubtedly be a disaster,' he proclaimed in his first prime ministerial statement.

Hume was thinking beyond the immediate crisis, which was not susceptible to such easy solutions as giving a few opposition MPs seats (or even salaried chairs) on Unionist-dominated parliamentary committees. He pointed out that Faulkner's package was not even new, being derived from an inquiry into local government. Hume asked in the Stormont debate on 23 June for more details, saying Faulkner's proposals were 'fine words, and we will match them with equally fine words. But we would want to see fine actions following those words, and then we will equally match the actions of the Prime Minister and his government with our actions.' He was willing to admit that changes had been made, but posed the question: 'What has failed in Northern Ireland, other than the system no one wanted? Surely that is the lesson that is staring us in the face. And, are the confines of our discussion on the problems of Northern Ireland not too narrow? Should we be not discussing the system itself rather than tinkering with it any further?'

His rhetoric was not answered, but the SDLP withdrew an amendment calling for a select committee to recommend constitutional change. The debate ended on a note of optimism. It lasted only days. Faulkner and high-ranking Cabinet colleagues secretly met Orange Lodge leaders in Lurgan, County Armagh, to reassure them there was no 'sell-out' and they could go ahead with their provocative 'Twelfth' marches the following month. Hume was furious. How could anyone expect the Prime Minister to deal with this issue impartially 'when we had the pathetic sight of half a Cabinet being summoned to a secret society to be told what to do?' he asked. An embarrassed Faulkner held talks with MPs of all parties that week, in which everyone praised the 'helpful and constructive spirit' that prevailed.

This cosy, if fragile, calm was destroyed by events in Derry the next day, 8 July. During overnight rioting, two Bogsiders, Desmond Beattie and Seamus Cusack, were shot dead by soldiers. They were the first civilians to die at the hands of the army in John Hume's Derry. The Army said Cusack had been 'levelling a rifle to fire at soldiers', while Beattie was about to throw a nail-bomb. Hume made exhaustive inquiries into the case, and then said: 'I personally, publicly challenge the British Army to face an inquiry which will prove that they are telling lies about these deaths.' Accustomed to the authorities setting up such investigations – the Cameron and Scarman inquiries had substantially vindicated his conduct – Hume might genuinely have thought he could get to the truth on this occasion.

Circumstances had altered. In what was now a shooting war, Faulkner was not going to investigate each and every civilian death. He had already told Stormont (to the dismay of SDLP members) that any soldier seeing any person with a weapon or 'acting suspiciously may ... fire to warn or with effect without waiting for orders'. This became known as the 'shoot to kill' strategy.

In the face of ministerial intransigence, Hume called a council of war of SDLP colleagues, including O'Hanlon, Currie and Ivan Cooper, in his home in West End Park, Derry, on the following Sunday. While they debated, the Provisionals held their first mass rally in the area, appealing for recruits who literally queued up to join.

Hume came out of his house while the Provo rally was going on a few hundred yards away, and threatened that if the Westminster government did not set up an official inquiry, the SDLP would withdraw from Stormont, leaving the Northern Ireland Parliament without a credible opposition. Hume knew that if he did not try to do something convincing, something dramatic, the leadership of the Catholic community would slide into the hands of the Provisional IRA. Touring the Bogside earlier, he had been told scornfully, 'You'll never get anywhere, Johnnie, by doing the Stormont crawl.' Maudling refused to set up an inquiry, and withdrew an offer to ensure that soldiers testified at the inquests when the idea was leaked to the press. So there was nowhere to go but out.

On 16 July, the SDLP formally withdrew from Stormont. In a statement drafted by Hume, delivered to a press conference in a

Belfast hotel, the party said that as responsible public servants unable to secure action on an issue that had outraged their constituents, they felt no role was left for them in the present parliamentary system. If British troops had shot dead civilians in a riot in Birmingham, what would have been the reaction of the British public? Would there have been an inquiry? The statement complained of 'the virtual disappearance of due process of law and democratic checks on army excesses'.

Hume accused the Heath administration of having no real policy beyond reacting to events and hoping that the problem would run away. 'Insofar as we can detect any definite policy, it would appear to be the maintenance of Stormont in its present form carrying out minimum civil rights reforms and involving the Opposition only to a point where the Unionist right-wing would not be alienated. In other words, British policy is still governed as it always has been, except for a few short months in 1969, by the threat of a right-wing backlash. There can be no solution until the right-wing is confronted.'

There was more to the withdrawal than tactics. Hume was also pursuing a strategy of undermining the corrupt Stormont system. Pulling out was a calculated blow, designed to rob the fifty-year-old 'statelet' of its credibility. 'We have now been driven to the point where we have been faced with a clear choice: either to continue to give credibility to the system which is itself basically unstable, and from which derives the unrest that is destroying our community, or take a stand . . .' he said. Henry Kelly, northern editor of the *Irish Times*, was in no doubt about what had happened: 'From the day the SDLP left Stormont, the whole future of the parliament, the government and the entire system, was in serious and escalating doubt.'[15]

The province's top civil servant, Ken Bloomfield, later agreed with this analysis. Hume's decision, he said, may well have been strategic rather than tactical 'since of all Northern Ireland politicians he has been the most inclined to think in grand conceptual terms and in long-term time scales'. In spite of Faulkner's olive branches and the SDLP's participation in the all-party talks only days before, 'Hume may well have come to the conclusion that the situation demanded more radical change than could be delivered by even the most able Unionist leader within the Stormont system."[16]

Conscious that the vacuum created by their withdrawal from Stormont would be filled by the IRA, Hume and his fellow-parliamentarians set up an 'alternative assembly', which would be charged with being (in Devlin's words) 'a new and effective forum, to keep up a political output to the media and maintain leadership of our constituents'. It met only twice, amid much media derision, in the ballroom of Dungiven Castle. Nevertheless the very fact of its existence proved a continuing goad to Faulkner, and a reminder of lost opportunities.

With Stormont in summer recess, and the violence escalating – bombings virtually doubled from June to July – the Unionists began casting around for solutions. John Taylor, the hardline Home Affairs Minister, openly canvassed the re-introduction of internment for terrorist suspects without trial. Hume had already warned against this draconian step, arguing that the security situation needed an 'acceptable police force' rather than a round-up of the usual suspects.

The trouble was that this time the authorities did not know who the real suspects were. Their intelligence was dated and inadequate. Gerry Adams has recorded that after a three-day army curfew in the Falls Road in July 1970, 'recruitment to the IRA was massive'. Internment *had* worked before, in the 1950s, when the identities of veteran republicans, often living in rural border areas, were well known. But the Provisionals' new cadres were drawn from the warrens of the city streets. Moreover, they were an organic part of a minority population that (rightly or wrongly) felt itself under threat, initially from the RUC and now from the British Army. Nor, given the withdrawal of the SDLP (the largest body of non-Unionist opinion) from Stormont, could Faulkner expect the Irish government to introduce reciprocal internment south of the border, as it had before.

Those were the arguments ranged against internment. But Faulkner was under pressure from his own people to act, and by the end of July a majority in favour of locking up the Provos existed in his Cabinet. The Northern Ireland Prime Minister flew to London on 5 August in conditions of great secrecy. He was hustled into the back door of 10 Downing Street for talks with Heath, his senior ministers and security chiefs. Unfortunately, an Irish journalist spotted him being whisked back to RAF Northolt, and in very short order press speculation about the imminent imposition of internment was rife. Security chiefs brought forward the round-up by twenty-four hours to 9 August.

They were too late. Most of the birds had flown south, over the border. Of the 452 republicans targeted throughout the province, 342 were arrested. Of these, 105 were released within two days. In Dublin, the IRA boasted that only thirty-five of its men had been 'lifted'. Militarily, the internment operation was a failure. Politically, it was a disaster. No Loyalists were seized, confirming in the minds of the Catholic community the one-sided nature of the exercise, and hardening support for the Provisionals. Mayhem ensued. Within three days, twenty-two people had died in riots, and 7,000 people – mainly Catholics – had been driven from their homes by arson. The pogrom forced more than 2,000 Catholics to flee to makeshift refugee camps in the Republic. As a means of diminishing the violence, internment was hopelessly counter-productive. Previously, thirty-four people had died. Afterwards, the figure rose to 140.

In Derry, Hume was dismayed. Woken during the night by relatives of men who had been taken away, he tried to get answers from the RUC, but failed. Working on information received, he drove out to Magilligan Point, a flat sandy promontory at the mouth of the river Foyle, and was just in time to see a furniture van full of internees being driven through roadblocks into a disused Second World War army camp. For days, anguished constituents came to the door of his house overlooking the teeming streets of the Bogside with harrowing stories of what had happened to their menfolk. There was little he could do. Hume led peaceful protests, including a sit-down when he and the other demonstrators were sprayed by the Army with purple dye. The days of street dissent were over. Hume was arrested.

The SDLP still had political clout, however, if only in a negative form. Hume and his colleagues broke off all links with the Faulkner administration. In the words of John Campbell, Edward Heath's biographer: 'The search for a political solution was suspended, since the SDLP leaders John Hume and Gerry Fitt, had no option but to refuse any co-operation with Faulkner as long as it [internment] continued.'[17] Nor could Heath himself move on the half-envisioned next step: the abolition of Stormont and the imposition of direct rule from London. This was the declared aim of the IRA, in its projected plan for the reunification of Ireland. Heath could not possibly be seen to be making concessions to the Provisionals, and in talks at Chequers with Faulkner on 19 August, he 'utterly ruled out' intervention by Westminster.

Meanwhile, the barricades were back up in Derry and a rent and rates strike was in full swing. The SDLP leadership threw its weight behind a campaign of peaceful civil disobedience, and withdrew councillors from local government and its representatives from other official bodies. Internment had united middle- and working-class antagonism towards the state, the very reverse of Faulkner's stated aim – confirmed in a Green Paper that October – of broadening the basis of Northern Ireland government by involving the minority.

Hume ignored these blandishments and went ahead the same day with his much-vaunted 'Catholic parliament for a Catholic people', the Alternative Assembly. It met for the first time on 26 October. About fifty 'moderate' Nationalists turned up to hear Hume say: 'Today, we do not recognize the authority of the Stormont parliament, and we do not care twopence whether this is treason or not. Ever since partition, we have had government without consensus, because the free consensus of all the people has not been given by the system of government, and when you have a situation like that, you have a situation of permanent instability, and when you have permanent instability, you have recurring acts of violence, and surely that has been the history of fifty years of this system of government.'

Four days later, the Rev. Ian Paisley began predicting the end of 'this system of government'. Launching his new Democratic Unionist Party (DUP) at Belfast City Hall on 30 October, he forecast the end of Stormont and the imposition of direct rule from Westminster. In default of the SDLP, the Democratic Unionists formed an opposition composed of Paisley and Desmond Boal, a brilliant but quixotic lawyer. Boal sought a broad-based opposition to Faulkner's government, and in mid-November invited Hume and his fellow-SDLP MPs to talks at his home on the County Down coast. This was the start of an unlikely pragmatic partnership. The strange relationship survived Paisley's sneers of 'Saint Hume', and Hume's assertion that Paisley's church 'will die', right up to the preparations for elections for the Northern Ireland peace forum, in mid-1996. In late 1971, according to Paisley's biographers, the two groups 'found broad areas of agreement in their opposition to internment, support for state investment and belief in better cross-border relations'.[18]

Another initiative came from the Labour Party, whose leader Harold Wilson was asked by Heath to sound out the SDLP's willingness to join in a round of political talks on the future governance of Northern Ireland. Wilson had himself put together a twelve-point plan to restore balance, which envisaged a Cabinet minister based in Belfast reporting to Westminster, and proportional representation for all elections in the province. This was a precursor of the concept of a Northern Ireland Secretary, and alarm bells began ringing in Stormont Castle. Cabinet Secretary Ken Bloomfield prepared papers for Faulkner on possible responses to Westminster moves to curtail the powers of his government, or even its complete suspension. At the close of the year, the death toll from the Troubles was 174. There had been, 1,756 shootings, and 1,515 bombs had been planted.

Nor were the SDLP leaders immune from the violence; indeed, they were prime targets. At least one plot to assassinate Hume had been exposed. Loyalists from the notorious Burntollet area were detected watching him as he drove through the area at night from Belfast to Derry. There was also a melodramatic bid on his life at Belfast's Aldergrove airport, when Hume and Paddy Devlin were en route to London to brief MPs before a debate on Northern Ireland. As Devlin later told the story, the pair were waiting in the lounge for their flight, when a 'wild-eyed' young man pulled a gun on them from inside his bomber-jacket. One of the two plain-clothes RUC officers escorting them knocked him down and the other retrieved the gun as it went spinning across the floor. Hume and Devlin were naturally relieved, but as they went to the barrier for their aircraft, one of the detectives grabbed Devlin by the sleeve and begged him not to give their names to the newspapers. 'For Christ's sake,' he urged, 'if some of my relatives in Londonderry hear that I saved you and Hume, I'll never be able to go back home again.'[19]

SIX

THE DEATH OF STORMONT

THE NEW YEAR OF 1972 found John Hume in a state resembling political limbo. He was an MP, but boycotting parliament. He was still a respected figure in Derry, but his influence was being undermined among his own people by the Provisional IRA, which was engaged daily in violent clashes with the Army. His argument in favour of an Irish dimension had borne some fruit in the first meeting of British, Irish and Northern Ireland prime ministers, but the talks at Chequers had come to nothing. Edward Heath was musing about all-party talks at Westminster, but no invitations went out. It was a sterile period, and one fraught with danger. Faulkner presided over a government that was, in the words of one commentator, 'in the oldest, and strictest sense of the word, corrupt. It had no mandate from the people, no genuine support, and no ultimate hope of survival.'[1] In the absence of political initiatives, the IRA intensified its bombing campaign, injuring sixty people, mainly women and children, with one bomb in the commercial heart of Belfast.

With the detestation of internment so strong among Catholics, Hume and his colleagues in the SDLP leadership felt they simply could not talk to anyone. Gerry Fitt said on BBC radio: 'If we talked now, we would be representing nobody.' He had been intending to say that he would talk while internment was still on, but the others made him remove this modest proposal from his script. Internment dominated their thinking, and in this they were only taking their cue from their constituents, even though it stultified all political policy-making.

Hume decided to lead from the front in the opposition to internment. In mid-January, he marched at the head of an anti-internment rally on the sands of the Magilligan peninsula at the mouth of the Foyle. All marches and rallies had been banned for a year when internment was introduced, but Hume took 2,000 demonstrators on a five-mile route march across rough ground to the seashore. Dr Raymond McLean recalled: 'We started across the strand in determined mood, singing "We Shall Overcome". I had a vague, uneasy feeling that the words of the song might be a bit optimistic.'[2]

Barbed-wire barricades had been strung along the shore, right down to the water's edge, and soldiers in riot gear stood behind them. An army officer said they could proceed no further because 'this is Ministry of Defence Property', while the marchers argued that the sand belonged to all of them. They continued walking, while Hume 'spoke heatedly' with the officer in charge, demanding the right to demonstrate in his own country against 'the evil' of internment, which by this date had taken 882 men into its net.

Some marchers began walking into the sea to get round the wire, moving the barricade aside. 'Suddenly, the soldiers charged forward with batons waving, smashing everyone on sight. The crowd broke in panic and we started running back across the sand, through water, sand, seaweed and anything that came in the way,' recorded Dr McLean. The army action was brief, but vicious. Some soldiers shouted, 'fuck you, fucking Paddy bastard', and kicked those who fell while fleeing. Scores of marchers were injured, several suffering severe skull lacerations. Hume regrouped his marchers, but the soldiers charged again, firing rubber bullets and CS gas into the crowd, driving them off the strand. The whole scene was filmed by television cameras. Hume accused the army of 'beating, brutalising and terrorising the demonstrators'. As they nursed their wounds on the bus journey home, the marchers agreed that from the point of view of political profile Hume had done well, but the British had not paid much heed to him.

The soldiers belonged to the Parachute Regiment, operating in the Derry area for the first time. Dr McClean had served as a medical officer with them in Bahrain, and knew they were the elite corps of the British Army, hand-picked volunteers of fearsome combat ability. Their behaviour sparked intense speculation about a shift in emphasis and a much tougher line from the authorities. The still active

Northern Ireland Civil Rights Association had signalled its intention to hold an anti-internment rally in Derry eight days later, and Hume was deeply apprehensive. A new, shadowy body, the National Resistance Movement, formed by members of People's Democracy and Provisional Sinn Fein, was associated in the planning of the demonstration. He was approached to speak at the rally, but declined, warning that the Paras were in an ugly mood. The local SDLP branch also decided not to take part, though it allowed individuals to do so, after hearing from Hume that 'someone will be killed'. Rumours were rife that the Paras were being brought into the city for the day, though the IRA had privately assured the march organizers that they would stay away so that the people could make their protest.

The march that Sunday afternoon started in the Creggan, a bleak housing estate on the south-western outskirts of the city, and wound its way through the Bogside. These were both still 'no-go' areas to the Army and the RUC. About 15,000 marched, and they felt their numbers had made the point. The march ended in Rossville Street, by Free Derry Corner, where the police and soldiers were drawn up in force. What was described as 'a run-of-the-mill riot' ensued, with rioters throwing stones and soldiers responding with CS gas, rubber bullets and water-cannon spraying water dyed purple on the marchers at high pressure. Then, four sharp cracks in rapid succession were heard towards the back of the march, quite unlike the sound of rubber bullets. 'In an instant, with no warning, there was an inrush of terror as the Paras erupted into Rossville Street and the slaughter began,' recollected Eamonn McCann.[3] Minutes later, thirteen men and teenage boys lay dead or dying in the vicinity.

Hume had stayed at home, on call, in West End Park, overlooking the scene of the march. He clearly heard the shots ring out and turned to his wife Pat with the words: 'That's it. There it goes. The lid's really off now.'[4] It was, with a vengeance. Once more, his living room became a crisis centre. Paddy Devlin, who had been on the march, went at once to Hume's house and found him 'in deep shock'. He proposed throwing out the reporters who were commandeering the phone to file their stories and Hume assented: 'Go ahead. Get our own people in here to the parlour and let's agree a strategy on this.'[5] Later, he visited Altnagelvin Hospital to visit the wounded and break the bad news to distraught relatives.

The next day, Hume said in an Irish radio interview on the walls of Derry city: 'Many people down there [the Bogside] feel now that it's a United Ireland or nothing. Alienation is pretty total.' Unionists were not slow to pick up this comment, and turn it into Hume's own opinion, even into SDLP policy. He shrugged off this deliberate misrepresentation, but it came back to haunt him down the years at election times.

Hume also advised his people to have nothing to do with the public inquiry into the shootings announced on 1 February, to be conducted by the Lord Chief Justice, Lord Widgery, a former Lieu-tenant Colonel in the Royal Artillery, a regiment that regularly did tours of duty in the province. Hume wondered aloud why Widgery regarded himself as suitable for the role. It would be 'A British judgement on a British crime'. He wanted something more indepen-dent, preferably an international tribunal. Eventually, when nine priests decided to give evidence, most Catholics relented and fol-lowed suit. Widgery's report, rushed out two months later, blamed the organizers of the march for setting up a confrontation, admitted that none of those killed or wounded 'is proved to have been shot while handling a firearm or bomb', but paradoxically found that 'there is no reason to suppose that the soldiers would have opened fire if they had not been fired on first'. The report was regarded as a whitewash in Catholic Derry.

For now, there was an urgent political crisis. Heath decided to take the issue out of bumbling Maudling's hands and put it at the top of his own agenda. He called for all the papers and began the search for a political initiative. Douglas Hurd, then working in Heath's private office and later a Northern Ireland Secretary himself, said ministers 'went back to first principles' on Ireland. There was talk of 'discontinuity', some event that would draw a line and make possible a fresh beginning.[6] Heath was reluctant to impose direct rule, preferring instead to take away Faulkner's responsibility for security and leave him in charge of a county-council-style adminis-tration. Faced with this option the Northern Ireland Prime Minister decided that his government would rather resign *en masse*, and privately told Heath so.

Events, the old politicians' nightmare, forced Heath's hand. In Dublin, a mob burned down the British embassy. Ireland recalled its ambassador from London and declared a national day of mourning. In Westminster, Bernadette Devlin crossed the floor of the Commons and physically attacked the Home Secretary. In Armagh, the Official IRA shot John Taylor, the Home Affairs Minister of State, six times (mostly in the head), but he survived. In Aldershot, the IRA planted a bomb in the barracks of 16 Parachute Brigade, killing seven, including a Catholic army priest. In Belfast, the Provisionals tricked people into the vicinity of a 100lb car-bomb, killing four shoppers and two policemen.

It could not go on like this. On 22 March, over scallops mornay, roast beef and fine wines at Downing Street, Heath told Faulkner that his ideas for political reform were not good enough. There must be a constitutional referendum, a move towards ending internment, the appointment of a Secretary of State for Northern Ireland, and 'open-ended talks' with the SDLP aimed at agreeing a community government. Worst of all, Stormont must hand over law and order to London. Faulkner refused, and Heath suspended Stormont two days later. A quarter of a century later, it still lies empty and unused, a testament to the vanity of 'No Surrender' Unionist hegemony. With the resignation of the Faulkner administration, William Whitelaw became Secretary of State for Northern Ireland. He had visited the province only twice, the first time before the Second World War to attend a birthday party and the second to play golf in the 1950s. He brought an open mind. On the day his appointment was announced, he told a meeting of Harrow Conservatives: 'The solution will not be found by military means alone. It will only be found in the hearts and minds of men and women.'[7]

John Hume could scarcely have put it better, but he was still keeping up the SDLP's boycott of public office and political contacts. Whitelaw wanted to 'give hope to the Catholics of a new standing in the community'. It was difficult for him to do so without further enraging the Protestants, who were furious about the suspension of 'their' parliament. Nevertheless, Whitelaw began a cautious programme of internee releases, and lifted the ban on marches and demonstrations.

It was clear he would go further if the climate improved, and indeed it did, prompted by the Official IRA committing a murderous political blunder. Private William Best, a nineteen-year-old Royal Irish Rangers soldier on home leave in the Creggan, was abducted, 'tried' by a kangaroo court and shot in the back of the head. His murder shocked Derry people, including the Catholic community. Four hundred women besieged the local headquarters of the Official IRA, who called off their limited involvement in the violence.

Hume seized the opportunity of an emerging peace movement to proclaim the end of his party's boycott of public office 'as a demonstration of our determination to bring about community reconciliation', and to appeal for a ceasefire. 'We ask those engaged in the campaign of violence to cease immediately in order to enable us to bring internment to a speedy end and in order to make a positive response to the British government's proposals. We also ask for an immediate cessation of political arrests by the British Army and the RUC,' the SDLP leadership said. They also made overtures to the Protestants, saying: 'We do not regard our political achievements as a victory over you.' Rather, they were an opportunity for all. 'We recognize that many of you feel isolated in present circumstances. You are not. You are our fellow-countrymen and we are yours. Together a great opportunity awaits us.'

The Provisionals did not agree to a ceasefire, but did outline their terms for a truce: a release of all internees, still numbering around 400; the withdrawal of British troops to barracks; and an amnesty for acts of violence already committed. At a press conference behind the barricades in 'Free Derry', Sean MacStiofain, the Provos' Chief of Staff, offered a seven-day ceasefire if the army ended arrests, halted searches and stopped harassing civilians. Hume knew from his contacts that the Provisionals were serious about a truce. They had not made the ending of internment a pre-condition for a ceasefire, but they did have two demands before talking: the granting of 'political' status to a group of IRA prisoners who had gone on hunger strike in Belfast's Crumlin Road gaol, and the temporary release from detention of Gerry Adams, then aged twenty-five, brilliant but virtually unknown outside Republican circles, so that he could take part in any negotiations.

Hasty arrangements were then made with Whitelaw's private office for a meeting between the Northern Ireland Secretary and Hume, who took Paddy Devlin with him. The talks took place in London on 15 June, and concentrated first on how to remove obstacles preventing talks between the SDLP and the new occupant of Stormont Castle. Then, Whitelaw said internment could only be fully ended after a two-week break in the violence. An amnesty was not ruled out. Whitelaw was also willing in principle to grant 'special category' status to the prisoners, but not while the violence raged. Furthermore, he and the security forces would respond to any genuine end to violence.

Hume and Devlin flew to Dublin to meet the other four SDLP Stormont MPs, convinced they had the makings of a ceasefire deal. Over lunch at the Royal Dublin Hotel they secured the backing of their colleagues and, so armed, set off to find the Provos. Initially, they had no idea where to find them, and were passed from one emissary to another. Eventually they were told to go to a pub in Donegal town; here they were told to go to Hume's house in Derry and await further directions.

'The Provo leadership exists on the run, so getting the runaround like this was not unusual,' recalled Devlin.[8] He was catnapping on the sofa when a messenger came in the early hours of Saturday, 17 June, to take the pair to a safe house in the nearby Creggan estate. There, Hume and Devlin met MacStiofain and Daithi O'Connaill, Northern Ireland's two most wanted men. O'Connaill, wounded in a gun battle with the RUC during the 1950s' IRA campaign, was the more impressive of the two. Hume and Devlin explained their mission, outlined Whitelaw's message and answered questions as best they could. Later that morning, they reported back to Whitelaw in Belfast.

From Hume's standpoint, the mission was highly successful. The British government agreed to 'special category' status for convicted prisoners, which allowed more visits and the use of civilian clothes. Astonishingly, Whitelaw also agreed to meet the Provos face to face, even offering to use a house near Derry belonging to a relative. This suggestion was vetoed, and Northern Ireland officials were chosen for the preparatory talks. Devlin rounded up a number of senior Provisional figures, and brought them to Belfast with the aid of safe conduct letters from the Army. Hume and Devlin met Whitelaw again to discuss the ceasefire terms. Adams was released temporarily, with thirteen others alongside him to disguise what was really happening. The IRA high command held a strategy meeting in Belfast, and then took part in talks with Whitelaw's civil servants at the house near Derry. Position papers were exchanged, and two days later the IRA in Dublin announced a ceasefire operational from midnight, 26 June. The statement said that hostilities were being suspended 'provided that a public reciprocal response is forthcoming from the armed forces of the British crown'. The IRA called for 'meaningful talks between the major parties in the conflict'.

The ceasefire was a major coup for Hume. He had been obliged to prevaricate about his role in the negotiations, simply saying he was engaged in 'a public dialogue'. He would not say he was meeting the Provisionals, and he would not say he wasn't. 'They hear what I'm saying,' he teased reporters.

Talks between the British government and leaders of the Provisional IRA took place on 7 July. The IRA men were flown to London in an RAF aircraft, and smuggled into the London home of Paul Channon, Minister of State at the Northern Ireland Office and scion of the Guinness family. The meeting was, in Whitelaw's own words, 'a non-event'. It was over in less than an hour. The IRA made impossible demands, including a commitment that British troops leave the province within two years, a public declaration of the Irish people's right, North and South, to self-determination and an amnesty for 'prisoners of war'. Whitelaw told them the British government would never concede such impossible demands. The ceasefire held for a few more days, then failed amid sectarian violence in Belfast over the allocation of houses to Catholic families in the Lenadoon area. Hume rang O'Connaill in Dublin, angry and mystified that the IRA could 'throw this whole thing away' over a housing issue. O'Connaill snapped back: 'We're on a new plane now and we won't need you next time. It'll be Heath and us next time.'[9]

The killing resumed immediately, thirty-three dying in the first week of renewed hostilities. On 'Bloody Friday', 21 July, the IRA set off twenty-two bombs in Belfast in little over an hour, and the television pictures of policemen shovelling bits of bodies into plastic bags at a bus station so repelled Whitelaw that he ordered a military strike forthwith. After giving several hours' warning, the army deployed 1,200 troops to destroy the barricades and end the 'no-go' areas in Derry and Belfast. Operation Motorman was a success, in that the authorities could now patrol areas that had been off-limits for a year. 'Free Derry was finished, for the time being anyway,' said McCann. Hume said the local people were 'resentful but resigned', and called for continued restraint.

The whole episode of the ceasefire and the IRA's mishandling of an opportunity created by hard work and patient diplomacy initially filled Hume and his colleagues with deep dismay. They could scarcely believe the Provisionals' political naïvety and negotiating incompetence. For the SDLP, remarked Devlin, it was a salutary lesson, for it showed that the IRA was incapable of engaging in the political process. However, the Provisionals' intransigence opened more doors for Hume. Now that the IRA had ruled itself out, he had a freer hand. Since the Provisionals had engaged in dialogue while internment continued, so could he.

The day after Operation Motorman, Hume and his fellow-MPs gathered at a hotel in Lifford, in the Irish Republic, to map out their strategy for the future. They were united in their resentment of 'increased militarization', but drew back from criticizing the security forces for fear of playing into the hands of the Provos. Instead, they issued a statement praising the calm response to what was unquestionably a military invasion of the Catholic areas, saying: 'In the present situation, restraint and silence are the best expressions of resentment.'

The rural calm of County Donegal was interrupted by a telephone summons from the Irish government to attend urgent talks in Dublin. An Irish Army helicopter collected Hume, Ivan Cooper and Paddy Devlin from the hotel car park for a meeting with ministers at the Foreign Affairs office. Hours later, the trio was whisked back to Lifford by car, some of them irritated by the suspicion that they had been used as pawns in the Fianna Fail party's bid to bolster its faltering electoral fortunes. Nevertheless, they were back in the poker game.

The day after this mystifying trip, Whitelaw arranged for talks with Hume and the other SDLP leaders at the government's clandestine 'safe house', Laneside, a secluded villa on the south shore of Belfast Lough. There, on 7 August, Whitelaw began his search for 'community government' that would involve the Catholic minority. The chief obstacle was still internment. The Northern Ireland Secretary offered the SDLP a new system of judicial tribunals, with no juries and presided over by three judges, before which the internees would appear to prove they were not engaged in terrorist activity. Hume and his colleagues instantly rejected this proposal, because it overturned the principle of assuming innocence until guilt was proven, and the SDLP could not be party to a further erosion of justice. A disappointed Whitelaw refused to give a date for the phasing-out of internment.

Soon after, Whitelaw wrote to all seven parties that had MPs in the suspended Stormont Parliament, inviting them to a round-table conference in the northern English town of Darlington. In a move designed to sell this conference to the SDLP, Heath invited Hume and his fellow-MPs for talks at Chequers. On 12 September they ranged down on one side of a magnificent dining table with the Prime Minister in splendid isolation on the other side. The SDLP leaders complained bitterly about internment for three hours, but Heath, while hinting at radical political concessions, would not give a commitment on a date for the ending of detention without trial. In the absence of that pledge, Hume's party said it would boycott the Darlington conference.

They did not have to be there in the flesh, however, to influence its deliberations. Hume wrote the final version of a definitive policy paper to be tabled for the government and for the three parties – the Ulster Unionists, Alliance and the Northern Ireland Labour Party – which did attend. This document, *Towards a New Ireland*, contained seven proposals for a new basis for the governance of Ireland. Foremost among these was a call for Britain to declare that it would positively encourage a united Ireland, but only on terms acceptable to both North and South. That is, the UK government would join the ranks of the 'persuaders' for a united Ireland. Until unification was achieved, the whole country would be run as a UK-Irish condominium, with London and Dublin controlling their own areas of foreign affairs, defence, security, finance, and the police. It further proposed an eighty-four-member Assembly, elected by proportional representation and joint action 'to plan the integration of North and South'. The Union flag and the Irish tricolor would be flown side by side, and Northern Ireland would have its own flag. The document was published with a flourish simultaneously in Belfast and Dublin, and SDLP leaders believed it would dominate the conference even though they were not there, by locking the other parties and the government into their agenda. Substantially, that proved to be the case.

Darlington brought Hume's ideas to the forefront of political discussion. To a remarkable degree, they were reflected in a Green Paper, *The Future of Northern Ireland*, published by Whitelaw the next month. Looking at the form of government in the province, the discussion paper said: 'There are strong arguments that the objective of real participation should be achieved by giving minority interests a share in the exercise of executive power.' There must be a search for 'a much wider consensus than has hitherto existed', and any new Assembly to replace Stormont must be capable of involving all its members constructively in ways which satisfied them and those they represented. As a minimum, minority groups would have to believe they would have an effective voice and 'a real influence'.

This was the language of power-sharing, and it was music to Hume's ears. So, too, was the insistence on an Irish dimension, another priority for Hume, which was now spelled out clearly. Whatever arrangements were made for the future, the administration of Northern Ireland 'must take account of the province's relationship with the Republic', the Green Paper insisted. And it was 'clearly desirable' that any new plan would be acceptable to and accepted by, the Republic. One element in the Whitelaw blueprint that the SDLP did not like was the proposal for a plebiscite in Northern Ireland on the future of the border, to be held the following year. However, having seen so much of his thinking incorporated into the Green Paper, Hume thought it was now necessary to drop the boycott of formal contacts with the government. At the SDLP's third annual conference in Dungiven in November, he appealed to delegates: 'I think the time has come for us to come out and say frankly we are prepared to talk to anyone and to talk now.' His strategy was endorsed by delegates.

Nineteen seventy-two had been the most bloody year of the Troubles, with 467 shootings and the planting of 10,628 bombs. More than 500 people had been charged with terrorist offences.

On 1 January 1973, both Britain and the Irish Republic became members of the European Economic Community. This accession, achieved by Edward Heath with the active support of many Labour MPs, brought a new dimension into the seemingly eternal Ulster question. Henceforth, the UK and Eire would be working together as partners in the great European project, with unforeseeable implications for the border. Hume, a fluent French-speaker who had taken European social democratic parties (particularly the German SPD) as models for the SDLP, was a genuine European. He was, by now, as well versed in coping with continental television and press interviews as with the domestic media. Going into Europe, he believed, would put the 'Irish problem' in a new perspective from which moderate Nationalists like himself could only gain. For the same reason, some Unionists were deeply suspicious of this development.

Reaping the benefits of this shift in perception was going to take some time. The SDLP's first priority in the new year was to get itself in shape for three polls: the referendum on the border, set for 8 March; local government elections in May; and the election, by proportional representation, of an Assembly proposed in a White Paper by William Whitelaw setting out the government's intentions for the future. These would be a critical test of the new party, which was fighting under its own colours for the first time. Membership was climbing respectably, though it was top-heavy with middle-class professionals (particularly teachers) and remnants of the old Nationalist Party. Many were political novices, and would need knocking into shape before they went anywhere near a voter's front door. Hume was instrumental in putting together briefing papers on every aspect of party policy: law and order, the economy, health, social services, education and so on. These documents served as the basis for a seminar for prospective candidates held in Donegal.

Before the border poll could be held, a brief but intimidatory episode darkened the scene. Early in February two men held in connection with the murder of a Catholic workman in Belfast became the first two Protestant internees. The Loyalist Association of Workers called a general strike for their release, and power cuts hit much of the province. Transport, industry and schools were disrupted, and there were violent clashes with the security forces in which five died. The strike lasted only a day, but it was a foretaste of what hard-line Loyalists could do. That they had the muscle to do it was well understood. 'If Protestants ever want to bring Northern Ireland to its knees, all they need to do is strike,' wrote Henry Kelly, northern editor of the *Irish Times*.

Hume and his colleagues urged SDLP supporters to boycott the border poll, but they did seek to extend the hand of amity towards the Protestant community with an unprecedented, full-page advertisement in the *Belfast News Letter* just before polling day. The advertisement explained party policy and asked, 'What is the alternative to partnership?' The predictable answer in the border poll was a 97.8 per cent 'Yes' to the question 'Do you want Northern Ireland to remain part of the United Kingdom?' The turnout was a shade under 58 per cent, which showed that most Catholics had supported the boycott.

Having given the Unionists this risk-free reassurance, Whitelaw unveiled his plans for the province twelve days later. His White Paper provided for an Assembly of seventy-eight members, elected by proportional representation, as Hume had argued. It would be elected for four years, and it would have an Executive which could not be controlled by any one party if it drew its support from only one side of the community. This sentence spelled the end of Unionist ascendancy. Given the disposition of the electorate, it was inevitable that some SDLP politicians would serve on the Executive, to which the former powers of Stormont (with the exception of security, law and order and the conduct of elections) would be restored. Power-sharing had arrived. The White Paper also proposed further anti-discrimination laws and discussions with Dublin on an All-Ireland

Council to be set up in concert with the Irish Republic. The Unionists grudgingly agreed to give the White Paper a chance to work. Hume, while unhappy that the Irish dimension did not go far enough, none the less pledged his party's involvement in the experiment.

In the run-up to the Assembly elections, the SDLP did well in the local elections in May. The party fielded 166 candidates, and eighty-three were elected, making the SDLP – at its electoral debut – the second largest party in Northern Ireland after the Unionists, with 13.4 per cent of the poll. Labour co-operated with the government in rushing through the Northern Ireland Assembly Bill, and polling day was set for 28 June, just fourteen weeks after the White Paper was published.

The SDLP campaigned vigorously on a platform of making the proposed Council of Ireland work, as a preparatory stage towards unification. Hume also aroused the wrath of Protestants by taking out full-page advertisements demanding a new police force reflecting both sides of the community in the place of the RUC, an end to internment and an amnesty. He also remarked on the folly of expecting a miracle from power-sharing. 'There is no point in trying to fool the people that if Brian Faulkner and Gerry Fitt sit down in an Executive together the Northern Ireland problem will be solved.'[10]

Despite the inevitable toll of violence in the election campaign – Paddy Wilson, Gerry Fitt's election agent, was one of the victims – turnout on polling day was high, at more than 72 per cent. The SDLP confirmed its place as the second largest party, taking 22 per cent of the first preference places to win nineteen seats. The Unionist camp was split between Faulkner's Official Unionists, who supported power-sharing, and anti-White Paper Unionists. Faulkner, with twenty-one seats, would have to rely on Hume's SDLP and the smaller parties to make the new system work.

Months of political horse-trading ensued. It was October before the main parties met at Stormont Castle under Whitelaw's chairmanship to share out the Executive portfolios. Hume's work in preparing the Donegal policy papers was influential in convincing Faulkner, the Chief Executive, that the SDLP could handle big ministerial jobs. When the division of the spoils was finally agreed, Hume's party had four of the Executive seats and six of the fifteen ministerial posts. Gerry Fitt became Deputy Chief Executive, and John Hume was appointed Commerce Minister.

The SDLP made a bid for the Finance portfolio but Faulkner resisted strongly. Devlin said later: 'The job would have been Hume's and, if he had really wanted it, I am sure we could have forced the issue. Instead Hume set his sights on the Department of Commerce, where the prime task was to stimulate the economy by promoting investment and employment.'[11] The Dublin government privately intervened, urging the SDLP leadership to think again, but, according to Devlin, Hume was 'steadfast, clearly judging that the potential political advantages in Commerce were substantially greater than in Finance'. This was certainly unfair. Hume was an obvious choice for the post. With his experience in starting up a business, Atlantic Harvest, he had direct experience of the problems of commerce in the province. Encouraging, persuading and pushing business to invest and expand in the province has been a lifelong passion of Hume's and the prosperous waterfront of his native city is a testament to its success.

Hume was also in constant contact with the new Fine Gael–Labour government in Dublin, whose Foreign Minister Garret Fitzgerald he had known since the heady days of 1969. Those first contacts, when Fitzgerald travelled to Derry for a long de-briefing by Hume, had matured into a close political kinship. Dublin was anxious for the RUC to be broken up on lines of the British county forces, its name and uniform changed. Hume supported these reforms, but Whitelaw, fearing mass resignations, demurred. Equally, Dublin feared that progress on setting up the new Assembly would prejudice work on the inter-governmental Council of Ireland, a fear shared by Hume. The issue of the Council was to prove the first flaw in power-sharing and eventually led to its downfall.

The hurly-burly of all this high-level bargaining occasionally exasperated the participants. Hume, by now winning respect from Faulkner as 'a formidable political thinker with great personal integrity, but sometimes exasperating dogmatism', clashed angrily with Whitelaw when he accused the Northern Ireland Secretary of leaking details of the negotiations to *The Times*. Whitelaw, a former commanding officer in the Scots Guards, stood up and shouted, 'How dare you!'

Hume rejoined: 'Don't you start bawling me out. You'll listen to me whether you like it or not.' Whitelaw was back in the officers' mess. 'Will you have a drink?' he asked, and the quarrel evaporated.[12]

The formation of the power-sharing Executive was announced on 22 November. Apart from Fitt and Hume, Austin Currie took Housing and Paddy Devlin, Health and Social Services. Outside the Executive, but still of ministerial rank, were Ivan Cooper at Community Relations and Eddie McGrady, the party's first chairman, at Planning and Co-ordination. The news infuriated hard-line Unionists. At Stormont, on one occasion, the Speaker had to abandon proceedings amid insults of 'traitor' and 'out, out' hurled across the chamber at Faulkner by his one-time allies, now bitter enemies after his 'sell-out' to the Catholic minority. In early December, the police had to be called on to the floor of the House to remove fighting Unionist extremists. Outside, it was no different. Loyalist thugs circulated a scandal sheet calling the SDLP leaders 'Six Dirty Lousy Pigs'. A grenade was thrown into a bar owned by one of the party's Assembly members.

Preparations nevertheless went ahead for a joint conference of the Executive and the British and Irish governments at the Civil Service College in Sunningdale, Berkshire, a venue chosen for a rural seclusion that made security easier. The purpose of Sunningdale was to establish the political framework within which the new government would operate, and explore the 'Irish dimension'. Hume knew these vital negotiations would make or break the bold experiment on which they were engaged. He was still in close contact with Dublin, meeting Fitzgerald for a briefing on the Irish government's position only two days before the three-day conference opened on 6 December.

Unhappily for Whitelaw, who had teased the warring factions to the negotiating table, he was not there to see his work come to fruition. A second national pay strike by Britain's coalminers was imminent, with all that meant in terms of economic disruption. Heath calculated that a man who could get Irish politicians to agree might be able to avert a crippling pit strike. Whitelaw was brought back to London as Employment Secretary and replaced by Francis Pym, the Chief Whip. His loss was a serious blow to the government team. Pym was regarded as 'a cold fish, and certainly not as adroit a politician'. Furthermore, his abrupt removal to deal with a domestic dispute – admittedly one of great moment, for it would precipitate Heath's downfall – was interpreted as a signal to the people of Northern Ireland that their problems were peripheral.

The conference began on a high social note, with a 'very convivial' dinner at Downing Street where the drink flowed freely. In the cold light of dawn, however, things were very different. The Unionists tried to wriggle out of their commitment to a Council of Ireland, but Hume stopped them with a curt reminder that they had already agreed to it. Hume's strategy, in the words of another participant, was 'to get all-Ireland institutions established which, with adequate safeguards, would produce the dynamic that would eventually lead to a united Ireland'.[13] Unfortunately, the SDLP shared this view with varying degrees of intensity. Fitt and Devlin were anxious not to drive the Unionists too far, for fear of having them 'hung from the lamp-posts when they get back to Belfast'. Hume, in contrast, wanted a Council with executive powers, rather than the inferior intergovernmental body contemplated by Faulkner.

Once the principle of a Council of Ireland had been confirmed, at Heath's suggestion the conference divided into five working parties to deal with the issues at stake: finance, economics, the police, a common law-enforcement area, and constitutional matters. Fitt did not sit on any of the committees, a role he disliked, but acted as a co-ordinator. 'John loves that sort of thing,' he remarked dismissively.

Hume and O'Hanlon, a lawyer, were posted to the constitutional group. Policing, and the role of the Council of Ireland in this field, quickly emerged as the main point of contention. Hume wanted the Council to have a 'major role' in policing. The Unionists insisted that the Executive should control the police. The British government did not want to relinquish that power to either body. Hume privately told Fitzgerald that 'if the SDLP could not support policing wholeheartedly, they should not be in government at all, and the political reality was that they could support it only by having the police associated with the Council'.[14] The SDLP saw no way of overcoming Nationalist alienation from the police unless the RUC was seen to be in some way responsible to the Council of Ireland, in which the government of the Republic would have a key role. Unsurprisingly, Fitzgerald agreed.

The impasse over policing threatened to destroy the Sunningdale initiative. Hume joined in the work of the police group, and Devlin admitted later that 'our side of the policing sub-committee were proving intractable, especially when Hume had joined them'. A compromise was brokered on the third day. The Northern Ireland Secretary would establish a Police Authority in the province after talks with the Executive, which would in turn consult the Council of Ireland. It was not much to show for the thirty-six hours of exhausting negotiations, and it was never properly put into practice.

However, Sunningdale did produce an agreement, the centrepiece of which was a Council of Ireland, which would have seven ministers each from Northern Ireland and the Republic, a consultative assembly and a secretariat. Hume and his SDLP colleagues were satisfied that they had bested the Unionists, but some of them wondered if they had done too well, that Faulkner would have difficulty in selling the package to his people. For that reason, Hume refused to crow over his achievement, and instructed an ambitious SDLP assemblyman, Hugh Logue, to cut out a reference to the Council as a vehicle that would 'trundle' the North into a united Ireland in a speech he was due to make at Trinity College, Dublin. He was too late. The speech had already gone out to the press, and the anti-Sunningdale Unionists had a field day.

Faulkner regarded the Council of Ireland as 'essentially propaganda' that would not impinge on the powers of the elected Assembly. He was confident that Unionists, 'being basically practical people', would judge Sunningdale on a practical rather than symbolic level. He could not have been more wrong. Loyalist paramilitaries formed the Ulster Army Council, an umbrella group bringing together the most extreme armed opponents of power-sharing, which promised support for politicians who would wreck the Council of Ireland before it could begin operating. Anti-Sunningdale Unionists grouped under a new title, the UUUC, and Loyalist workers also began planning action to make the agreement unworkable. The Unionist community was in turmoil. Oliver Napier, leader of the moderate unionist Alliance Party, asked in an open letter in the *Irish Times*:

'Do you really want a Council of Ireland ... if you do nothing in the next few weeks, history will judge you and its judgment will be harsh and unforgiving.'[15]

SEVEN

POWER SHARED AND LOST

'DEVOLUTION-DAY' came on 1 January 1974. The new Executive took office amid great expectations from the politicians and determined moves by hard-line Unionists to destroy it at birth. John Hume was sworn in in his 'Sunday best' with the other ministers at noon on New Year's Eve before the Lord Chief Justice, Sir Robert Lowry, and Northern Ireland Secretary, Francis Pym. All but Paddy Devlin took the oath. They had a brief meeting before formally taking office, and agreed a statement calling for an end to the killing. In 1973 250 people had died in the Troubles. There had been more than 5,000 shootings and over 1,500 bombs had been planted. More than 3,000 cases of intimidation had been recorded, and 1,414 people were charged with terrorist offences. The Executive called for action to make 1974 'the year of reconciliation'.

The year began badly. Most Catholics were willing to give power-sharing a chance. It was, after all, what their leaders had been demanding for years. True, Pym had refused to set a date for the ending of internment, but he outlined to the SDLP leaders new concessions: a parole scheme, and a more liberal regime within Long Kesh, the detention camp. But, as the Executive's Permanent Secretary, Ken Bloomfield, noted, neither Fitt nor Hume could guarantee the support of a united Nationalist community, and 'the IRA continued to operate, with very substantial open or covert support'.[1] The Provisionals would 'bend every effort' towards sabotaging the new settlement, which fell far short of their demands.

On the Protestant side, first indications were little short of disastrous. On 5 January 1974, before the ministers had time to settle into their offices, the Ulster Unionist Council, governing body of the Unionist Party, rejected the Sunningdale Agreement, and Faulkner was obliged to resign as the party's leader two days later. From that point on, he was a lame duck.

To compound the problems, Edward Heath was losing his pitched battle with the coalminers, whose industrial action had forced Britain to go on a three-day working week. Not even Willie Whitelaw's negotiating skills could avert a confrontation. The country was under an official State of Emergency, with rota power cuts hitting home and industry as the colliers piled on the pressure. The Cabinet was divided over the wisdom of calling a 'who rules?' snap general election, fearful of getting the wrong answer. As a result the problems of Ulster were pushed to one side.

In Belfast, matters went from bad to worse. When the Assembly met for the first time on 22 January, anti-Sunningdale Unionist members occupied the seats reserved for Hume and other members of the Executive. One hard-liner stood on the table with a microphone, another removed the ceremonial Mace and carried it off. Amid uproar, the session was suspended. Eighteen Unionist Assemblymen were bodily removed by policemen. Their disruptive behaviour not only shamed the new parliament, it made MPs at Westminster shake their heads. Was the game worth the candle?

Hume attended the first inter-ministerial meeting between the Executive and the Irish government at Hillsborough on 1 February, which set up joint groups of civil servants to determine what 'executive functions' might be given to the Council of Ireland. Faulkner was determined to limit these to tourism, conservation and animal health, but even these modest beginnings were put on hold as Heath ignored the advice of Pym and Whitelaw and called a UK general election on 7 February. Hume had begged him not to, when he had twice been called to Stormont Castle to talk to Heath on a confidential telephone line. The first time he warned of the 'dreadful consequences' for Northern Ireland if all the work that had gone into creating the power-sharing arrangements came to nothing because they had no time to deliver. The second time, Heath said his options had run out and he had to go to the country.

While the economy and the power of the unions dominated the campaign in Britain, in Northern Ireland the election inevitably became a referendum on Sunningdale. Anti-Sunningdale Unionists ran under the slogan: 'In Britain, they are asking, Who Governs Britain? We in Ulster ask, Who Governs Ulster? The Irish Republic – the IRA – the SDLP – a Council of Ireland?' The SDLP, now a much smoother electoral machine, fielded candidates in all twelve constituencies. Polling day, 28 February, was predictably violent. The outcome was eleven seats for the anti-Sunningdale MPs, and one for the SDLP, Gerry Fitt narrowly staving off a Republican challenge to retain his West Belfast seat. Ian Paisley entered Westminster at the expense of a traditional Unionist.

The overall result was just as pregnant with danger for the fledgling power-sharing administration. Heath failed to survive, and a minority Labour government, once more under Harold Wilson, took office on 4 February. Merlyn Rees, who as Shadow Northern Ireland Secretary had met IRA leaders in Dublin with Wilson in 1972, was appointed to Stormont Castle. He took with him Stan Orme, a veteran supporter of the Ulster civil rights campaign and friend of Gerry Fitt, as his Minister of State.

Rees had met Hume on a number of previous occasions, the first time being on 13 June 1972 when he was in Derry at the same time as Sean MacStiofain, the Provisionals' Chief of Staff. Hume and a doctor met Rees outside Ebrington barracks to take him home. 'As we drove down the hill towards "Free Derry Corner" with its barricades and armed masked men, John and the doctor agreed that as usual they were not going to stop. We drove straight through and as I looked back I could see a Provisional with a gun raised in aim at the car. He did not fire!'[2] Rees discovered only later that Hume had been instrumental in getting the IRA to cease fire that month.

After that hair-raising experience, Rees met SDLP leaders in London on a regular basis. He found Hume 'positive' about the chances of power-sharing succeeding, whereas Whitelaw, in private, had been gloomy, arguing that Hume had overplayed his hand on the Council of Ireland. Now, even Faulkner's supporters in the Assembly decided that no further steps should be taken towards ratification of Sunningdale. Whatever the wider political difficulties, Hume set to work on his commerce portfolio with a vigour. Rees noted that he 'took to his work as if born to it', while Bloomfield said, 'with his linguistic skills and earnest eloquence, John Hume made a natural minister of commerce'. He talked to the banks, to the business community, to foreign investors, to anyone who might be able to bring work to the 25,000 men and women on the dole in the province. He travelled to Europe and the USA, and set up shop in Brussels. Within four months, he was able to show results in the form of a promise of at least 4,000 jobs. He even worked with Stan Orme to bring urgent aid to Harland and Wolff, the Belfast shipbuilders known to Catholics as 'the Protestant soup kitchen'. The Executive was working tolerably well, meeting weekly in the old Cabinet room at Stormont. The SDLP had shown its commitment to responsibility in power by calling off the anti-internment rent and rates strike.

Beneath the surface, however, Unionist resentment was simmering. Only four days after Rees's arrival, 2,000 anti-Sunningdale demonstrators descended on Stormont to proclaim their intention of bringing down the Executive. The hardliners had been organizing for months. As far back as November 1973, the extreme Loyalist Vanguard organization met sympathizers from key industries in the province to set up a militant new alliance whose sole objective was to destroy power-sharing by a political strike. A date of 8 February was initially set, then abandoned when the Westminster election was called. Later, more anti-Sunningdale politicians, including Ian Paisley, became involved, and the Ulster Workers' Council (UWC) was formed. Members of this shadowy body met Rees shortly before polling day to warn that they would bring the province to a halt if the Executive and Sunningdale were not scrapped. He sent them packing. The UWC spread its shopfloor tentacles discreetly. On 23 March it went public, issuing a statement threatening widespread public disobedience unless new elections for the Assembly were held immediately.

On 8 April, Rees met the UWC again and warned Harold Wilson in a confidential minute of his 'overall scepticism' about Sunningdale. In talks with Hume and the other SDLP leaders, Faulkner was demanding a watering-down of the Council of Ireland. Rees told the Cabinet two days later that a crisis could 'hit unexpectedly'. Wilson set in train contingency planning, while publicly insisting that there was no alternative to Sunningdale.

During a Stormont debate on ratification of the agreement on 14 May, a Vanguard Assemblyman, Ernest Baird, warned that if Sunningdale was approved, Loyalist workers would bring industry to a halt. Electricity supply would be cut from 730 megawatts to 400 megawatts. It would be up to the Commerce Minister to ration power supplies. If power cuts caused hardship to hospitals, essential services or old people, 'the responsibility will lie entirely on the shoulders of John Hume'. That this threat was as cruel as it was illogical did not alter its reality. The Loyalist workers had learned from striking miners that electricity was the lifeblood of civil society, and cutting off the supply could bring a government to its knees very quickly.

Despite the dire warnings, the Assembly voted to ratify Sunning-dale, with its unmodified Council of Ireland, by forty-four votes to twenty-eight. The UWC immediately called a strike. At first, the response was limited, but it grew as the Loyalist paramilitaries moved in, threatening to burn the cars of those who turned up for work. Barricades went up. The port of Larne, a key link with Britain, was closed by armed men. Hume was appalled that Rees did not move quickly to dismantle the barricades and provide protection for those who wanted to work. It did not help that an order legalizing Sinn Fein and the outlawed Ulster Volunteer Force (a Loyalist private army) was coincidentally passed at Westminster the same day.

Hume, accused by the Loyalists of wanting to 'squander' dwindling electricity supplies on industry, was obviously a key political target for the UWC. He said he could not guarantee to maintain domestic supplies. The UWC met Orme, who unwisely denounced them as bigots, and said the troops would grind them into the ground if they did not call off the strike. Shipyard worker Harry Murray rounded on the minister, accusing him of being in league with the Derry civil rights campaign. 'You slept in John Hume's house for a fortnight,' he railed, calling Orme 'a committed man, a United Irishman'.[3]

At this stage, the Northern Ireland Office believed that the strike would fizzle out like the one called the year before, but the Orme meeting created an ugly mood among the UWC hardliners. Intimidation of workers intensified, though in the unusually warm early summer many did not need bullying to stay at home. They were on Social Security benefits, paid out by Paddy Devlin's civil servants.

Postmen had been exempt from the strike because they delivered the Giro cheques. Businessmen wanted Hume and Faulkner to urge the authorities to take steps to enable those who wished to go to work to do so. The Commerce Minister and his Chief agreed, and for good measure added in the message to Rees and Orme a demand for the barricades to be removed. By now, there were physical barriers even within the grounds of Stormont, and Faulkner could get to his office only by helicopter.

Food shortages grew, farmers had to pour milk down the drains and patients had to be discharged from hospital. Hume tried to combat the Loyalist stranglehold on power supplies by boosting output from Coolkeeragh generating station outside Derry. Hume believed the substantially Catholic workforce at Coolkeeragh could supply all the north-west's needs. He issued instructions allowing the workers to run the station. The Coolkeeragh men even said they would work alongside army technicians if they had to. Hume was over-ruled by the top brass of the Northern Ireland Electricity Service who claimed he was over-stepping his general ministerial responsibility for the service by issuing detailed operational instructions. Rees recorded later: 'It was forcefully explained to him that for technical reasons there could never be any question of this.'[4] Harold Wilson came up with a ludicrous idea to moor a submarine in Belfast Lough to supply power. The army politely advised it would not work.

With 30,000 troops and policemen in the province, Hume found the Northern Ireland Office's dithering in the face of intimidation difficult to stomach. Then Rees appeared to realize that he was losing. He called in Faulkner, Fitt and Hume (who had to travel from Derry by helicopter) on the morning of Saturday, 18 May. Hume complained that the NIO and the Executive were meeting and acting in different spheres. They should act in concert. Accordingly, Rees set up an emergency committee, of which Hume was a member. A second-tier committee of civil servants was also established. Yet the system never worked properly, because, as Hume well knew, individuals on both bodies – actually strike-busting organizations – were leaking sensitive information to the strike leaders. Hume could not get home that night, because his driver was on strike. He was in

Belfast for further talks when Rees went to see Wilson at Chequers and proclaimed a State of Emergency the next day.

On his return, Rees met the Executive and told them more troops were being drafted in, but they would not be used because such action might erode the little support there was for power-sharing. On 20 May Fitt gloomily passed Hume a note saying that the Executive might fall that evening. Rees then suddenly called on them to decide what they were going to do about the Council of Ireland. In fact, an Executive sub-committee, of which Hume was a member, had been discreetly negotiating a modified version of the Council, with fewer trappings, no Assembly, and no full-time secretariat. Effectively, it would be reduced to a joint ministerial talking-shop, with no real powers. Any further reforms would be put off until after the next Assembly elections. In-fighting between the parties was fierce, and John Hume 'became so depressed as the battle raged around him that he buried his head in his hands on the table'.[5]

Eventually, the SDLP negotiators conceded that the 'full Sunningdale' could not be implemented, and accepted a watered-down version of the Council of Ireland. They then had to sell it to their back-benchers. Unprepared for the scale of the concessions, the rank-and-file Assemblymen were hostile. Fitt warned that without the agreement, power-sharing would collapse. Hume told them: 'I know we will be in trouble with the constituencies for agreeing to a phasing, but if we do otherwise, everything will be gone. We can't carry the Council of Ireland at the present time, and that is the reality.' The SDLP Assemblymen could not bring themselves to accept the proposal, which robbed them of their hard-won opportunity to bring about Irish integration, and voted the package down. The Executive then convened, and Faulkner signalled his intention to resign. Fitt tried to reverse his party's vote, and failed. The Executive paid tribute to a tearful Faulkner, and Hume said: 'We have made a terrible mistake, but that's the way it is.'[6] Still Fitt refused to accept defeat. He called in Orme who appealed to the SDLP Assemblymen not to do the Loyalists' work for them. That did the trick. They voted for the diluted Council, and power-sharing was saved for a few more days.

Hume went back to work. He produced a fuel plan drawn up in

1972 that would take control of transport out of the hands of the UWC by providing supplies from selected petrol stations. It would require army involvement and protection. The Army was uncomfortable because it thought it would make soldiers easy targets for terrorists of either stripe. There were other strategic considerations: if the Army moved in to deliver petrol, it was virtually certain that the remaining power workers would leave their posts, and service personnel would have to take their place. Rees was supportive, and sought Wilson's backing. He said it would have to go to Cabinet.

The beleaguered Executive, conscious that its authority was slipping, demanded a meeting with Wilson. The three main party leaders were flown to Chequers on 24 May, and the Hume plan formed a major part of their five-hour-long talks. It was decided to go ahead. The oil project would be synchronized with a television address by Wilson. From that point, the situation began to unravel. First, Wilson delayed his speech. Then the Army General Officer Commanding in Ulster, Sir Frank King, warned that use of the Army to break the strike would almost certainly make things worse, given the general hostility of a substantial section of the population. A planned round-up of Loyalist paramilitaries failed to take place, and, finally, the UWC itself announced an oil distribution plan for the province which was exactly the same as the Hume plan. The strike leaders had been alerted to the top-secret preparations, and retaliated first. When Wilson did go on television, he completely misjudged the mood, excoriating Loyalists as 'thugs and bullies' and accusing them of 'sponging on democracy'. The speech merely increased support for the strike.

According to his biographer Ben Pimlott, Wilson had by this time 'come to the conclusion that the Executive was certain to fall'.[7] He told Rees to go ahead with the oil plan, while simultaneously preparing for the reimposition of direct rule. As they chatted on the tarmac at RAF Culdrose, 'Harold advised me to prepare for direct rule and questioned me on the necessary House of Commons procedure,' Rees recorded.[8] The oil initiative was no more than a sop to moderate politicians struggling to retain office in Northern Ireland. Only a token operation was mounted.

On 27 May, the Executive met in a mood of 'total depression'.

Overnight, the SDLP ministers had threatened to resign *en masse* if the government did not take action to allow the Executive to carry out its responsibilities. Faulkner, equally dismayed by the Wilson government's pusillanimity, suggested that an intermediary should be found to seek terms with the strikers. This was unacceptable to the SDLP group. Yet, according to Rees, John Hume said that the Chief Executive was 'absolutely firm, which was clearly not the case'. The power-sharing administration was falling apart. Rees rejected the proposal of a third-party negotiator – as did Hume and his SDLP colleagues, in the only vote ever taken on the short-lived Executive – and Faulkner said he would have to resign.

A bleak report to ministers the next morning showed that power cuts were getting worse, lasting up to eighteen hours a day. Parts of Derry had no water supply, and the city had run out of gas. Soon, sewage would be coming up through the manhole covers. Hume was unmoved: 'I'll sit here until there is shit flowing up Royal Avenue and then the people will realise what these people are about and then we'll see who wins.'[9]

Ministers were quarantined in their offices, because Stormont itself was blocked by demonstrating farmers and their tractors. There was no petrol in the ministerial car pool for them to go anywhere, even if they could leave. Faulkner quit. Over drinks in his office, as they surveyed the jeering Loyalist crowd, Hume said: 'Do you know what Carson said once? He said that Unionism's last fight would be between the forces of the right and the forces of the crown. That's it all started now. Once a confrontation between the loyalists and the British begins, it's all over for what you would call Unionism.'[10] Faulkner was inclined to agree.

In a bizarre twist that afternoon, Hume, Fitt and Currie refused to resign and stayed at their ministerial posts, but Rees told them they were 'ignoring reality'. At 2 p.m. on 28 May, Rees announced that Faulkner and his fellow-Unionist minister had gone, and there was 'no statutory basis' for the Northern Ireland Executive. The Assembly met half-heartedly for less than thirty minutes, and adjourned *sine die*. Ministerial drinks cabinets emptied swiftly. Dismissal notices came in the post the next morning. The strike was called off, and Westminster reimposed direct rule.

Power-sharing had vanished after little more than six months, the victim of a complex train of events that sometimes favoured Hume, but finally held him and his party at the mercy of the Unionist majority and its historic legacy of fear of a united Ireland. Many, indeed most, Protestants felt that if John Hume was so keen to have a Council of Ireland, then it clearly was a step towards unification. Equally clearly, the belief that giving the Catholic minority a say in the governance of Northern Ireland would 'deprive the IRA fish of water in which to swim' had been misplaced. The Provisionals continued to bomb and shoot, reinforcing the Unionist view that they had been conned into giving concessions for nothing. 'Thus the strike was to win back what had been lost, which was Protestant control,' argues Don Anderson, chronicler of the strike.

Hume and the SDLP insisted then, and still insist today, that if only the British government had stood firm against the Loyalists in the first two days of the stoppage, when it was still lukewarm, Sunningdale might have been sustained, if only in a diluted form. Rees disputes this analysis, pointing out that the RUC was not organized to respond quickly to such a situation, and the dispute was a political one 'that in their hearts they supported'. Nor could the Army take their place. 'It is one thing to fight the IRA and quite another to fight a whole community. Sunningdale had been pushed down the throats of the loyalists. It had been a London/Dublin solution that had ignored the reality of the situation in the North of Ireland.'[11]

Sunningdale had also, of course, been negotiated by a Conservative government, and although the Wilson–Rees axis promised to continue Heath's policies, the Labour government never exhibited the same degree of commitment to power-sharing. Orme was solidly supportive, but Rees brought a certain hauteur to the scene. He viewed the SDLP as 'neither Social Democratic in the European sense nor Labour in the British sense'.

The perspective from Dublin was different. The government shared Hume's analysis. Garret Fitzgerald subsequently disclosed that 'years later, a member of that British Cabinet confirmed to me that fear of the army failing to carry out orders was a significant factor in the way events turned out'.[12] At the first post-strike contact with the Irish government, Rees said the Executive, with the exception of Faulkner and the 'magnificent Hume', had virtually ceased to govern.

Looking back, SDLP leaders saw little to apologize for in their short reign. It had demonstrated, argued Paddy Devlin, that power-sharing could be effective, and that would be a mandatory principle in any formula to create peace and political stability. Whitelaw (who also believed that Wilson gave in too early to Loyalist violence) shared this view, expressing the hope that sooner or later another effort would be made to establish a broadly-based administration in Northern Ireland. Hume put a brave face on the loss of the only ministry over which he has presided in more than three decades of political life. He told reporters: 'To be honest, being a minister had very little effect on me. When the Executive resigned, I didn't miss anything. I didn't lose anything. To me it was a job that had to be done.'

In the aftermath of the UWC strike, the Nationalist community was in deep shock. Rumours abounded of a 'doomsday scenario' of Loyalists putting on another show of strength to win outright independence for Ulster, even at the risk of civil war. The Catholic church set up a shadow welfare state to handle such an emergency. Hume refused to recant, arguing in a speech to the Irish Transport and General Workers' Union that power-sharing had not been a failure. Catholics and Protestants had shown they could work together. The experiment was suspended, but rather than 'wrap our respective flags around us and beat our popular drums', the country required a more sane approach. 'It is much more difficult to give real leadership and say that we do not seek victory for our point of view, but that we rather sought a solution to the real problems of this country. We cannot crush the aspirations of our fellow Protestant countrymen in the North, and any solution has to be founded on the basic belief that everyone has the right to their aspirations.' This was the credo on which he intended to take the struggle forward, though he knew it was not the time for his own community to be receptive to it. In talks with the Irish government a few weeks later, he spoke of 'deep anger' among northern Nationalists. Significantly, and indicating their political closeness, he added that the SDLP and

Dublin shared identical objectives. Only the means to be employed were under discussion.

Merlyn Rees held ritual consultations with the parties on the possibility of reviving power-sharing, but nothing came of them. Hume and his colleagues went to Downing Street in June 1974 to remind Harold Wilson of the minority's continuing wish for a role in governing their country, and for some form of 'Irish dimension'. The government moved instead towards the idea of an elected Convention, which would allow the people of Northern Ireland to resolve their own constitutional problems. Rees published a White Paper outlining his ideas on 2 July, offering an elected Constitutional Convention of seventy-eight members (the same as the ill-fated Assembly) presided over by an independent chairman.

This body would seek a broad consensus on political structures. It would still tacitly be anchored to some form of power-sharing. 'There must be participation by the whole community', the White Paper maintained, because no political system would survive without widespread acceptance within the community. And, more as an observation of geographical reality than an expression of political intention, it added: 'There is an Irish dimension.' Hume thought the White Paper did not go far enough, but the SDLP could not boycott the elections and agreed to give it a try.

Before this poll could take place, Wilson judged it opportune to hold a second Westminster general election in the hope of winning a clear mandate from the voters. Hume decided to run this time, knowing that in the wake of the strike it would be a struggle to succeed in the huge Westminster constituency of Londonderry whose 90,000 voters took in much of the rural, solidly Unionist hinterland as well as the city. Willie Ross, the anti-Sunningdale sitting member, had beaten the SDLP's Hugh Logue (the 'trundler') by almost 9,500 votes in the February election. On a slightly lower turnout, Hume improved on Logue's vote, chiefly at the expense of the Republican candidate, but Ross also increased his vote and the outcome was practically identical: a Unionist majority of 9,020. It probably did not help that the party's manifesto called on Britain to declare its intention to withdraw from Northern Ireland.

Overall, the SDLP popular vote was marginally down at 22 per cent from 22.4 per cent in February, but Hume's party was confirmed as ranking second only to the Unionists, under whatever banner they fought. Rees moved somewhat from his initial judgement that the SDLP was 'a party of protest', with potential but not yet ready for government, predicting that it would not lose ground to Sinn Fein and would remain the main voice of the Catholic, Nationalist community. Faulkner's reconstituted pro-Sunningdale party attracted only 2 per cent of the vote, in an election that showed the voters had retreated into their religious camps.

Around this time, the SDLP began to pick up indications that the IRA might have decided to go for an all-out bombing campaign in Britain to push public opinion into demanding withdrawal from Northern Ireland. Indeed, Rees later admitted that the Cabinet Northern Ireland sub-committee had 'seriously considered' withdrawal.

Hume was anxious enough to raise the issue with Irish Foreign Minister Garret Fitzgerald, suggesting that London and Dublin reach an agreement to set up 'new agreed institutions' and for the Army to stay in Northern Ireland until they were established. His concern over a precipitate pull-out sat strangely with his party's election demand for a declaration of withdrawal. In the event, the Republic refused to raise the idea with Rees and Wilson, nervous that to do so might create a self-fulfilling prophecy. IRA bombs exploded in Birmingham pubs weeks later, on 21 November, killing twenty people and ushering in the Prevention of Terrorism Act, which allowed for detention without trial for seven days and expulsion orders from Britain.

The Provisionals unilaterally declared a temporary Christmas ceasefire to run from 22 December to 2 January. The day it began, and in secret contradiction of its official policy of not talking to terrorists, the government began a dialogue with Sinn Fein, political wing of the Provos. Senior officials from the Northern Ireland Office met SF representatives at Laneside, the government 'safe house'. The talks continued until 17 January, after the IRA extended its ceasefire to that date. Rees ruled out substantive talks until there had been 'a genuine and sustained cessation of violence'. Bombs in

London and Manchester marked the resumption of hostilities, but the IRA then called an indefinite truce on 9 February.

There appeared to be a twelve-point deal between the Provisionals and the British government, involving monitoring mechanisms for the ceasefire, a lower profile on the part of the Army, the phasing out of internment, freedom of movement for some top Provisionals, 'incident centres' manned by Sinn Fein and other measures. Hume was alarmed. Any break in the violence (which in 1973 claimed 216 lives) was welcome, but a secret Provo–government deal was not. Despite government denials that any agreement had been *signed*, it was clear that an understanding had been reached, or the IRA would not have called a truce. Any deal enhancing the credibility of Sinn Fein would, of course, undercut the SDLP's standing among its own people.

The party went into the Convention elections in May 1975 on a platform of power-sharing and an internationalized 'Irish dimension'. It looked to the Convention to seek a solution through trust and agreement. Seeking to address Unionist fears, Hume's manifesto said: 'The best security that can be provided is through a system that commands the loyalty of all. The SDLP would not hesitate to pledge full support and loyalty to the police service of a fully agreed government.' The campaign was a joyless affair. Hume attacked the anti-Sunningdale Unionists for their links with Loyalist paramilitaries, which had been exposed after the UWC strike. The Alliance Party accused both Unionists and the SDLP of operating a 'postal vote factory' using the names of people who had died. In the event, the electorate divided along traditional tribal lines. The SDLP won seventeen seats, two fewer than in the old Assembly, and there was a marked swing against power-sharing among the Unionist majority.

In London, Edward Heath had been deposed by Margaret Thatcher, whose views on Ireland were a virtually unknown quantity. They did not remain so for long. She appointed Airey Neave, her campaign manager and a war hero (he was the first British officer to escape from Colditz), as her Northern Ireland spokesman. He was an influential 'Friend of the Union', who came out strongly against power-sharing. Neave was later assassinated within the precincts of the Palace of Westminster, the INLA, a splinter terrorist group, claiming responsibility.

All in all, this was not an auspicious period for John Hume. An aside on television describing RUC officers as 'scoundrels' merely confirmed what many Protestants wanted to believe, that the SDLP was the Nationalist Party in civil rights clothing, unfit to participate in government. In fact the party's annual conference in Belfast earlier that year had voted to modify its tough line on disbanding the RUC, a vote brushed aside by Hume as unrepresentative because only a third of the delegates were in their seats – a not uncommon feature of SDLP conferences.

The anti-power-sharing Unionists, in overall control of the Convention with forty-seven of the seventy-eight seats, were in no mood to make any concessions to the minority. Members agreed without a vote to commit themselves to devising a system of government that would have the most widespread acceptance throughout the community, and voiced many similar warm words before giving themselves a six-week recess. Hume's contribution to the debate on the province's future, however, was a landmark speech that impressed both sides. Developing his theme of Unionist identity, he said: 'The real security your tradition has rests in your own strength and numbers and in nothing else. It does not rest in Acts of a British Parliament. The history of Anglo-Irish relations is littered with Acts of the British Parliament giving promises to the Irish Protestant population, every one of which has been broken.'

He was plainly touching a raw nerve. Ian Paisley had complained of a disillusionment with both London and Dublin, and Hume called for a partnership between Loyalists and Republicans. This would involve a re-examination of attitudes in the North and South, where 'the government, the political parties and the people ... have to ask themselves where their political dogmas or political commandments have led them or led us in the North'. Hume pointed out that 'power-sharing' and 'Irish dimension' were both British phrases (Paddy Devlin preferred 'responsibility-sharing'), and he was candid about the basis for his thinking. 'We are under no illusion, and never have been, that power-sharing is an unnatural form of government. But we are living in an unnatural situation.'[13]

Hume was always willing to give any initiative a try. Inter-party talks ensued, amid excitable talk of a grand coalition of anti-Sunningdale Unionists and SDLP that would govern Northern Ireland in the manner of the wartime Churchill coalition or the National government of the 1930s. Naturally, the Unionists would be in charge. Hume joined in these talks, and on 3 September the two sides asked the chairman of the Convention, Sir Robert Lowry, the Lord Chief Justice, to prepare a paper on how such a coalition might be effected.

The possibility of a Southern Irish involvement, modelled on the loose economic ties of the Benelux countries, was even mooted. Hume and his colleagues recognized that the Provisionals would mount a bloody campaign to destroy any such creation. One SDLP participant is said to have told a Unionist negotiator: 'De Valera had to shoot Republicans, and we may have to do the same.'[14] William Craig, the man who banned the Derry civil rights marches and who now led the Unionist delegation to the talks, believed the SDLP was serious. On hearing the news, Paisley pumped his hand, saying, 'Bill, we have saved Ulster.'[15]

Not for long. An IRA atrocity in Newtownhamilton, when masked men machine-gunned elderly men meeting in an Orange Lodge hall, killing four and wounding seven, gave the Unionists the ideal pretext for a retreat. In truth, they were also under intense pressure from hard-line church ministers and the Ulster Workers' Council to have no truck with coalition. The idea was ditched by the Unionists, and Craig had to resign from the leadership of his Vanguard Party and the Convention itself. Barry White recorded that anxious SDLP observers breathed a sigh of relief that the coalition proposal had failed. 'Hume himself admitted privately that the plan was "dynamite", and could have split the party, as it would have forced it to become part of the establishment.'[16] With it went any real hope of making the Convention work.

With the only serious move towards power-sharing out of the way, the 'bury Sunningdale' Unionists moved to consolidate their position. On 7 November, in the teeth of opposition from Hume and his colleagues, they pushed through the Convention a report recommending a return to majority rule, subject only to scrutiny by all-party committees of the kind suggested by Brian Faulkner four years previously. The Northern Ireland Prime Minister would choose whom he liked for his Cabinet, with no obligation to the minority. Good neighbourly relations with the Republic should be welcomed, but there could be no 'imposed institutionalized association'. The report was not what the government wanted.

The 1975 tally of death and destruction was 247 people dead, 1,805 bombs planted, and 1,197 people charged with terrorist offences.

Rees tried to keep the Convention alive, and Hume supported him. The SDLP believed some Unionists could be persuaded to amend the report so as to make it more palatable to the minority. The Northern Ireland Secretary decided to recall the Convention in the new year, but the Unionists told him there was no point in doing so if they had to discuss power-sharing with 'republicans' or consider an institutionalized Irish dimension. Equally, Hume told him on 8 January 1976 that they wanted power-sharing: 'Nothing else will do.' Rees responded by recalling the Convention for a four-week period, in the hope of extracting from the Unionists a wider element of power-sharing.

Before it sat, there were further inter-party talks (though, by this time, Rees felt he was 'becoming more Irish than the Irish – we were talking for the sake of talking').[17] The crunch came at a private, but Hansard-minuted, meeting on 12 February between the hard-line Unionists and the SDLP. John Hume argued yet again that the only way to create circumstances in which the whole community could support a Northern Ireland government was for both sections of the community through their elected representatives to work together 'for the betterment of all the people'. Fitt tried to pin down Harry West, leader of the majority United Ulster Unionist Council on this issue. Was it right to say they would *never*, in government or opposition, co-operate with the SDLP? West vacillated. Hume asked point-blank: 'Are we to understand Mr West as saying that there are no circumstances in which the UUUC would serve in a Cabinet with the SDLP?' West replied: 'That is right.'

It was, as Rees admitted, all over. The meeting adjourned, leaving Hume to work out how the SDLP would conclude. He did so by saying the talks had not got to grips with the Northern Ireland

Secretary's agenda, which sought a 'wider element' of power-sharing. Hume added: 'We will be here at any stage if anybody wants to talk to us about it.' Nobody did. The Convention met one last time, on 3 March, when Ian Paisley's wife Eileen called Hume 'a twister, a political Jesuit twister'. The Convention was dissolved two days later. Its report was pigeon-holed.

A fortnight after that, the ceasefire, which was being honoured more in the breach than the observance, came to an end when the Army raided the IRA's Falls Road incident centre. On 16 March, Harold Wilson resigned and was replaced by James Callaghan, who as Home Secretary had had responsibility for Northern Ireland when the Troubles first began. One of his first moves was to take Stan Orme, Hume's political ally, out of the Northern Ireland Office and replace him with Don Concannon, a one-time British Guardsman.

As is his nature, Hume refused to accept that the end of the Convention meant an end to the talking. He and Paddy Devlin accepted an invitation from two Unionist politicians, Rev. Martin Smyth and Austin Ardill, for discreet talks at the latter's house at Greenisland, near Belfast. They met half a dozen times, in the spring and early summer, combing the Convention report for possible fresh points of departure. Hume detected a willingness to compromise, but the SDLP pair feared that the Unionists were only looking for cosmetic changes that would allow them to go back to the government with a credible demand for their 'majority rule' report to be reconsidered. Even these tentative moves were stymied by Ian Paisley, who affected not to know that they were going on, then proceeded to leak the details. Devlin, who believed progress was being made, concluded bleakly: 'It only demonstrated what it was possible to achieve by compromise, without actually achieving anything.'

When the talks were formally abandoned in September 1976, Hume disclosed just how far he had been prepared to travel in order to win a consensus. The SDLP had proposed a greater measure of devolution; an assembly or parliament to give effect to that principle; a power-sharing Cabinet reflecting the proportional strength of those assembly parties willing to form a government; a review of the working of the new constitution after two parliamentary sessions; the transfer of the functions of the Secretary of State to a Lord President; and a 'positive and freely negotiated' agreement between North and South on matters of common concern.

This was a far cry from Sunningdale, and the Official Unionists to whom he was talking appreciated as much. However, they demanded full majority rule subject only to a two-fold restraint of the executive: all-party back-bench committees and a Council of State, appointed on a basis of proportional representation. This body would have powers to block legislation for up to a year, and would have executive responsibility in the field of human rights. Hume saw some merit in such a restraint on the executive, but it fell with the talks. Later that month, Rees was recalled to London as Home Secretary, and his place was taken by Roy Mason, a short, pipe-smoking toughie who never forgot his origins in the Yorkshire coalfields.

The new Northern Ireland Secretary found that politics in the province had taken on a new and wholly unexpected dimension: a women's peace movement. In mid-August, the army shot dead an IRA man, Danny Lennon, as he was driving through the strongly Republican Andersonstown area of Belfast. His car ran off the road and ploughed into a family walking by. Mrs Anne Maguire was seriously injured. Three of her children, ranging in age from six weeks to eight years, died. The televised grief of Mrs Maguire's sister, Mairead Corrigan, gave rise to an enormous, spontaneous outpouring of emotion. More than a thousand women in Republican Andersonstown demonstrated for peace, a figure which had grown tenfold at a march on 14 August.

A week later, the Women's Peace Movement (later the Peace People) was launched at a rally attended by 20,000 people, Catholic and Protestant, in Ormeau Park, Belfast. Mairead Corrigan said: 'Everybody has so far failed to get the two sides together and to bring us peace. I believe it is time for the women to have a go.' More marches and rallies throughout the province followed, and the movement spread to Liverpool and Glasgow. Yet within a month, the founders found themselves under attack by a mob in the Turf Lodge area of Belfast, scene of the death of a thirteen-year-old boy from an army plastic bullet. Republicans had denounced the movement as a tool of the British. In November, Mairead Corrigan and Betty Williams, the Peace People leaders, were at the head of a 30,000-strong peace march through London, attended by the American singer Joan Baez. Corrigan and Williams shared the Nobel Peace Prize for 1976, a year in which 297 people died in the Troubles.

EIGHT

LEADER

THE COLLAPSE OF THE CONVENTION, the failure of discussion with the Ulster Unionists and the arrival of a new Northern Ireland Secretary decidedly less sympathetic to moderate Nationalism conspired to marginalize John Hume as a politician and leader of his people. Still only thirty-nine years old, he was not only out of the frame, but also out of work. The Convention salary may not have been much – at £2,500 little more than half the pay of a Westminster MP – but it kept house and home together. He and Pat had five children: Therese, Aine, Aidan, John and Maureen. He earned a little from freelance writing, particularly in the *Irish Times*, whose editor Douglas Gageby was a confirmed admirer, but it was imperative to find something more reliable. To make ends meet, Pat Hume went back to work, teaching at St Anne's Primary School in the Rosemount district, just a street away from where John had been born.

Hume continued to act as an unpaid 'constituency representative' in Derry, a city still beset by the Troubles; the Army's behaviour gave rise to complaints, and shootings and bombings were commonplace. He was particularly distressed by the IRA murder of Jeffrey Agate, the English manager of the Du Pont factory in County Londonderry. However, the prominence that the Troubles gave to his regular media appearances and speeches in favour of non-violence paradoxically worked to his advantage. He was known in Europe and the USA as the foremost advocate of a constitutional settlement of 'the Irish problem'. And his brief period in office as Commerce Minister in the power-sharing administration had brought him into contact with leading public figures abroad.

The American connection had been forged as early as 1969, when the young Senator Edward Kennedy grasped the identity of interest between the American civil rights movement and the similar struggle in Northern Ireland. In June, he telegraphed the NICRA chairman: 'Today, the Irish struggle again, but not alone. Your cause is a just cause. The reforms you seek are basic to all democracies worthy of the name. My hopes and prayers go with you.' That year, Hume made his first propaganda foray to the USA, beginning a campaign of influence that grew steadily into a small industry over the decades. As an MP in Stormont, and as Commerce Minister, he travelled widely down the Eastern seaboard and inland as far as Wisconsin, drumming up investment and urging Irish Americans not to be gulled into giving money to the Provisionals. He asked them if they themselves would be prepared to fire a gun or throw a bomb 'for that is what their dollar will do'.

In April 1974 on a visit to Boston, capital of Irish America, he rounded on 'so-called patriots' who contributed to Noraid, a new support group for hard-line republicanism: 'In three hundred years, violence has not solved our problems. It will not do so now.' In Washington, he impressed seasoned politicians with his sanity: 'The conflict is not between unionism and nationalism, between Britain and Ireland or, still less, between Protestant and Catholic. It is a struggle between those who believe in the political process and those who do not. I am not interested in the removal of lines, however arbitrary, from a map, or in the reunification of square miles of territory. Ireland without her people is nothing. The only unity I cherish is that which has the whole-hearted and freely-given consent of my Protestant fellow-countrymen. Unless that consent is forthcoming, unless there is a union of heart and mind, there can be no unity.'[1]

Hume's original, articulate outlook made him talked about. He was interviewed by the right-wing commentator William Buckley, to whom he expressed frankly his hopes for an Ireland united by agreement. He appeared on Barbara Walters's *Today* celebrity show. He became a regular visitor to the USA, extending his political network through the Kennedy clan to the Boston Democrat Tip O'Neill, whose accession to the post of Speaker made him one of

Washington's most influential politicians. O'Neill's ancestors hailed from Buncrana, the resort on Lough Swilly close to Burt, where Hume's own forebears had lived. The two became firm friends. He spent Thanksgiving Day in November 1976 at O'Neill's home on Cape Cod, and joined Teddy Kennedy's senatorial campaign in Massachusetts.

Hume's high profile and his political philosophy made him a natural choice in late 1976 to become an associate fellow at Harvard University. For a term, he studied and lectured on conflict studies at the Center for International Affairs. Teddy Kennedy was influential in landing him the job; it did not pay very well but it offered huge dividends of another kind in the years to come.

It was as well for Dublin that Hume was spreading his wings. In Washington, the British embassy had long had the upper hand in dealings with the strongly Anglophile State Department over the Irish question. Furthermore, the Irish embassy's antagonism towards the IRA had sidelined Dublin in the eyes of many Nationalist Irish Americans. In 1975, the Nationalist lobby in the USA, working very effectively through the Irish National Caucus, had persuaded Jimmy Carter to include a proposal for an international commission for Northern Ireland in his presidential manifesto. He also publicly suggested a more active role for the USA in achieving a settlement of the Troubles.

On St Patrick's Day 1977, the Big Four – Kennedy, O'Neill, Hugh Carey and Moynihan – issued a statement, appealing to all those organizations engaged in violence to renounce 'their campaigns of death and destruction'. They added: 'We appeal as well to our fellow Americans to embrace the goal of peace and to renounce any action that promotes the current violence or provides support or encouragement for organisations engaged in violence.'

This was a political coup for Hume. The St Patrick's Day statement led to the formation of a Friends of Ireland movement in Congress, and the announcement on 30 July 1977 of the Carter initiative, shortly after Jack Lynch became Taoiseach. Carter's presidential statement exploited the popularity of the Big Four, asking all Americans to 'refrain from supporting, with financial or other aid, organisations whose involvement, direct or indirect, in this violence

RIGHT Meeting Harold Wilson and
Labour leaders (note Tony Benn in
background).

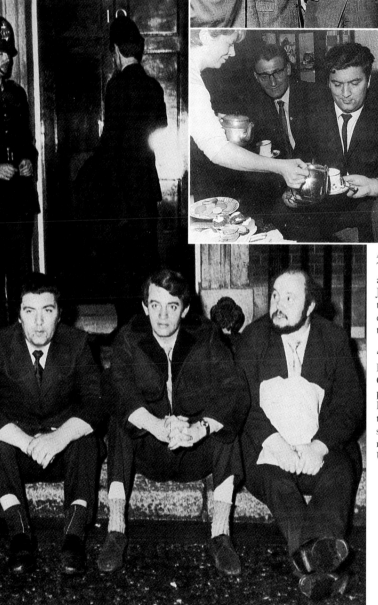

ABOVE Taking tea in the
Troubles: John Hume
and Home Secretary
James Callaghan discuss
the Ulster crisis over a
cup of tea in a Bogside
terrace home, 1970.

'Hunger Striker 1971':
Hume, Currie and Paddy
O'Hanlon sitting on the
pavement outside No 10
Downing Street during
their 48-hour hunger
strike against the government's handling of the
Ulster crisis.

Water cannons were turned on protesters during this demonstration in Derry, August 1971. John Hume – holding his hand to his head in the centre – was later arrested.

Hume addresses a mass sit-in at Brandywell football ground in August 1971, held to further the campaign of passive resistance in Londonderry.

LEFT
On 8 September
1971 Hume leaves
the courthouse
in Londonderry
after being fined
£20 in charges
under the Special
Powers Act.

Confrontation: leading an anti-internment march on Magilligan Strand,
Lough Foyle, January 1972.

RIGHT A testing time: John Hume, Commerce Minister in the short-lived power-sharing government at Stormont, in the control room during the 1974 Ulster Workers' council strike that brought down the administration.

ABOVE The Minister of Commerce at the controls of a powerboat on 21 February 1974 when he looked at exhibits in the Sportsman's Show at Balmoral, Belfast, after announcing details of a £600,000 pleasure-and-leisure package of tourist amenity schemes.

RIGHT At the Guildhall on 4 October 1978, arriving to give evidence to the investigatory commission which inquired into allegations about the placing and management of contracts by the Northern Ireland Housing Executive.

delays the day when the people of Northern Ireland can live and work together in harmony'.

In admittedly cautious terms, President Carter endorsed the idea of a broadly-based administration – thus implicitly recognizing the right of the Catholic minority to participate – saying: 'We support the establishment of a form of government in Northern Ireland which will command widespread acceptance throughout both parts of the community.' In the event of such a settlement, he pledged US government readiness 'to join with others to see how additional job-creating investment could be encouraged to the benefit of all the people of Northern Ireland'. Months of horse-trading between the three governments, in which Hume played a key role, preceded delivery of the final compromise. The statement avoided mention of the 'Irish dimension', but clearly envisaged that any 'just solution' would require the support of Dublin as well as London. President Carter also avoided using the term 'power-sharing', in deference to thin Unionist skins. But the inducement of substantial US investment, variously reckoned at between $100 million and $500 million, was very much Hume's idea.

Garret Fitzgerald, out of office but now Fine Gael Leader of the Opposition in Dublin, said the embassy 'with John Hume's help' had shown how the Irish government could move from what had hitherto been an essentially defensive position, fighting IRA propaganda, 'to one in which we held the initiative and could influence Congress and even the Administration in our interest'.[2] To secure the full value of this breakthrough, he persuaded Lynch to send Sean Donlon, a brilliant civil servant who headed the Anglo-Irish Division at the Department of Foreign Affairs, as Irish ambassador to Washington. Donlon was still well under forty. Not the least of his qualifications was that he had a particularly good relationship with John Hume, and had worked very closely with him in penetrating and commanding the attention of the US Congress.

However, the Unionists were at best unimpressed by and at worst downright hostile to Hume's transatlantic diplomacy. They were more interested in buttressing their position by winning greater representation for the province at Westminster. Prime Minister Callaghan, with at least half an eye on his government's disappearing majority, was inclined to oblige a potential parliamentary ally.

Against strong protests from the SDLP, which correctly divined that an increase in the number of seats in Northern Ireland would serve not only to increase the Unionist presence but also to bind the province more closely to the 'mother country', Callaghan referred the issue of representation in the province to an all-party Speaker's Conference in May. Local elections held that month in the wake of a failed Loyalist attempt to repeat the 1974 strike found the Unionists deeply divided, with the SDLP still garnering more than 20 per cent of the popular vote. On that basis, Hume's party might hope to pick up one or more parliamentary seats.

The party was going through a period of deep soul-searching. Paddy Devlin, chairman of the SDLP parliamentary group, argued that its character had changed. Its few Protestant members had become disenchanted, and it was openly identified in the media as 'the mainly Catholic' SDLP. The strongly anti-clerical Devlin complained that its members were straightforward Catholics who were conservative in economic and social policies. He objected to the close links with Charles Haughey's hardline wing of the Fianna Fail party in the South, and even more so to reading about new developments in the newspapers about which he claimed he had not been consulted.

'More and more the party was being autocratically run from Derry by John Hume and his cronies,' Devlin recalled bitterly. He accused Hume of formulating policy on the spur of the moment and of pursuing his own initiatives such as 'building up his contacts in Washington DC' and securing Carter's financial commitment. 'Again, without formal party nominating procedures taking place, Hume announced that he was going to stand for election to the European Parliament in 1979.'[3] Devlin was furious at the way the party was 'being stripped of its socialism and being taken over by unadulterated nationalists'. He even suggested that the party's response to IRA violence was 'sometimes doubtful', citing its silence in the aftermath of the most horrific outrages.

Some of this criticism owed much to political jealousy. Fitt was still the leader, but Hume was unquestionably calling the shots. He could scarcely have submitted every twist and turn in the preparations for the Carter initiative to his party hierarchy back home, nor could he be blamed for looking to Europe as his next political venture. Yet there was some truth in the criticism: the SDLP *was* becoming more like a bourgeois version of the Nationalist Party.

A Hume policy document adopted by SDLP leaders on 25 August, calling for a greater emphasis on the Irish dimension in response to the perceived 'integrationist' policy of the British government, brought matters to a head. Devlin quit his chairmanship of the 'parliamentary group' of former MPs who were the core of the leadership, dismissing the document as 'a hastily-drafted piece of froth' published to coincide with the US President's intervention. Certain leading members of the SDLP had been given prior sight of the presidential statement, he said, and they hoped to exploit its content and timing. They could not resist the temptation of making a public demonstration of their connections. For 'certain leading members', we may read 'John Hume'.

Devlin's resignation statement made some telling points, however. It was true that, under pressure on one side from a British government increasingly uninterested in political reform, and on the other from Sinn Fein, the SDLP was shifting to more traditional Nationalist ground. The move was later accentuated by the formation of the short-lived Irish Independence Party in the North, by former Unity MP Frank McManus, a leading figure in the civil rights movement in Fermanagh. Hume found it necessary to shift towards the right, towards 'green' (Nationalist) politics, in order to stay in the middle, ran the joke of the day. To Hume's dismay, a move to demand straight British withdrawal from Northern Ireland, backed by the increasingly important figure of Seamus Mallon, had gained substantial support at the 1976 annual conference. It was defeated by a majority of only forty-seven votes out of 269 cast.

Devlin further questioned whether it was wise to push the Irish government into the forefront of any new political initiative. Such a policy would only goad the Unionists to invoke their veto on progress, prompting 'collision politics on a grand scale – the ingredients of total warfare'. He also singled out the party's Article 2, which promised that the party's aims and objectives were based on left-of-centre principles: a just distribution of wealth; support for the unions; promoting co-operatives; a minimum wage; equal pay; public ownership of fishing rights; and the setting up of state industry in areas of high unemployment.

With one or two notable exceptions, none of the SDLP leaders had done anything to promote these policies since the collapse of power-sharing in 1974. Despite the province's hideous unemployment statistics, 'we have rarely heard a cheep of protest' from the men who until recently had ministerial responsibility for such matters. This was another jibe at Hume, as was Devlin's disclosure that during the 1975 referendum on Europe the party had issued pro-EEC advertisements 'which we did not pay for'. Having issued his credo, he reaffirmed his intention to continue as a rank and file member. Not for long. A few days later, the executive expelled him. He insists that Ivan Cooper, veteran of the Derry protest days, followed him soon after, though this is denied by Hume who claims that his old comrade of the streets still supports the SDLP.

Even before the Devlin interlude, Hume had moved on. In June 1977, he was appointed political adviser to Richard Burke, formerly Education Minister in the Republic's Fine Gael administration and now Ireland's EEC Commissioner with responsibility for Consumer Affairs. It was only a part-time post, but the work brought him into the inner circle of European politics. The money was a big boost, too. 'I was unemployed, I had no income', he explained, 'apart from some freelance journalism. I had a column in the *Sunday Press*, which brought in, I think, £50 a week. The only income was my wife's as a teacher.'[4]

Burke was uniquely placed to help Hume's European political ambitions. As Commissioner responsible for liaison with the European Parliament in Strasbourg in the run-up to the first direct elections, he was constantly travelling to the capitals of the member nations and the Parliament itself. Hume was at his side, learning the ropes of the European system, and incidentally setting up the new relationship between Northern Ireland's Catholic community and the EEC that was to prove so fruitful. 'I made a lot of very powerful contacts in the European Commission over that period, which I still have,' Hume recalls. In particular, he noticed the painfully inadequate scale of the Community's regional fund, and determined that it should be improved, and that Ireland's depressed north-west should have at least its fair share.

There was also a bigger picture: 'Europe has been central to my political thinking. I regard Europe as the best example in the history of the world of conflict resolution. Areas of conflict everywhere should study how it was done. Consider the bitterness of the European conflict over the centuries, and the 35 million dead in 1945; yet fifty years later there is a European Union. But the Germans are still German and the French are still French,' he argued. 'How did they do it? Exactly as I am trying to do here, by building institutions that respect their differences, gave no victory to either side, but allowed them to work together in their common interest, to spill their sweat, not their blood, and thereby break down the barriers of centuries. As a result of that, a real healing process began. The divisions of centuries cannot be healed in one decade, in Ireland or anywhere else. There has to be a healing process and the task of politicians is to create the framework in which that process can take place.'[5]

The British government, harried on one side by an increasingly confident Tory opposition under Margaret Thatcher, whose Northern Ireland spokesman Airey Neave was deeply inimical to power-sharing, and by a powerful trade union movement disillusioned with its 'social contract' with Labour, was not minded to risk its fragile parliamentary position by upsetting the Ulster Unionists. In late 1977, Roy Mason unveiled a Five-point Plan, which proposed partial devolution as a stepping-stone to a devolved legislative body with a wide range of powers. It smacked too much of the Unionists' ideas for the gradual restoration of 'their' Stormont to be taken seriously by Hume and his colleagues, and it was left to gather dust.

The Northern Ireland Secretary congratulated himself at the end of the year that 'the tide had turned against the terrorists'. His message for 1978 was 'one of real hope'. In 1977, 112 people died in the Troubles. There were more than 1,000 shootings, and more than 500 bombs were planted. There were in excess of 3,000 cases of intimidation, two-thirds of them during the abortive Loyalist strike, and 1,308 people were charged with terrorist offences. Nineteen seventy-eight was to prove a less lethal year, though it opened in Derry with an IRA bomb that severely damaged the historic Guild-hall. It had been open for only seven months following an arson attack by the Provisionals in 1972.

To keep the Unionists sweet, Callaghan agreed to implement the Speaker's Conference recommendation for more parliamentary representation in Northern Ireland. In the teeth of SDLP opposition, he created five more seats for the province, bringing the total to seventeen. With the continuation of the Lib–Lab Pact, which gave Callaghan the support of Liberal MPs, he was able to soldier on for another year. However, Mason was anxious. 'We are out on a limb,' he warned a Cabinet meeting in September 1978, soon after Callaghan had ruled out an autumn election. The British Prime Minister, the same man who had been so well received by the people of the Bogside, admitted about this time that his government had 'no policy' on Northern Ireland.[6] This shortcoming, which he evidently regarded as inconvenient rather than dangerous, was to prove instrumental in his downfall.

Hume was increasingly setting his sights on Europe. He easily took his party's nomination for the Euro-poll in June 1979. Gerry Fitt recalled: 'I nominated him. We all did. There was no way anyone from Belfast was ever going to get that nomination because John Hume had the Catholic vote tied up.'[7] However, Hume still kept up the pressure for an 'agreed Ireland', the current SDLP slogan for reconciliation. He argued in the *Irish Times* that if Britain did not want to leave, but was weary of maintaining the statues quo, 'the third option for the British government is to declare that its objective in Ireland is the bringing together of both Irish traditions in reconciliation and agreement'.

There was no response from the government, and no new initiative from Mason, which was not surprising as the Callaghan government was deeply embroiled in the 'winter of discontent' from the end of 1978, facing strikes throughout the public services and in key private-sector businesses such as road haulage. In January 1979, Mason reported to the Cabinet that Northern Ireland was 'bleeding to death' because of a strike by petrol tanker drivers.[8] In late March, just as the European socialist candidates published their election manifestos – Hume's slogan was 'Your No. 1 for Europe' – Thatcher tabled a censure motion in the Commons. Fitt, the SDLP leader, refused to support the government. So did Frank Maguire, Independent Nationalist MP for Fermanagh and South Tyrone who made a rare Commons appearance 'to abstain in person'. The Labour government fell by one vote, the first time this had happened on a vote of censure since 1925.

On 29 March, Callaghan called a general election for 3 May. The next day, Airey Neave, who would have been Thatcher's Northern Ireland Secretary, was assassinated by a bomb planted in his car within the precincts of the Palace of Westminster. Neave had insisted that power-sharing was no longer 'practical politics', and his murder tore a gaping hole in the Conservatives' Ulster policy. The party went to the polls promising elected regional councils in the province, which was in line with Unionist thinking. The SDLP polled just over 18 per cent of the votes, retaining its sole seat for Gerry Fitt in West Belfast. Mrs Thatcher triumphed, and appointed Humphrey Atkins, a close adviser and her Chief Whip but an unknown quantity, as Northern Ireland Secretary. His first important decision was to ban the INLA, who claimed to have assassinated Neave.

Hume did not stand in the Westminster elections, preferring to throw his energy into winning a seat at Strasbourg. His election address stressed his academic background, his skill as a fluent French-speaker, his role as an adviser to Richard Burke and in the Credit Union, and his record of representing Derry in the Northern Ireland Parliament, Assembly and Convention. He also endorsed the European Parliamentary Socialist Group's strategy for combating unemployment.

In the aftermath of the general election, turnout in the Euro-poll was much lower at only 57 per cent. Paisley easily topped the list, with 170,688 first-preference votes (the election was conducted under the proportional representation system favoured by Hume). Hume came a good second, with 140,622 first-preference votes, almost a quarter of the total, easily ahead of the Official Unionist and other Nationalist rivals including Paddy Devlin and Bernadette McAliskey (née Devlin). He was also the only strongly pro-Europe candidate to be elected. Hume had campaigned as a supporter of the European Socialist Group, which emerged as the largest group in the Parliament. He was swiftly (and unanimously) elected Treasurer of the group.

Hume's election to the European Parliament put him back into the public gaze as a serious politician. He had secured support across the political divide ('It was indisputable that some Protestants had voted for him,' wrote Barry White),[9] and was now in a position to revive the influence of the party he had founded as well as to reform the system of funding depressed areas like Ireland's north-west. But soon after he took his seat in July came the murder of Earl Louis Mountbatten, the Queen's cousin and the last British Viceroy of India, blown up by an IRA bomb while on his boat off the County Sligo coast; the killing of eighteen British soldiers at Warrenpoint, County Down; and the downing of an army helicopter with the death of eleven members of the Queen's Own Highlanders.

This was the blackest day in more than a decade of the Troubles, and it led to a surge in anti-Catholic sectarian murders. It was also influential in eliciting an overt denunciation of Ireland's political culture of violence from Pope John Paul. On 30 September, at an open-air mass said before a quarter of a million Catholics outside Drogheda, Hume heard the Pope make an emotional appeal:

> To all of you who are listening, I say: do not believe in violence. Do not support violence. It is not the Christian way. It is not the way of the Catholic Church. Believe in peace and forgiveness and love, for they are of Christ. On my knees I beg of you to turn away from the paths of violence and to return to the ways of peace. You may claim to seek justice. I too believe in justice and seek justice. But violence only delays the day of justice. Violence destroys the work of justice. Do not follow any leaders who train you in the ways of inflicting death.

To politicians like Hume (who read a passage from the Bible during the service), the Pope spoke with equal urgency and intensity: 'Do not cause or condone conditions which give excuse or pretext for violence. Those who resort to violence always claim that only violence brings about change. They claim that political action cannot achieve justice. You politicians must prove them wrong.' The IRA immediately repudiated the papal message, arguing that force was the only means of removing 'the evil of the British presence'. The Pope had unquestionably begun a process of thought that would later lead to a realignment of Republican analyses about 'the armed struggle', bringing John Hume and Gerry Adams together in the search for a peaceful solution.

First, however, there was an unexpected crisis at the top in the SDLP, from which Hume emerged as undisputed leader of the minority community of Northern Ireland. Behind the scenes, pressure had been building up for some time. Fitt felt isolated in his urban, socialist stronghold, at odds with the rural, middle-class and increasingly Nationalist mainstream of the party. Hume's impressive showing in the European elections had created an alternative focus of power, which threatened to expose Fitt's tenuous hold on the leadership. The crunch came in late October 1979, when the new Northern Ireland Secretary unveiled yet another new political initiative. Atkins called all the constitutional parties in the province to inter-party talks, ahead of a White Paper on the governance of Northern Ireland to appear the following month.

The invitation presented the SDLP with a dilemma. Atkins's terms of reference for the talks specifically ruled out any discussion of the Irish dimension. Since this was a central tenet of the SDLP faith, Hume favoured a boycott of the conference. Fitt was opposed to this strategy, seeing in it a revival of the sterile Nationalist tradition of abstentionism. Hume, absent in Brussels, telephoned a warning that the party members would not tolerate ditching the Irish dimension. Fitt, widely thought to have signalled his party's readiness to talk to the Unionists despite the restrictive terms of reference, undertook to seek from Atkins a wider basis for the conference. Before he did so, angered by criticism from Seamus Mallon that upset his wife Anne, Fitt decided he had had enough. They could keep 'their' party. He called in the political correspondents at Westminster and announced his resignation from the SDLP leadership.

Hume was told of Fitt's resignation in a telephone call from BBC Radio's 'World at One' presenter Robin Day, and was surprised to learn that he was now acting leader of his party. In truth, he had been its inspiration for many years, though he had always had to play second fiddle to the street-wise Belfast politician who could charm the voters and the media with his rollicking sense of humour. Fitt had clearly believed that he could sell the British government's limited terms of reference for talks to his party, but he had miscalculated. The Irish dimension, conceded at Sunningdale, was too firmly embedded in the SDLP psyche for it to be set aside so lightly.

In the period between Fitt's resignation and the formal takeover by Hume, Garret Fitzgerald, leader of Fine Gael, made an extraordinary private intervention. Seeking a way out of the impasse, he asked the British ambassador in Dublin to convey a message to Foreign Secretary Peter Carrington. If, after he was elected to Europe, Hume was invited by Mrs Thatcher to meet him, and she told him that the Irish dimension could be added to the agenda after it had discussed the government's plans for devolution, then Hume might be drawn into the talks process. It was a convoluted idea, but it could have worked. 'Unhappily, nothing came of this initiative, to which only John Hume and I were privy,' recorded Fitzgerald.[10]

When it appeared in late November, Humphrey Atkins's White Paper excluded all discussion of new relationships with the Republic, while admitting that direct rule was not a satisfactory way of governing Northern Ireland. In December, under Hume's leadership, the SDLP voted to take part. He held out little hope of progress, but came round to the view that participation was more profitable than boycott.

Even in these dog days for the SDLP's long-term objectives, Hume refused to lose sight of what he was in politics for. In a seminal article entitled 'The Irish Question, a British Problem', written for the influential US quarterly *Foreign Affairs* while he was still deputy leader, but published in the winter 1979/80 edition, he recalled that the British government had recently brought back from retirement to work in Northern Ireland the man who reputedly furnished the model for George Smiley in John le Carré's spy novels. 'This may be symptomatic of a long-standing British inability to take the Irish seriously. It should be admitted that the reverse tradition also exists. However, events [the Mountbatten and army murders] recently unleashed a chilling shower, drenching Irish and British alike, from which the flippant, patronizing and slightly bemused attitudes of the past afforded no refuge whatever.

'It is beyond high time the British and the Irish took each other – and our common crisis – seriously. There is, I believe, an urgent need for the friends of Britain and Ireland to do likewise, and there is heartening evidence in fact that some of them have begun to do so.'[11] He was referring here not just to President Carter's pledge of economic aid two years previously, but to the visit a few months before of Tip O'Neill, the American Speaker. At a government dinner in Dublin Castle, O'Neill had shown his irritation with Britain by suggesting that Northern Ireland had become a 'political football'. Tory MPs close to the Unionists roundly denounced him as little better than an IRA sympathizer. This unwise response prompted Hume's 'Four Horsemen' to renew their campaign for a British initiative in Ulster, a by-product of which was a US State Department ban on the sale of American hand-guns to the RUC.

The British view of the problem as 'their quarrel, not ours', argued Hume, was fundamentally wrong. Britain was a protagonist and must be central to the solution. Yet the basis of British policy lay concealed under layers of good intentions, ingenious initiatives, commissions of inquiry, attempted reforms, financial aid and a good deal of genial bewilderment. 'I do not use the word "concealed" maliciously', he argued. 'Many sincere and concerned British politicians thought they had tried everything possible to bring the Irish into agreement with each other.' All that showed, he said, was how far they had lost sight of their basic aims.

The central tenet of British policy was the reiterated guarantee that Northern Ireland should remain a part of the United Kingdom so long as a majority of the electorate of Northern Ireland wished it to do so. 'That would seem, at first reading, to be an eminently democratic and responsible undertaking. The fact is, however, that it has not worked. It has not produced peace or stable government in Northern Ireland. Moreover, it has provided the basis for a half century of injustice, discrimination and repressive law, a situation in which the minority community (the one-third Catholics) have been the persistent losers and victims.'

Hume described this legislated undertaking as 'the British guarantee', a term which he was to popularize in the years ahead. The British guarantee, he went on, had proved to be a guarantee of permanent exclusive power to one side, the Unionists, and a guarantee of permanent exclusion of power for the minority. Its existence undermined any hope of political negotiation between the two sides, and guaranteed the integrity of 'their' quarrel. While the guarantee continued, there was no incentive for the Unionists to enter into genuine dialogue with those with whom they shared the island of Ireland. 'The suffering and frustration of the people of Northern Ireland overwhelmingly attest to the fact that the guarantee was, to put it very bluntly, a tragic mistake. The price has been paid too long, and in too many lives.'

Hume paid tribute to the political courage and imagination of the previous Conservative government in establishing power-sharing and a North–South Irish dimension through the ill-fated Council of Ireland. He excoriated the Wilson government for committing 'one of the most squalid examples of government irresponsibility in our times' in surrendering to Loyalist paramilitaries in the strike of 1974. This show of pusillanimity, he argued, had not only restored the British guarantee after Sunningdale, but had reinforced it. Unionists now believed they could resist and subvert any British moves to concede power to the minority.

'My hope is that Prime Minister Thatcher, in coming to grips with the problem, will commit all her vaunted capacity to reversing the blind momentum of British public policy, all her vaunted steadiness of nerve in the face of contrary pressure to secure and maintain a success,' he wrote. Failure, either to take a serious initiative or sustain it under Unionist pressure, would mean 'a spreading field of white crosses' in front of Belfast City Hall commemorating those who died at the hands of political violence.

Hume was 'encouraged' by what he took to be a resurfacing of traditional Unionist realism, brought on by a series of factors: the rapid economic growth of the Republic, which was poised to overtake the North economically; the growing importance of the European Community, in which Dublin (currently exercising the EC presidency) was treated as the equal of London; and a growing suspicion that total dependence on the British guarantee for long-term political survival may prove risky and unprofitable. He called on political leaders in Northern Ireland, in the Republic and Britain to re-examine their fundamental assumption. The two greatest problems remained the British guarantee, which inhibited such re-examination, and the Unionist dependence on it. However, given economic developments and a growing sense of realism about the future, 'this would seem a propitious juncture at which to take a serious initiative'. He could have added that the arrival of a new government also improved the outlook, but contented himself with saying: 'Only Britain can create the conditions in which Unionists can perceive and pursue their true interests.'

Hume then addressed the issue of the Provisional IRA, explaining why it still thrived in the face of rejection by the majority of Catholic opinion north and south of the border. The IRA's view that everything would be solved by the expulsion of the British and a unified independent state was a simple view of a highly complex situation, but its very simplicity gave the Provisionals 'strength and purpose'.

Their analysis also gained from affinities with the vision of the partially successful, and widely revered, insurgents of the 1916–22 period. A second factor in Provisional endurance was the encouragement they drew from British weakness and prevarication. He criticized the 'intermittent British dalliance with Provisional "political spokesmen" whose credentials have been forged by bombs and bullets'. This was provocative coming from the man who had acted as a go-between for the Provisionals and Willie Whitelaw, but Hume was addressing an American audience, and seeking to detach them from a romantic view of an historic problem.

The absence of political life in Northern Ireland, Hume pointed out, provided both an opportunity and an argument for the men of violence. They could play on the frustrations of the minority, asking in the face of British immobilism: who but we are doing anything about Northern Ireland? Finally, there was a politico-military argument. The Provos had hardened into a ruthless terrorist force able to make up in experience and technique what they had lost in political support. Mao's dictum about guerrilla fish swimming in the water of popular approval no longer applied. 'We can now see that the fish need less water than we thought,' he noted grimly.

Hume none the less saw 'no hope of success' for the IRA campaign. 'It is, I suppose, conceivable that it might eventually frighten a feeble British government out of Northern Ireland before any process could begin,' he added. 'What would undoubtedly follow would be a serious risk of a bloodbath. This would quickly spread to the south, and, after thousands of deaths, would finally resolve itself by the division of the island into two bristling, homogeneous sectarian states, neither stable, both sunk in the obscurantism of their most extreme supporters.' He followed this chilling picture of Ireland sunk into barbarism (so prescient of events in Bosnia) with the ringing assessment: 'No military victory followed by a political settlement is possible in Northern Ireland. That is true not for the Provisionals alone but for the Loyalists and the British government as well.'

If not, then how could the problem be solved? Hume called for a 'positive and decisive' initiative, taken by London and Dublin acting together. 'They should first make it clear that there are no longer any unconditional guarantees for any section of the northern community. There is only a commitment to achieving a situation in which there are guarantees for all.' They should agree that there was no easy solution, only a process leading to the ultimate goal: 'An agreed Ireland with positive roles for all.' Drawing on the examples of the United States and the European Community, where constitutions able to harness great differences for the common good had been forged, he observed that they had created a 'unity in diversity'. Was it too much to ask that two responsible governments begin to declare themselves now in favour of such a process? 'Can we too build a unity in diversity?'

It was a challenge issued at the conclusion of his most acute and passionate analysis of events to date. Hume got his answer in the shambles of the 'Atkins Talks' in January 1980. The Northern Ireland Secretary, originally greeted as 'Humphrey Who?' by the *Belfast Telegraph* several months previously, was making slow progress with his plans for a constitutional conference. A genial but unimpressive figure, he had already earned the wrath of the Official Unionists who were boycotting the talks on the grounds that devolution might loosen ties with Britain. Hume had agreed to attend, along with Paisley's DUP and the moderate Unionist Alliance Party.

Unhappily, far from meeting to create 'unity in diversity', the parties were all busily pursuing their own exclusive agendas. Paisley was there chiefly because Jim Molyneaux, the Official Unionist leader, was not. He saw a clear opportunity to take over the entire Unionist constituency, and kept Atkins interested with private hints of compromise. Hume complained at the opening of the conference that North–South dialogue had been excluded from the terms of reference, and successfully insisted that the Irish dimension be discussed at 'parallel' talks. Privately, he did not believe that Paisley was willing to make any concessions, and he wanted Unionist intransigence to be seen for the destructive influence that it was. Atkins proposed various complicated ideas for devolved administration in the province, including weighted majorities and co-ordinated groups of committee chairmen, and a secondary chamber holding a minority veto. Anything, in sum, that was not called 'power-sharing'.

Paisley basked in the new-found approval of the liberal British press for his 'statesmanlike' attitude. Hume advised scepticism, which was fully justified when the DUP turned the full force of its unyielding bigotry on the hapless Atkins. 'Maybe you'll believe me now,' Hume told him. The talks were formally adjourned indefinitely on 24 March 1980. Hume kept up the pressure in private, urging the Northern Ireland Secretary in an intense de-briefing to consider a joint London–Dublin initiative to circumvent the Unionist veto. The new Taoiseach, Charles Haughey, had made the same plea at his Fianna Fail conference a month before, but Mrs Thatcher said at Westminster on the eve of her first meeting with him: 'The future of constitutional affairs of Northern Ireland is a matter for the people of Northern Ireland, this government and this parliament and no one else.' In other words, the British guarantee was not a matter for negotiation.

However, beneath the ice, inexorable pressures were building up. For the past two years, IRA prisoners in the 'H-blocks' at the Maze prison had been engaged in a 'dirty protest' to win political status, substantially granted by Willie Whitelaw but revoked by Merlyn Rees in 1976. Protests in the prisons began immediately, and in 1978 after a riot in which beds and other cell furniture were destroyed, the authorities made it a condition of good behaviour for their return.

The inmates refused, and were left in bare cells with nothing but blankets and mattresses. They would not leave their cells and the warders refused to clean them. As human excreta began to pile up on the floor, the prisoners began smearing it on the walls, so as to clear a space for their mattress and to diminish the foul smell. As fast as the prison authorities cleaned the cells with steam hoses, the IRA men went back on the 'dirty protest', despite vomiting and plagues of maggots. Dr Thomas O'Fiaich, Hume's teacher at Maynooth who was now Archbishop of Armagh, visited the prison and said: 'One would hardly allow an animal to remain in such conditions, let alone a human being ... The stench and filth in some of the cells, with the remains of rotten food and human excreta scattered around the walls was unbearable. In two of them I was unable to speak for fear of vomiting.'[12]

With the collapse of his 'rolling devolution' ideas, Atkins now announced the phasing out of 'special category' status from 1 April 1980 for all prisoners convicted of terrorist offences. The IRA inmates, whose campaign of non-co-operation was aimed at winning the right to wear their own clothes and associate freely within the compound, more generous remission of sentences and freedom from prison work, began to discuss a new weapon: an organized mass hunger strike. Detailed preparation went on all summer, while Atkins busied himself with another futile discussion paper. *The Government of Northern Ireland: Proposals for Further Discussion* appeared in July, just before the marching season opened. Atkins proposed either an executive with seats allocated by proportional representation, or a majority-rule executive counter-balanced by a Council of the Assembly with a Catholic majority. Hume, who had already urged his own views on Mrs Thatcher in a face-to-face meeting at Downing Street in mid-May, found little to be commended in the document. The Unionists, for their own, entirely different reasons, agreed with him.

NINE

HUNGER STRIKE

ON THE MORNING OF 27 October 1980, seven Republican prisoners in the Maze camp refused breakfast, so beginning the hunger strike that was to polarize Northern Ireland yet further and exacerbate the violence, particularly in Britain. The 'fast unto death' is not unknown in Irish history; the practice of achieving justice by self-starvation had a place in the medieval civil code of Ireland, and legend dates it back even further. St Patrick is said to have gone on hunger strike against God, and the deity is said to have conceded – 'capitulation in the face of such self-sacrifice being seen by early Christians as a godly quality'.[1]

In modern times, the practice was resurrected for political purposes by Irish Republicans incarcerated for their part in the war of independence that following the abortive Easter Rising in 1916. Prisoners held at Mountjoy gaol, Dublin, rejected food in protest at the brutal treatment meted out for refusing to do prison work or wear prison clothes. These two issues became core objectives in the IRA's search for status as political prisoners. Thomas Ashe, a thirty-two-year-old Republican leader, died in 1917 after the authorities force-fed him, but his death was eclipsed by the hunger strike of Terence Mac-Swiney, Lord Mayor of Cork, who refused to recognize British rule in Ireland. MacSwiney, forty-one, a noted literary figure, was gaoled for two years on a sedition charge (he had been caught attending an IRA meeting in his own town hall) and promptly offered himself to 'the bravest test'. He died in Brixton prison, south London, where the authorities had transferred him, after starving himself for seventy-four days. Huge crowds greeted the return of his coffin, and the Pope sent a blessing to his funeral service.

MacSwiney's words – 'It is not those who can inflict the most, but those who can suffer the most who will conquer' – have filled Republican hearts to bursting point down the generations. So it was not surprising that the IRA revived the tactic half a century later. Veteran Republican Billy McKee's threat to 'fast unto death' in 1972 was instrumental in prompting William Whitelaw to introduce 'special status' after little more than five weeks. The Price sisters, Doloures and Marian, convicted for their role in a London car-bombing, won the right to serve their sentences in Ireland after a hunger strike lasting 200 days, during which time they were force-fed.

The action of Brendan Hughes, commanding officer of the IRA inside the H-blocks of the Maze, in refusing breakfast that morning must be seen within this historical context. For John Hume, already beset with political difficulties after the collapse of the Atkins initiative, the prospect was calamitous. Nothing was more guaranteed to boost popular support for the Provisional IRA and the political prospects of Sinn Fein than a long, drawn-out hunger strike engaging the deep sympathy of the Catholic community. 'It was', he admits, 'a very serious period.'[2] The prisoners said they were willing to meet an agonizing death to establish that they were political prisoners. Mrs Thatcher was adamant. Within twenty-four hours, she had ruled out any concessions.

An anxious Hume appealed to the Northern Ireland Secretary to investigate the possibility of using a recent report of the European Commission for Human Rights as an avenue to settle the growing crisis. That report was an adjudication in June 1980 on a complaint by Republican prisoner Kieran Nugent, the first Provisional to be refused special status and the man who began the 'blanket protest'. Nugent claimed that his treatment was inhuman and degrading, but the Commission held that the 'dirty protest' conditions were self-inflicted to enlist sympathy for political aims. However, the report also accused the British government of an 'inflexible approach', arguing that the prison authorities were more interested in punishing the Provos' offences against prison discipline than in exploring ways of resolving 'such a serious deadlock'.

Hume believed that if the Northern Ireland Office showed itself to be flexible, then so would the hunger-strikers. He opened up a line of contact between the prisoners and Atkins, using the Maze chaplain as a go-between. 'I got involved trying to bring the hunger strikes to an end,' Hume recalled. 'I was approached by a priest who was working with the prisoners. I went to Atkins with a proposal that would end the hunger strikes that a spokesman for the prisoners had agreed.'[3] This compromise is understood to have involved concessions on freedom of association and freedom for prisoners to wear their own clothes. Atkins was delighted, and asked him to stand ready. Hume sent a message into the Maze: 'If I come in and I am there when you are told the plan, you can take it this is the one I have agreed.' In other words, Hume acted as a personal guarantor.

Unknown to Hume, however, Atkins was also working on another plan, one which offered fewer concessions and risked less loss of face. Events were going his way. The Provisionals were concerned that one of the seven, Sean McKenna, was close to death. He was losing his sight when the authorities took him to the Royal Victoria Hospital, Belfast, on 18 December. Simultaneously, a British government official and a Redemptorist priest brought into the Maze a long document detailing peace terms. The hunger-strikers seized on this paper, and came off the strike. It was not until the Provisional inmates scrutinized the document closely that they appreciated it was no more than a verbose reiteration of a thirty-two page explanation of prison rules that had been given to them – and rejected – earlier. The prisoners could wear their own clothes during recreation time, but had to 'come off the blanket' and wear prison uniform during 'working time'. In the first biography of Hume, Barry White recorded the SDLP leader's suspicion that 'Sinn Fein had insisted on taking charge. Some at SF headquarters were by no means convinced that a hunger strike was in their interests.'[4]

Talking to me a decade later, Hume was more specific. 'The government sent in their plans through another priest, and in a sense when they [the prisoners] got the plans, they were conned by [Gerry] Adams. And that led to Bobby Sands, which led on to . . .'[5] At this point he shook his head and lit another cigarette. 'This was an incredibly difficult period.' In fact, Adams had already condemned the hunger strike, writing that Sinn Fein was 'tactically, strategically, physically and morally opposed'.[6] What would have happened if

Hume had been able to carry through his initiative is more than idle speculation. A settlement closer to the prisoners' demands might have avoided what followed: the death by self-starvation of ten Republican prisoners and of many more civilians at the hands of the IRA. The Provisionals inside the Maze quickly realized they had been taken in, and under a new commanding officer – the stubborn hardliner, Bobby Sands – preparations began almost immediately for a new hunger strike.

Hume had not been politically idle. At the November conference of the SDLP in Newcastle, County Down, his first since taking over from Gerry Fitt as leader, Hume put his imprimatur on a clear statement of party policy on Northern Ireland. The twelve-point discussion document, *Strategy for Peace*, intended for wider circulation than the delegates gathered by the seaside, rehearsed the attempts at partnership, in particular the 'noble experiment' of 1974. It asked whether any agreement could ever be reached within the context of Northern Ireland 'as it is presently structured' and argued that responsibility for finding a solution must be shared with the politicians and people of Britain and Ireland.

Turning to the British guarantee, the document developed, for the first time in such a formal context, the notion that Britain 'has no longer any interest in remaining in Ireland'. This formula, later to be expanded to 'selfish economic or strategic interest', was the real intellectual beginning of the peace process that led on to the Hume–Adams talks and the ceasefire of 1995. It was to be dignified (or debased, depending on your point of view) with the description of 'Humespeak', as though it were an Orwellian slogan rather than a genuine and intelligent means of persuading Nationalists and Republicans alike that Britain could be drawn into a process of reconciliation in an 'agreed Ireland' (the phrase of the *Foreign Affairs* article) rather than blasted out of the country by Semtex.

The Hume–SDLP document went on to propose joint talks between the British and Irish governments, leading to a constitutional conference. This would, in turn, 'provide the forum in which the necessary negotiations for a New Ireland and for new forums of Anglo-Irish co-operation can take place'. Apart from the two governments, all major political parties would be invited to attend, and table their own proposals for the future. The SDLP would concentrate on three areas: constitutional structures for a New Ireland; a Bill of Rights and possible structures for developing Anglo-Irish Relations. The first might yield a unitary, or a federal, state; the second would safeguard human and civil rights; the third would encourage development to the mutual advantage of both peoples – an expression of reconciliation between Ireland and Britain. The word 'reconciliation' appeared again twice in the final section, presenting the SDLP policy paper as a challenge to parties and people alike to forge 'the consent' necessary to make any political agreement work.

Like Britain's 'interest' in Northern Ireland, these two key words, 'reconciliation' and 'consent', underpin Hume's political philosophy. Neither is attractive to the Unionist majority, who fear they are being enticed into giving up their culture and their hegemony by warm words. 'Reconciliation' has religious echoes only to be expected from someone of Hume's strong Catholic background, but if it is to mean anything other than an expression of hope that ancient wrongs will be forgotten (or at any rate forgiven), then a dramatic change of heart will be needed on both sides of the sectarian divide in Northern Ireland. There were no signs of it in 1981, and there are precious few today. Consent is an even more difficult word. Conor Cruise O'Brien, the Irish diplomat turned politician, famously said 'consent means the right to say no'. Hume has crossly argued: 'That's clever, but doesn't get us any further ahead.'[7] He conceded that a 51–49 vote for a changed constitutional situation would not be good enough, because the large minority would resist change, just as the Catholic minority has resisted the status quo. He spoke instead of the broad consent of the Protestant community, without defining what proportion would be necessary or acceptable to both sides.

These problems of definition and meaning took second place for the moment to the noisy reality of the hunger strike. Delegates at the Slieve Donard Hotel were barracked by chanting Sinn Fein demonstrators, and the conference adopted a motion critical of the British government's 'inept' handling of the crisis. The SDLP agreed that prisoners should be allowed to wear their own clothes and serve their sentences under a regime based on human dignity. But Hume's underlying political message from the conference resurfaced with remarkable speed and gravity within a month, at the Conservatives' first Anglo-Irish summit in Dublin on 8 December 1980.

Mrs Thatcher indicated the importance she attached to the occasion by bringing with her Lord Carrington, her Foreign Secretary who had just brought the long-running war of independence in Rhodesia to a successful diplomatic conclusion, her Chancellor Geoffrey Howe and Humphrey Atkins, the Northern Ireland Secretary. Haughey, 'the Boss', who had called for a British withdrawal from Ireland, took his top team to the conference at Dublin Castle. The communiqué at the close of the talks spoke of 'extremely constructive and significant' contacts. Moreover, it promised joint studies on 'the totality of relationships' between the two countries. There was even reference to 'new institutional structures'. Haughey saw this as an 'historic breakthrough', and suggested there were no limits to the arrangements that might be agreed. Mrs Thatcher was more cautious, insisting that there was 'absolutely no possibility' of a confederal Ireland.

The two governments agreed to hold similar meetings twice a year. Hume and the SDLP were hugely encouraged. The Unionists were understandably alarmed, particularly when Haughey unwisely (but characteristically) made the extravagant claim that the whole constitutional position of Northern Ireland as part of the UK was now in the melting pot. When they next met, on the fringes of an EC summit at Maastricht in the spring of 1981, Mrs Thatcher attacked him so severely that the normally loquacious Haughey was unable to defend himself before she walked out on him.

Haughey's political faux pas had serious implications for Hume. The Dublin summit probably *did* point the way towards the genuinely historic Anglo-Irish Agreement signed five years later; but in the short term the unreasonable expectations placed upon it raised Hume's party's hopes and then dashed them again, just as events in the Maze were approaching their climax. For the sake of appearances Hume went along with Haughey, while privately confiding his fears to Garret Fitzgerald, leader of the Fine Gael opposition and a sworn political enemy of the Taoiseach. In late 1980, Fitzgerald suggested to a senior SDLP figure that if Hume wanted to make his closeness to Fine Gael known beyond question, all he had to do was tip off the 'Backchat' gossip column in the Dublin *Sunday Independent* that he had spent a holiday with Garret and Joan Fitzgerald in the south of France that summer. 'When this idea was put to John shortly afterwards he immediately rejected it,' recollected Fitzgerald. 'But within a fortnight the story appeared in "Backchat" – and it was not I who leaked it.'[8]

Two days after the Anglo-Irish summit, Humphrey Atkins, speaking in the Commons in a debate on the continuation of the Emergency Provisions Act, denounced the protest movement inside prison as an 'important arm in the strategy of the Provisional IRA', saying that it was aimed at securing political legitimacy for a movement whose only weapon was violence. They were words he perhaps came to regret. On 1 March 1981, Bobby Sands, a member of the IRA since he was eighteen and at that time serving a fourteen-year sentence for firearms offences, began the Provisionals' second hunger strike. It was designed to be a rolling protest. As commanding officer inside the H-blocks, Sands went first, and he would be joined by the second a fortnight later. Thereafter, a new hunger-striker would join the campaign every week.

Initially, the resumption of what had seemed to be a failed strategy had little impact. A Sinn Fein rally in West Belfast attracted only a third of the turnout that had greeted the first hunger strike. Dr Edward Daly, the Catholic Bishop of Derry, condemned the action as morally unjustified. Atkins ritually reiterated the government's refusal to grant political status. Sands was adamant that he was prepared to die, telling a Republican-minded priest, Fr Denis Faul, 'Greater love than this hath no man than he lay down his life for his friend'. For all the melodrama, however, the second hunger strike seemed destined for more ignominy than the first.

On 5 March, with Sands only five days into his strike and still writing poetry, Frank Maguire, Independent Republican MP for Fermanagh and South Tyrone, died of a heart attack, triggering a Westminster by-election. 'Big Frank', the MP who had turned up to abstain in person and help bring down the Labour government a year before, bequeathed a Nationalist majority of 4,987 over the combined opposition – including Austin Currie who had stood as

Independent SDLP, taking third place with a respectable 10,785 votes. Gerry Adams spotted a tremendous opportunity for publicity for 'the struggle' and suggested that Sands run as a parliamentary candidate from his bed in the Maze prison hospital. Local opinion was lukewarm, but SF strategists decided to go ahead anyway, and announced his candidature as 'Anti H-Block/Armagh Political Prisoner' on 26 February.

Their move placed Hume and his party leadership in a quandary. If they fielded a candidate in an area where their strength was limited the SDLP would be accused of splitting the Nationalist vote and letting in a Unionist at the expense of a man starving himself to death for the cause of a united Ireland. If they failed to put someone up, the SDLP would be accused of cowardice. At first, Hume's executive voted to stand against Sands, prompting a private condemnation from the IRA inside the prison as 'devious pro-Brit bastards'. They then retreated when Noel Maguire, Big Frank's brother and heir-apparent for the seat in the customary dynastic Irish fashion, lodged his nomination papers. Austin Currie was ready to stand again as Independent SDLP to show the Social Democrats meant business in their hostility to the men of violence, but he stayed his hand to give Maguire a clear run against Harry West, the hard-line Unionist contender.

Republicanism runs deep in the constituency, a border area that has seen more than its share of political bloodshed, and Noel Maguire came under intense pressure to withdraw his nomination. He did so just a few minutes before the deadline, frustrating Currie's plans. Maguire told reporters, 'I just cannot have the life of another man on my hands' and urged his supporters to vote for Sands. There was more than a suspicion of Sinn Fein intimidation.

Hume justifies to this day his party's decision not to offer a formal challenge. 'Sometimes in politics you are faced with two wrong choices, and you take the lesser. The atmosphere was so emotional at that time, the danger was that we would have been wiped out. We would have suffered so severely, it would have damaged the party right across Northern Ireland.'[9] Officially, his explanation is that Noel Maguire's late withdrawal gave the party 'no time to enter the fray', though it is clear that the SDLP had hesitated and was outfoxed

by Sinn Fein. To his critics who argue that he was at best pusillani-
mous and at worst complicit, he retorts: 'You can only make judgements about the past if you have lived in it. The massively emotional
atmosphere made decisions very, very difficult. The results were that
we retained our strength as a party and kept building. In the very
first election we contested, we got 14 per cent of the vote. In the
last election, we got 29 per cent. In every election in between our
vote has risen steadily.'[10]

On polling day, 9 April, with the eyes of the world's media focused
on an obscure Northern Ireland by-election, Sands triumphed with
a majority of 1,446. It was a propaganda calamity for the government,
though Mrs Thatcher sought to nullify the result by insisting: 'It is
not political. It is a crime.'

Recognizing the harm being done not just to his own party but
to any hopes of a peaceful resolution of the prison crisis, Hume
turned desperately to Dublin and Europe for help. With the support
of Irish Prime Minister Haughey and Derry's Bishop Daly, he sought
the intervention of the European Commission on Human Rights. In
June 1980, the Strasbourg-based Commission had ruled out Kieran
Nugent's claim for political status, but criticized Britain for inflexi-
bility in ending the crisis. Hume, working his contacts, tried to organize an informal mediation by two senior members of the Commission.
When this initiative foundered through internal hostility, Haughey
persuaded Sands's sister Marcella to lodge a formal complaint with
the Commission. This move allowed Hume's contacts – the Danish
acting president, Professor Carl-aage Norgard, and a Norwegian
professor, Torkel Opsahl – to visit Sands. He refused to see them
without the presence of high-ranking Republicans, and later slipped
into a coma. On 5 May, the sixty-sixth day of his hunger strike,
he died.

Three more hunger-strikers followed him to their deaths that
month, amid rising tension in Catholic areas. Others took their place,
and Catholic Primate O'Fiaich warned the government that it faced
the wrath of 'the whole nationalist population' if a solution were not
found.

Hume struggled to make Mrs Thatcher understand that a vote
exceeding 30,000 for a Provisional convict represented more than 'a

crime'. He was granted a meeting with her in Downing Street on 13 May, a meeting described in a letter smuggled out from a leading Provo in the Maze as being between 'Jack and Tin-knickers'. The talks were postponed for four hours by the Northern Ireland Office, and to make good use of his spare time Hume went to see Michael Foot, Leader of the Opposition. Hume tried to obtain his support, but Foot equivocated. Labour was holding to a bipartisan position with the government on the hunger strikes. Hume's departure from the Labour leader's office coincided with the arrival of Gerry Fitt, who had publicly condemned the hunger-strikers as 'brutal murderers'. Fitt, once Hume's party leader but now politically at odds with him, persuaded Foot to ignore the SDLP leader and stick to supporting Thatcher. Hume was now without a party colleague at Westminster, Fitt having changed his party denomination to Independent Socialist.

It was not an auspicious start to his third visit to Downing Street. The Prime Minister gave him (and herself) a Scotch and listened to his litany of complaint. Hume warned that deaths and the success of Sands at the ballot box presented a real danger to constitutional nationalism in Northern Ireland and the Republic. The people in the Maze did have public sympathy. He suggested a compromise: if the government would allow the prisoners to wear their own clothes and make other minor concessions, he would seek to bring about an end to the crisis. It was more or less the settlement he had sought from Atkins six months previously, and he was no more successful on this occasion. Mrs Thatcher reiterated her views, and refused to become involved. Hume found it difficult to control his temper, lecturing the Prime Minister on her inability to understand the situation. Democracy in Northern Ireland was at stake, he argued. It was a wasted hour. The Prime Minister's considered response was an amendment to the Representation of the People Act prohibiting prisoners from standing for parliament, and a sharp denunciation of Hume's 'Four Horsemen'.

In the local elections on 20 May, Hume's assertion that the SDLP increased its share of the vote every time proved not to be wholly accurate. In common with other parties of the centre, the Social Democratic and Labour Party saw its share of the vote fall from

20.6 per cent in 1977, to 17.5 per cent, while the Nationalist Irish Independence Party took 3.9 per cent. The SDLP tally of seats on district councils fell by ten to 103.

The effects of the hunger strike were being felt everywhere, as Hume discovered in mid-July. Martin Hurson, a twenty-four-year-old 'country boy' serving twenty years for conspiracy to murder, possession of firearms and membership of the IRA, began to sink after only forty-two days of fasting. His brother Francis heard the news from a hotel receptionist in Donegal. The next person he bumped into was John Hume, to whom he confided: 'I think Martin's dead.' Hume replied: 'God, he's not,' and telephoned the Maze on his behalf. Francis Hurson made it to the prison just hours before the last rites were read.[11] A week after Hurson's death, Hume was involved in telephone diplomacy with Atkins, who assured him that 'the whole matter is under reconsideration'. If it was, the rethink came to nothing.

Sands's death forced another by-election in Fermanagh and South Tyrone. More than three months had passed since that date, but the government was reluctant to order a poll for fear of another Republican victory and a further wave of unrest. Eventually, the writ for the by-election was moved by a Welsh Nationalist MP. The hunger-strikers continued to die – the tenth followed Sands to his grave on polling day, 20 August.

Hume, distressed that his European initiative had come to nothing, again decided that discretion would be the better part of valour in the by-election – even though the Republican candidate was Owen Carron, Sands's election agent, standing on an avowedly Provisional platform. Hume later defended himself, arguing that with ten men dead and more prepared to die, a split Catholic vote would give Thatcher a Unionist victory. 'The SDLP would have been accused of lifting the siege of pressure on the British,' he said. 'That would have reverberated through other elections. It was a no-win situation. We would have drowned in the deluge. Politics is not only about principles but about the ability to put principles into practice. The second is as important as the first.'[12]

Hume's political discretion did not save him from his critics. The Unionists accused him of a lack of political courage and an abdication of democratic responsibility. It is certainly arguable that the SDLP's act of expediency – which allowed Carron to win with a bigger majority than Sands had – both lost the party valuable credibility and gave Sinn Fein the boost it needed to re-enter politics. Three days after Carron's victory, Provisional Sinn Fein announced that it was now ending its boycott of Northern Ireland council elections, and would also seek to unseat Gerry Fitt, the SDLP ex-leader in West Belfast, who had been fiercely and publicly critical of the hunger strike. The political damage did not end there. To those remaining moderate Protestants who might have been attracted to Hume's party, the double failure in Fermanagh and South Tyrone was a catastrophe. To confirmed Unionists it merely reinforced the Paisleyite image of John Hume as a Republican wolf in sheep's clothing, which continued to undermine him in the years to come when he began the peace process with Sinn Fein.

By mid-1981 there was a new Fine Gael administration in office in Dublin, headed by Hume's long-standing friend Garret Fitzgerald. He had reinforced Hume's warning of growing sympathy for the hunger-strikers and now appealed to London for a fresh understanding. A period of intense political activity ensued, but nothing came of it. In fact, the hunger strike was beginning to collapse, as relatives of those nearing death intervened to have them taken off the fast. It took the arrival of a new Northern Ireland Secretary, James Prior, to break the deadlock. Prior, a gentleman farmer and a Tory of the old school, had as Employment Secretary introduced the first of the labour law changes that were to curb the power of Britain's trade unions. However, he was regarded as a leading Conservative 'wet', on the left of the Cabinet and a possible rival to Thatcher for the party leadership. He was reluctant to go to Stormont Castle, and relented only when he was allowed to remain on the Cabinet's influential Economic Committee and to take his political chums – Lord Gowrie, Nicholas Scott and John Patten – with him as ministers.

Within four days of taking up the post, Prior made the first visit to the Maze by a Secretary of State for two years, spending three hours in informal talks with Republicans. Soon after this he met Hume and other community leaders, including Fr Denis Faul. Prior disclaimed all talk of victory over the hunger-strikers, appealing to them directly to give up. If they did so, he would 'amplify' on government promises of reform within the H-blocks. On 3 October, the last six hunger-strikers ended their fast. They blamed 'mounting pressure and cleric-inspired demoralization' of their families. Three days later, Prior conceded one of their key demands: the right to wear their own clothes at all times. He also made partial concessions on lost remission, freedom of association with the H-blocks and on prison visits by families. On the outstanding issue of prison work, he pledged further possible changes. Ten men had died for this package, which plainly did not amount to 'prisoner of war' status, but the hunger strike had ushered in a serious political rival for Catholic votes that perturbed Hume.

The hunger strikes unquestionably changed the nature of political warfare in Ulster. In future, Hume could no longer be seen as the unchallenged leader of the Nationalist community. Even Margaret Thatcher noted that 'the SDLP was losing ground to the republicans', believing that this was partly a reflection of 'the general ineffectiveness' of John Hume's MPs.[13] Around this time, the British ambassador to Dublin even suggested that Cardinal O'Fiaich and other members of the Catholic hierarchy could be conscripted as substitute representatives for the Northern minority. Sean Donlon, at the Department of Foreign Affairs, left him in no doubt that both main parties in the South saw the SDLP as the legitimate leader of the Nationalist community, and 'trying to substitute the Cardinal for John Hume would get the British nowhere'.

By showing that their prisoners were willing to suffer for their cause as well as to kill for it, and encouraged by their success in the Westminster by-elections, Sinn Fein and the IRA began to broaden their struggle into what became known as the 'bomb and ballot box' strategy. Only three weeks after the hunger strikes ended, Danny Morrison, former internee and Sinn Fein spokesman for the fasting prisoners, told Sinn Fein's annual conference: 'Who here really believes we can win the war through the ballot box? But will anyone here object if, with a ballot box in one hand and the Armalite in the other, we take power in Ireland?'

Hume was well aware of the dangers of polarizing Catholic

Nationalists between working-class adherents, often unemployed, living in the rural Republican heartlands or the urban enclaves of Belfast, and the traditional middle-class supporters of the SDLP, secure in their professional jobs. If this potentially damaging drift was to be halted, there needed to be tangible progress on the constitutional front. In Jim Prior, Hume found a generally supportive figure. Lord Gowrie, his deputy, scion of a Protestant family in the South who spent much of his early life in Donegal, was even more sympathetic. 'Gowrie knew the problem well, coming from his own Irish background,' recalled Hume.[14] The two sides engaged in a 'very interesting' dialogue. Hume was much encouraged by the setting up of the Anglo-Irish Inter-Governmental Council on 6 November 1981, even if its role was exaggerated by Dublin and Mrs Thatcher continued to insist that Northern Ireland 'is part of the UK – as much as my constituency is'.

A week later, Hume took some – indeed, much – of the credit for the new joint body, arguing that the balance of power in Britain in relation to Ireland had shifted substantially. 'The Anglo-Irish political initiative, originally an SDLP concept, as the Taoiseach said in the Dail, has been formally launched by the Irish and British governments. In a major development, Mrs Thatcher agreed with Garret Fitzgerald in London to commit her government to "efforts to heal the divisions within Northern Ireland, and to reconcile the two major traditions in the two parts of Ireland".'

With this step taken, Hume was able to insist: 'Our long-standing policy on the way to promote agreement in Ireland has at last been adopted by a British government. These are important political advances in which you and I, as members of this party, can take considerable satisfaction. They are the first rewards – not the last – of years of patient, unfaltering efforts on the part of everyone here, in arguing the rationale of the politics of a divided Ireland.'[15]

Hume pinned his party's hopes on the determination of London and Dublin to make progress together. 'There must be no faltering, no diversion, no failure of nerve. We should expect progress to continue with a step-by-step, relatively unspectacular rhythm.' Here, consciously or not, he was drawing on Prior's 'step by step' philosophy in the reform of the trade unions. Less convincingly, he began to lay out his view of 'the growing reality of Britain's intentions'.

He maintained: 'The British will to territory, to power and to solidarity in Northern Ireland is simply no longer real. It doesn't exist any more. There is no positive commitment, merely a bothersome obligation.' Of course, the guarantee in the 1973 Act 'so dear to Mrs Thatcher's heart' remained; but what the British government was saying 'was tantamount to a man saying to his wife, "I will stay with you as long as you like, because I am obliged to do so under the guarantee clause of the '73 Marriage Act; but the very instant you agree to a divorce, you shall have it; and, what is more, I wish you to know that I have my lawyer on permanent retainer, so that there will be no delaying in arranging the separation." That is what the London communiqué says, like it or not.' Unfortunately, that is not at all how Mrs Thatcher, whose own instincts were 'profoundly Unionist' read the communiqué, as events were swiftly to prove.

Hume could none the less look back with some satisfaction on his achievements as a Member of the European Parliament. After he tabled a resolution within the Socialist Group for a serious analysis of the EC's role in revitalizing Northern Ireland, the Commission agreed to invest heavily in the province. The initial package of £16 million was earmarked for housing in Belfast, with more promised. The money was additional to UK government spending. Northern Ireland also benefited substantially from the EC Small Farm Plan, 'another SDLP initiative'. Europe's politicians were at last taking an interest in Ulster, which came out second to bottom in a survey of the EC's most deprived regions, just ahead of Calabria, on the heel of Italy.

He could take some comfort, too, from the SDLP's heightened profile in local government. The party now had 104 councillors, an increase of three on 1980. For the first time it had taken overall control of Derry, where social democracy in Northern Ireland had been born. Membership was up by 16 per cent. It may have been an appalling year for politics, but 'the reports of our demise are indeed somewhat exaggerated'.

In private talks with Hume, Jim Prior pushed ahead with his proposals for a new form of government for the province, partly borrowing from the SDLP proposals put forward to the Unionists for an American-style division of power between an appointed executive and an elected legislature. Hume was stimulated by his open-mindedness, and by Lord Gowrie's optimistic talk of 'people living in the North who regard themselves as Irish administered by Ireland and Britain'. There was much talk of 'rolling devolution' which the Loyalist hardliners could not veto, because the Secretary of State would appoint the executive from the parties in direct proportion to their voting strengths. Here were the renewed beginnings of power-sharing.

When Prior's White Paper, *Northern Ireland: A Framework for Devolution*, was published on 5 April 1982, however, it was a bitter disappointment for Hume. Mrs Thatcher, unhappy about the exaggerated expectations placed on the Anglo-Irish Inter-Governmental Council, had taken an axe to the original wording. She cut out an entire chapter on relations with the Irish Republic to appease Unionist sentiment. She also insisted on a blocking mechanism, so that no powers could be devolved to local politicians unless 70 per cent of those elected to a seventy-eight member assembly agreed. This ploy handed the Unionists a veto on political progress, and Charles Haughey, back in office as the Irish Prime Minister, dismissed the White Paper as 'an unworkable mistake'. Hume rejected the plan as 'largely unworkable' and warned Prior that the SDLP would not participate in the business of the assembly.

Britain's defence of the Falkland Islands that month relegated Northern Ireland to the political sidelines. Relations between London and Dublin were frozen when Haughey publicly opposed Britain's sending of a military task force to retake the islands. This was Thatcher's 'finest hour', and Haughey's 'unhelpful stance' was punished by a complete cessation of talks. Prior managed to navigate his proposals through the Commons, however, with the aid of the Labour opposition, despite the hostility of the Official Unionists and twenty Tory MPs who voted against the measure. Three junior ministers resigned from the government in protest. During the Commons debate, Prior told MPs that direct rule of Northern Ireland 'does not offer a long-term answer' and warned that the alternative to a gradual devolution of power would be complete integration of the province into the UK – the path preferred by Enoch Powell.

Preparations for an assembly went ahead, and in late August Hume's party decided to contest the elections but not take their seats – a resumption of the old Nationalist Party's abstentionist strategy that Hume had come into politics to get rid of for ever. However, even this delicate political footwork could not save him from the wrath of hooligan Republicans. Late on the night of 26 August, his large terrace home in West End Park, Derry, was stoned and fire-bombed by youths who recognized him when he went to the aid of a neighbour whose lorry had been set on fire. Pat Hume and the couple's two youngest children, John, then aged thirteen and nine-year-old Maureen were in the house when it was attacked. 'They were obviously very frightened as nothing like this has ever happened before,' Hume told the *Belfast Telegraph*.

The newspaper pointed out that the current issue of *Republican News*, the Provisional Sinn Fein paper, contained a strong attack on the SDLP leader. The article described Hume as 'a dangerous collaborator', and blamed him for influencing the SDLP executive to take part in the assembly elections. It was true that Hume had been powerfully instrumental in winning over the SDLP executive to a two-to-one majority in favour of his compromise: stand for the assembly on a platform of a New Ireland, but boycott the assembly's work on the grounds that it was structured to ensure continued Unionist dominance. This was a classic Hume compromise between outright boycott, as urged by hardliners, and acceptance of Thatcher's empty promises.

Naturally, Thatcher blamed the SDLP's tactics and 'negative attitudes' for the subsequent electoral outcome. Sinn Fein, standing for the first time in a Stormont election and riding a wave of sympathy after the hunger strikes, outflanked the SDLP with a simple demand for British withdrawal. Despite some vicious terrorist attacks in England (including the killing of eight soldiers with bombs at the Changing of the Guard and at the bandstand in Regent's Park in London) the Provisionals' political wing polled 10 per cent of the popular vote and took five seats. Hume's party was the main loser, taking fourteen seats – five down on the 1973 Assembly and three down on the 1975 Convention. The only consolation for Hume was a slight improvement on the previous year's local council result: the SDLP share of the popular vote rose 1.5 per cent to 18.8 per cent, finishing in third place behind the Official Unionists and Paisley's DUP.

Most commentators focused on the strong showing by Sinn Fein, echoing Hume's fear that they might displace the SDLP as the representatives of Nationalism in the North. The figures were genuinely alarming. The SDLP's first-preference vote had fallen by around 40,000 from previous similar elections to 118,891, while Sinn Fein had polled 64,191 at their first attempt. An exasperated Thatcher shared the fears expressed by Garret Fitzgerald, now returned to office, about erosion of electoral support for the SDLP. However 'uninspiring' Hume and his colleagues might be, they were the minority's main representatives and an alternative to the IRA. 'They had to be wooed,' she admitted.[16] Accordingly, she revived the talks with Dublin through senior civil servants. In the meantime, neither Hume nor any of his thirteen successful colleagues took up their seats, allowing £20,000 a year each in salary and expenses to go uncollected. With Sinn Fein taking the same line, the Unionists and a few Independents had the chamber to themselves. They had little to do, though they were officially charged with scrutinizing the work of government departments. Even this role was abandoned by the Ulster Unionist Party within a month. The year ended, as it had begun, in blood, with the INLA bombing of the Droppin' Well disco at Ballykelly, County Londonderry, in which seventeen people died, eleven of them soldiers.

TEN

THE ANGLO-IRISH AGREEMENT

POLITICS IN NORTHERN IRELAND may have returned to an all-too-familiar stalemate in early 1983, but John Hume was not the kind of man to let matters rest there. If nothing could come of Stormont and Westminster, then he must look elsewhere: specifically, to Dublin. Garret Fitzgerald was Irish Prime Minister again, and even while in opposition he had shown considerable sympathy for Hume's ideas. In his Dimbleby Lectures broadcast by the BBC in May 1982, Fitzgerald shadowed Hume's ideas about new structures that would respect the diversity of the two traditions in Ireland. What the parties should be looking for, he argued, was a structure, 'however novel', that would enable the people of Ireland to manage together matters that could not be managed so well separately, such as security and the pursuit of European ambitions. He took up the theme again in October, with a speech in Pittsburgh on reconciliation. In this address, he proposed consultations between the Irish government 'and all those in Northern Ireland who might be willing to talk to us – whether they sought, opposed or were indifferent to Irish unity'. Hume did not hesitate. He talked by telephone to Fitzgerald in the USA, and the two agreed to meet.

Six weeks later, Fitzgerald was back in office, having ousted Charles Haughey at a general election in coalition with Dick Spring's Labour Party. Hume had already honed his ideas into a political package. He was looking for a Council for a New Ireland, in which all the constitutional politicians would together define 'what we wish this new Ireland to be'. He looked to politicians in the Republic to 'join us in abandoning rhetoric and, by placing their cards on the table, show what sort of role there will be for the Protestant community, what share of power, what safeguards, what sort of economic situation and what would be the relations between Church and State'.[1]

Hume pressed his case in talks with Fitzgerald in January 1983, while the Irish government was privately warning London that it saw no future for the new Stormont Assembly. Events were moving his way. Peter Barry, rightly regarded as one of the more Nationalist members of the Irish Cabinet and who enjoyed a good working relationship with the SDLP, had become Foreign Affairs Minister. With the Republic facing a financial crisis, however, Fitzgerald initially had difficulty persuading his Cabinet to give the right priority to the North. In late February, he proposed to his government a New Ireland Forum, in which all constitutional parties in the island, including the Unionists, would be invited to participate. Its objectives would be an ending of the violence, reconciling the two traditions in Ireland and securing peace and stability. The terms of reference excluded Irish unity.

Fitzgerald was shocked by the 'almost uniformly negative' reaction of his ministers, who voted twelve to two against proceeding with the initiative. The Taoiseach then intensively lobbied his Cabinet, one by one, arguing cleverly that if they did not accept his plan the opposition Fianna Fail would outmanoeuvre them by announcing acceptance of John Hume's concept of a Council for a New Ireland. This ruse succeeded, and Fitzgerald proposed talks on long-term peace and stability. Hume was impatient for swifter progress on his own formula, and flew from the European Parliament meeting in Strasbourg to Dublin on 10 March to argue his case. Fitzgerald told him he could not stomach his version of a 'Council'; the word smacked too much of the failed Sunningdale Agreement. Instead, he proposed the Forum, open to all constitutional parties, not just the Nationalists. He asked Hume to back this compromise, and the SDLP did so 'without further demur'.

This interpretation, according to Haughey's biographer Bruce Arnold, is too simplistic. He notes that there has always been competition between Fianna Fail and Fine Gael for the co-operation of the SDLP, and that Hume's original idea had been for 'a "Council" for a new Ireland, which would bring together the nationalist parties without all the other parties becoming involved'.[2] Fitzgerald 'had his work cut out' persuading Hume; however, his commitment, once obtained, was the deciding factor. Fitzgerald was able to enlist the support of the wily Haughey, pointing out that he had the critical backing of John Hume. However, argues Arnold; 'It was something of a botched job.'

Hume later asserted his paternity of the Forum, which led, critically, to the Anglo-Irish Agreement with Mrs Thatcher. The Council for a New Ireland had been floated in his Assembly election manifesto in October 1982. 'My party took a fresh initiative at that stage, designed to break the log-jam and carry our analysis into practical politics.'³ The New Ireland Forum was a deliberative body of elected representatives of the four major constitutional Nationalist parties, North and South, representing more than 90 per cent of the Nationalist population of Ireland (i.e. excluding Sinn Fein). The function of the Forum, in Hume's view, was to hold consultations on the manner in which lasting peace and stability could be achieved in a new Ireland through the democratic process and to report on possible new structures and the way in which these objectives might be achieved. 'In other words, we sought to outline a modern, up to date and formal statement or blueprint, setting out the principles and structures on the basis of which the constitutional Nationalist dream of a new Ireland could be achieved.'⁴ It was, he pointed out, the first time since 1920 that Nationalist Ireland had sat down to examine intensively its attitudes to the problem.

Unfortunately, that was precisely how the other parties saw it. Within days, the Ulster Unionists, Ian Paisley's DUP and even the moderate Alliance Party all rejected invitations to join in the Forum's deliberations. Undeterred, Hume and the Irish government pressed ahead. The SDLP was given five seats on the twenty-seven-member body, which began its meetings on 30 May amid the splendour of Dublin Castle. Its terms of reference looked towards a report by the end of that year, paving the way for substantive negotiations with the British government early in 1984. At the outset, Margaret Thatcher was sceptical about the Forum. She thought that it 'complicated' things, and was not impressed by Dublin's argument that it would buttress John Hume's position within his community, which was being subverted by Sinn Fein. Mulishly, she argued that Hume could do this by taking up his party's seats in the Northern Ireland Assembly, completely misreading political realities. Neither could she see any merit in involving the Unionists in the exercise. That way lay a terrifying revival of the 'Sunningdale ghosts'.

These were exhilarating days for Hume, however. In early May, capitalizing on her victory over General Galtieri's Argentine forces in the Falkland Islands, Mrs Thatcher had called the long-awaited general election. Hume was in with more than a prayer this time. The boundaries for Westminster parliamentary seats had been redrawn, and Northern Ireland would now return seventeen MPs, five more than at the 1979 election. In his election manifesto, *Build a New Ireland*, Hume recalled that in the Assembly elections the previous October, he had proposed a Council for a New Ireland, set up in conjunction with the Irish government, to produce a blueprint 'so that a debate on real alternatives can begin within the Anglo/Irish framework'.

Since that poll, he pointed out the SDLP had delivered. Hume had secured the agreement of the parties of the South. The Forum had begun meeting. The committed efforts it represented were a source of unity, strength and hope. 'Such an approach will effectively challenge the Unionist and British assumptions which underlie their unwillingness to change,' he insisted. 'It is potentially the most significant political initiative since 1920. The SDLP is determined that its potential shall become reality.' The Northern Ireland problem, he predicted, would be at the centre of the next Westminster Parliament. The presence of strong SDLP voices would be crucially important to a positive outcome of these developments. He pleaded for 'a strong, clear manadate' on 9 June, the date of the election.

Hume exploited the opening ceremony of the Forum to gain vital air-time for his ideas, appealing to Unionists to believe that the Nationalist community understood their convictions, and took them seriously. 'Our aim is neither conquest nor coercion,' he argued. 'It is primarily to understand each other so that we can solve this crisis with your agreement and support.' Hume looked beyond opportunism and orthodox politics with an almost missionary determination to 'move mountains' and avoid the province becoming engulfed in 'a furious torrent of hatred, violence and despair'.

In the ensuing poll, the SDLP rejected any idea of a pact with Sinn Fein and fielded candidates in every constituency, the only party to do so. But if this was a test of voters' faith in the heady expectations of the Forum, the results were inconclusive. Hume easily triumphed in the new Foyle constituency, taking 24,071 votes, a majority of 8,148 over his Paisleyite Unionist rival Gregory Campbell in a 77.6 per cent turnout. Martin McGuinness, for Sinn Fein, ran a poor third with fewer then 11,000 votes. However, elsewhere the story was less encouraging. In West Belfast, the intervention of Hume's former party leader Gerry Fitt, running as an Independent against the SDLP candidate Dr Joe Hendron, split the constitutional Nationalist vote, allowing in Gerry Adams, the Sinn Fein president. Overall, the SDLP's share of vote had fallen slightly to 17.9 per cent, while Sinn Fein scored a menacing 13.4 per cent; in plain figures, 137,012 votes to 102,601. 'This was the stuff of political earthquakes,' commented Brendan O'Brien. 'The Republican Movement had finally demonstrated it could fight an armed struggle *and* win elections at the same time.'[5]

Despite his appeal for a strong manadate, Hume was to be his party's only voice at Westminster, facing a reinvigorated Official Unionist Party with eleven seats, the Democratic Unionists with four and the 'popular' Unionists who had one. Since Adams was precluded from taking his seat at Westminster under Sinn Fein's abstentionist policy, Hume was effectively outnumbered fifteen to one. Moreover, his scornful critic Mrs Thatcher had been returned with a breathtaking Tory majority of 144 over all other parties, the biggest since the Labour landslide of 1945. It was a forbidding prospect as he took the oath of allegiance (which, he privately admitted, 'stuck in his throat').[6] Hume took his seat on the second row back of the opposition benches, just in front of the Unionists and directly behind David Owen's Social Democratic Party.

Shortly before seven in the evening on 28 June, Hume rose during a debate on foreign affairs and defence to make his maiden speech.[7] On all sides, it was judged 'remarkable'. He spared no one and no party. Introducing himself as the representative of a new constituency in Ireland's north-west, containing the ancient city of Derry and the town of Strabane, he told the House: 'It is a commentary on the politics of the north of Ireland – or the fact that there is a problem there – that never before has someone with either my religious or my political persuasion stood in this House to represent the city of Derry.'

Pointing out that his constituency had the highest unemployment rate of any in the UK – 38 per cent in Strabane and 28 per cent in Derry – Hume argued that these statistics interacted 'seriously and severely' with the political crisis in Northern Ireland: 'People have wondered about the rise in the political strength of extremism in the north of Ireland. There is no greater example of the reasons for extremism in that area than that we now have a generation of young people who were only four years old in 1969 and 1970 and have grown up in a society in which they have always seen security forces and violence on the streets, in which they have been searched simply because they are young people, and in which, when they reach the age of 18, they have no hope of any employment because they happen to have come of age during the deepest economic crisis for a long time.'

Therefore, Hume told an attentive House, there was resentment among the young, 'and there are people who play upon those resentments, point to a British soldier and say, "Get rid of him and all your problems will be solved". This simplistic message has an appeal to young people.' If the government took seriously the economic crisis in Northern Ireland, and made a determined attack on youth unemployment, it would also be making a determined attack on the problems of extremism.

Turning to Mrs Thatcher's oft-misquoted remark that the people of his province were 'as British as Finchley', Hume tried to put the horrors of Northern Ireland into an English context. 'Imagine 2,000 people being killed on the streets in Yorkshire, 20,000 people maimed and injured, and £430 million spent on compensation for bomb damage; two new prisons built and a third under construction; the rule of law drastically distorted, with the introduction of imprisonment without trial; senior politicians and policemen murdered, and innocent civilians murdered by the security forces and by paramilitary forces. Imagine a shoot-to-kill policy for people suspected of crime being introduced from time to time instead of their being arrested.

Imagine jury courts being disbanded, plastic bullets used on the streets and innocent children being killed. Imagine paramilitary organisations engaging in violence and the type of interrogation methods that led to the British government being found guilty in the European Court of Human Rights being introduced. Imagine hunger strikers dying in prison in Yorkshire and representatives of the paramilitary being elected to this House to represent Yorkshire.'

If those things had happened on what was commonly called the mainland, he asked caustically, would any MP deny that such events would have been a major issue in the general election? Did any MP honestly believe, in their hearts, that the people of Northern Ireland were as British as those in Finchley? 'The truth is,' said Hume grimly, 'that if every Hon. Member spoke his heart, he would say that he has psychologically withdrawn from Northern Ireland. The truth is that Britain has psychologically withdrawn from Northern Ireland. Britain and Northern Ireland would be healthier places if that psychological reality were translated into political reality.'

The extent of the province's problems could be summed up by the 'desperate indictment' of the brick wall that had been built between the two sections of the community in Belfast to keep them apart and to protect them from each other. That wall, he argued, was 'an indictment of anyone who has governed Northern Ireland in the past fourteen years'. It was also an indictment of every political party in the province, and of everyone who had any part to play in the problem. 'It is an indictment of the Unionist tradition, the Nationalist tradition and the British who govern from this House.' But it was also a challenge, 'because the only truth that has emerged out of all the suffering of the past decade is that all our policies have led us to that wall in Belfast'. The real challenge was now to re-examine urgently the traditional approaches to a solution.

MPs representing the Loyalist tradition had a lot of thinking to do, he warned. Their consistent stance in Northern Ireland had been to protect the integrity of their minority tradition. 'I have no quarrel with that objective,' said Hume. 'Any country is richer for diversity. I quarrel with the methods of protecting the integrity. Put crudely, that method dictates: "We must hold all power in our own hands." That is precisely what has been said. It is a violent attitude. It is an attitude which demands the exclusive exercise of power.' Moreover, it invited violence, because it was not possible permanently to exclude an entire section of the population from having any say in the decision-making process.

His own community did not escape censure. 'The Nationalist tradition has also taken rather a simplistic approach,' Hume acknowledged. 'Its argument has often been presented in emotional and romantic terms.' Its definition of Irishness was extremely sectional, based on two powerful strands of tradition – the Gaelic and the Catholic – to the exclusion of Protestants. Such a definition made the Protestants feel unwanted. 'In its more extreme form, it is thought right not only to die, but to kill, for that version of Ireland.' He admitted that 'my tradition' had deepened Irish divisions.

'When one considers the streets of Belfast and examines the performance of the organisation that represents itself as the ultimate in Irish patriotism – the Provisional IRA – and one considers the bitterness it has created by its campaign of destruction and killing, one can see how much rethinking and examination we must do if we are to bring about a settlement of the Irish problem and bring forward a definition of Irishness which is inclusive, not exclusive,' Hume added.

The third element in the equation, he concluded, was the British government: 'As matters stand, it now has all the power over Northern Ireland.' Its only policy, consistently reiterated in the House, was that Northern Ireland would remain a part of the United Kingdom as long as a majority so wished. 'On the face of it, that seems to be a democratic statement and guarantee,' he conceded. 'However, if one looks behind that one sees that the majority that is being guaranteed was created artificially by a sectarian headcount. When one tells the majority that it can protect itself only by remaining in majority, one invites it to maintain sectarian solidarity as the only means of protection. Therefore, one makes sectarianism the motive force of politics.' Northern Ireland had demonstrated the validity of that argument over sixty years of elections.

'If we are to break the sectarian mould and divisions, we must recognise that they cannot continue for ever,' Hume urged. Drawing one more upon Europe's example, he pointed out that a continent which had twice slaughtered its people by the million had found the wisdom and foresight to build new pan-European institutions. 'What is wrong with asking for that for our small island of five million people?' he pleaded. 'What is wrong with asking to be able to build structures whereby the different traditions can live in peace, harmony and unity in a new relationship with Britain? What is wrong with the government adopting that as a policy objective?'

To the discomfiture of the Unionists and their powerful friends on the Tory benches, Hume the historian surprised the House with a choice quotation from no less a figure than Sir Winston Churchill. On 7 July 1922, in a private letter to Michael Collins, Churchill had written:

> Meanwhile, in the intervals of grappling with revolts and revolution, I think that you should think over in your mind what would be the greatest offer the south could make for northern co-operation. Of course, from the imperial point of view, there is nothing we would like better than to see the north and the south join hands in an all-Ireland assembly without prejudice to the existing rights of Irishmen. Such ideas could be vehemently denied in many quarters at the moment, but events in the history of nations sometimes move very quickly.

As MPs digested this retrospective endorsement of SDLP policy from an unexpected quarter, Hume moved quickly to his peroration. Events 'often move quickly when there is a strong government in power who have the courage to grasp the nettle and face up to reality,' he said. In a naked bid to enlist Mrs Thatcher's personal commitment to the cause, he concluded: 'Ending divisions in Ireland has evaded statesmen for centuries. Ending the divisions requires strength and leadership.' The Prime Minister was not in the House to hear his gambit, but her actions later took the first steps down the Hume road. Hume was content that he had laid out, in the Commons, for the first time in contemporary British political history, an intellectually challenging assessment of the crisis facing his people and the Irish nation as a whole. The next speaker, Sir Anthony Kershaw, Tory MP for Stroud, paid tribute to 'a remarkable maiden speech', but hoped that Hume would modify his opinion about the absence of human feeling about Ireland in the chamber. 'If we seem to be indifferent,' he said lamely, 'it is because we are unable to decide what to do.'

Despite the political satisfaction of becoming the first Catholic to represent Derry in the Parliament, Westminster held few attractions for John Hume. He was uncomfortable with the sometimes sterile tradition of adversarial politics. However, he quickly made friends among the lobby correspondents, propping up the exclusive Annie's Bar with the best of them and enjoying the long drinking and yarning sessions that were an inevitable accompaniment of late-night sittings. His excursions into the chamber to speak were infrequent, however. He was on hand to hear a debate on housing in Northern Ireland, but his intervention at 2.25 in the morning was limited to a retort of 'nonsense' to a minister's assertion that the opposition did not understand the difference between public and private ownership.

It was a debate on the death penalty that brought him back into the limelight. Many back-bench Tories wanted to see capital punishment brought back for terrorist murders. Hume was strongly opposed to such a step. Pointing out that he lived in the Bogside, an area of Derry so ravaged by violence that normal life was not possible, he said: 'I think I can understand better than most the yearning for law and order ... The desire for order is innate in human nature. It is a deep and powerful instinct.'[8] No people yearned for law and order more than the deprived, the oppressed and the minorities, and if MPs did not understand that, they would not understand Ireland's awful history nor the passionate desire to stop terrorism for ever.

Hume asked: 'Will the death penalty for terrorism, will hanging terrorists, promote law and order in Northern Ireland?' His answer was simple: 'If the House wants the IRA to win, then hang them.' Refusing to give way to Conservative or DUP members, he demanded to know: 'Who are the terrorists who would be hanged?' He had his own definition: 'An Irish terrorist is a person who for good reason distrusts British democracy and its application to Ireland and for bad reasons thinks that violence can solve the problems of Ireland.' Distrust of British democracy was widely shared, he added. 'It is shared by me.'

In language verging on the apocalyptic, Hume warned that the introduction of the death penalty would destroy any hope of democracy. The current disaster would become an unmanageable calamity through Ireland, bringing many more deaths there and in Britain. Recalling that the previous night four UDR men had been killed by an IRA landmine in Tyrone – the heaviest casualties suffered by the regiment in a single incident – he claimed that the attack had been timed to influence the hanging debate. 'The leaders of terrorist organisations want to see the introduction of hanging,' he told MPs. 'I live among them and know their thinking. They would be delighted.' They themselves would not be hanged, but more and more young followers would be swept into terrorist activity as the stakes rose and the position became ever more desperate. If MPs wanted Ireland to be convulsed in a frenzy of hatred, and the prospect of peace removed 'once and for all', nothing would be more certain to bring that about than the hanging of Irish people under British law. 'For God's sake, do not do it,' he cried. The House listened to Hume, rather than the Unionist hardliners, who had secured a majority for hanging in the Assembly they dominated in Belfast, and rejected the idea of erecting a scaffold in his country.

In his new-found eminence – he was now a member of three parliaments, but was not taking his seat in one – Hume stepped up his activities as a roving commercial ambassador. In September 1983, he toured the USA and Canada, drumming up investment and jobs. On the Northern Ireland Industrial Development Board delegation with him was the Rev. Ian Paisley, whose presence sparked fury among SDLP activists at home. Hume had no regrets, even appearing on national television with 'the big fellow' whose American visa he had helped restore.

The critical issue of employment, he argued, bridged political divisions. Hume's old contacts in the Democratic Party proved invaluable on the trip. Against the wishes of the US-based Irish National Caucus, which leaned strongly towards Republicanism, he backed the US Air Force's move to buy Sherpa freighter craft from Shorts, the Belfast planemaker notorious for discriminating against Catholic workers. Hume's logic was withering. Putting Protestants out of work would not give jobs to Catholics. He urged Speaker Tip

O'Neill and Teddy Kennedy to support the deal, and six months later Shorts received a £115 million order that triggered wider international interest in its range of planes and missiles.

The New Ireland Forum, by which Nationalists of all shades set such store, was well into its stride by this time. After receiving written submissions from the parties, it began holding public sessions in St George's Hall, Dublin Castle. But even before these began in late September, Hume had caused a stir by circulating his own confidential briefing paper. *The Fundamental Problems*, which raised doubts about Irish Nationalists' grasp of the Loyalist mind and their ability to live with the Loyalist tradition. For instance, could they accept reform of the role of the Catholic church in family law, education and health?

Developing his analysis, he proposed three possible models for a New Ireland: a unitary state, a federal or confederal system, and some form of joint sovereignty. He also suggested in-depth studies of the cost of violence, and the impact on the economies of North and South of implementing change. Having learned bitter lessons from the over-ambitious expectations of the Sunningdale Agreement, Hume was deliberately low-key in his expectations of the Forum. He looked for a coherent analysis of the problem that could lay the ground for a new framework in which London, Dublin and the parties of the North could break out of the decades-old political impasse.

Margaret Thatcher remained derisive of the SDLP leadership (except for the 'courageous' Gerry Fitt, whom she ennobled at the suggestion of outgoing Labour leader Michael Foot after his defeat in West Belfast) and deeply suspicious of the Forum. However, in the summer of 1983, she deputed Robert Armstrong, head of the civil service and Cabinet Secretary, to take up Garret Fitzgerald's offer of informal joint talks on the future of Northern Ireland. From her point of view, the contacts were designed almost entirely to improve security, particularly along the border. She ruled out any discussion of 'joint sovereignty' and was anxious that the Forum – 'this collection of nationalists, North and South' – might attract international respectability 'for moves to weaken the union'. She was 'intensely wary of them'.[9] As well she might be, for that was indeed their long-term aim.

Thatcher and Fitzgerald met at Chequers on 7 November. Anglo-Irish relations had been moribund for two years. The British side offered to come up with its own proposals, and secret talks got under way. This was to be the gestation of the Anglo-Irish Agreement. The Chequers summit also opened the door of No. 10 to John Hume. Fitzgerald had asked Mrs Thatcher to meet the SDLP, and she did so 'somewhat belatedly' on 9 February 1984. 'She was able to confirm for herself that he and I were on the same wavelength with regard to a future negotiation', wrote Fitzgerald later, 'for John and I kept in close touch on this matter throughout, and of course after, the Forum.'[10]

Hume emerged from the hour-long meeting with the Prime Minister uncharacteristically tight-lipped. He told Frank Curran of the *Derry Journal* that he was pledged to confidentiality about the subjects discussed, and therefore could not and would not expand on them. 'But it was obvious that he was pleased about the fact that the British Premier, whose attitude to Northern Ireland to date has been regarded as not particularly interested, has been prompted to invite him to a personal and private meeting.'[11] Mrs Thatcher, whose unflattering views of the SDLP are amply documented, was plainly less impressed. The meeting does not figure in her memoirs.

However, the *Derry Journal* speculated that Hume had availed himself of the opportunity to press the case of the New Ireland Forum, and to propose a Commons debate on the issue of Northern Ireland. The paper also reported that if the government would not make parliamentary time available, then Hume had won an undertaking from Neil Kinnock, the Labour leader, that the opposition would use some of its allocation to allow an airing for the Forum report. This item is the first indication of the growing entente between the two men: Kinnock, the newly-elected party leader, and Hume were to become firm friends.

In the early months of 1984, horse-trading between the Nationalist parties on the final version of the Forum report intensified. In private meetings of the party leaders, Charles Haughey insisted on a more 'green' model – a unitary state for the whole of Ireland. Hume wanted a more moderate formula, offering a series of options of descending desirability. Hume and Haughey did a deal. There would be three options for the future development of Northern Ireland: a unitary state, a federal/confederal arrangement and a joint Irish/British authority; with a fourth possibility, that the Forum would be open to 'other views that might contribute to political developments'.

The Forum report was launched in St Patrick's Hall, Dublin, amid the pomp and ceremony of the attending diplomatic corps, on 2 May 1984. It was four months late, but as the work of eleven months of hearings, and fifty meetings of leaders of the main political parties of the South and the constitutional party of the North, it was hailed as a unprecedented moment in Irish history. Hume had no doubt of its significance: 'The Report attracted widespread acclaim and support, including that of the then President Ronald Reagan and the United States Congress, in a concurring resolution of both Houses, the first on Irish affairs since the 1920s.'[12]

Hume regarded the report as providing the necessary framework for his long-desired goal of a new Ireland. It was deeply imbued with his concept of 'unity in diversity'. He identified one paragraph as its kernel:

The solution of both the historic problem and the current crisis of Northern Ireland and the continuing problem of relations between Ireland and Britain necessarily requires new structures that will accommodate together two sets of legitimate rights: the right of Nationalists to effective political, symbolic and administrative expression of their identity; and the right of Unionists to effective political, symbolic and administrative expression of their identity, their ethos and their way of life.

This was pure 'Humespeak'. It could have been lifted from virtually any of his speeches over the previous decade, and its appearance in the final version identified him as its intellectual progenitor.

The Dublin government had given Mrs Thatcher a sneak preview of the Forum report a week before publication. Garret Fitzgerald had kept the Prime Minister informed of the developing situation, and had formed the impression that she might find a radical new approach acceptable. It was a forlorn hope. She rejected as 'one-sided' the historical sections of the report, and said there was no reason to expect a majority of people in Northern Ireland to consent to any of the three forms of change in sovereignty. Later, she was dramatically to harden even this position.

Different parties put different emphases on the proposals of the Forum. Charles Haughey insisted that a unitary state was 'not an option, it is the wish of the parties of the Forum', while Fitzgerald desperately tried to win Margaret Thatcher round by arguing just as forcibly that they were only 'illustrative models' for discussion and debate. Despite her coolness and suspicion, Thatcher authorized her Northern Ireland Secretary to engage in exploratory talks with Dublin ministers. Jim Prior suggested that London might be willing to entertain the idea of joint authority if the Republic showed willingness to dilute its territorial claim to the Six Counties set out in Articles 2 and 3 of its constitution.

Hume was included in these extremely sensitive exchanges at the earliest stage. On 29 May 1984, less than three weeks after the initial contacts, Hume met Fitzgerald, Dick Spring and the Irish Foreign Secretary Peter Barry at the Taoiseach's home in Dublin for an intensive round of policy talks ahead of a meeting with British officials in Dublin the following day. The four agreed that if 'an adequate package' could be found, then it would be put to a referendum, as provided in the Irish constitution, thus opening up the constitutional issue. Hume also won round the Dublin political leaders to his idea of a locally recruited police force to operate in the Nationalist communities of Northern Ireland which were still no-go areas for the RUC.

While this discreet diplomacy was going on, Hume was also fighting his second European parliamentary election. The poll, on 14 June 1984, confirmed John Hume as the province's second most popular politician, after the redoubtable Ian Paisley. He increased his first-preference votes by 11,000, taking 22 per cent of the poll. However, with turnout significantly higher than 1979 at 65 per cent, Hume's share of the vote fell marginally against a strong showing by Danny Morrison, the Sinn Fein standard-bearer who came fourth with just over 13 per cent of the poll. In some senses, it was no bad thing for Hume that Sinn Fein managed to sustain a serious electoral following. The Irish government had consistently argued to Mrs

Thatcher that some form of agreement on the political future of the province was critical if John Hume's constitutional Nationalists were to prevail over the 'armalite and ballot box' strategy of Sinn Fein/ IRA. Garret Fitzgerald constantly raised the spectre of an IRA armed and financed by the Libyan leader Colonel Gaddafi destabilizing the whole of Ireland – and potentially the UK. Indeed, arms supplies were secretly coming to the IRA from Tripoli, as the subsequent seizure of the vessel *Eksund* proved.

In direct talks with Mrs Thatcher on the fringes of the European Council meeting at Fontainebleau later that month, the Irish Prime Minister again urged London to come forward with 'a substantial package' which could command the backing of Hume, whose party was 'a powerful influence on public opinion in our state'. In return, Dublin might be willing to downgrade its territorial claim to an aspiration. This was an historic opportunity, but Thatcher was uncharacteristically indecisive, and the exploratory talks dragged on for months, absorbing yet another new Northern Ireland Secretary, Douglas Hurd. Hurd, a former political secretary to Edward Heath, was promoted to the NIO from the Home Office when Prior was appointed chairman of the electrical conglomerate GEC, soon after telling MPs that neither Westminster nor Britain was 'particularly concerned' about the Forum report.

The pace of talks was slowed yet further by an IRA bid to murder the entire British government during the Conservative Party conference that autumn. In the early hours of 12 October, a Provo bomb devastated the Grand Hotel, Brighton, killing five and injuring thirty more. Thatcher was only two minutes away from death: the bathroom of a bedroom she had been using moments before the explosion was wrecked. Not surprisingly, a few days after the bombing the Prime Minister ruled out any 'sudden new initiative', but a month later she hosted an Anglo-Irish summit at Chequers at which Dublin and London agreed that the identities of both the majority and the minority communities in Northern Ireland should be 'recognised and respected and reflected in the structures and processes' of the province.

In private, she was still peeved that Hume would not take up the SDLP's seats in the virtually moribund Northern Ireland Assembly.

Then, without warning, she spoiled any attempt to put a constructive veneer on the summit.

At a press conference at the close of the Chequers gathering, Thatcher was asked about the three options for the future government of Ireland outlined in the Forum report: unification, confederation and joint authority. Each of them, she thundered, was 'Out!' This became known as the 'Out! Out! Out!' policy.

Hume and his party were 'in a state of shock, their morale shattered'.[13] Her brutal condescension also made it much less likely that Hume and his colleagues – some, like his deputy Seamus Mallon, more 'Nationalist' than their leader – could accept any diminution in the Irish Republic's territorial claim to the North. Unification was, after all, their Party's stated political objective.

Thatcher, evidently realizing that she had gone too far, issued a New Year's Eve invitation to John Hume, asking him to attend talks on 17 January 1985. It was a political boost for the SDLP leader, confirming that whatever her private opinion of his leadership qualities, she had to deal with him as the unquestioned political head of his community. Hume met the Irish Prime Minister en route to the meeting, and was warned not to write off 'the perceived menace' of Sinn Fein in his dealings with Thatcher. In the event, according to Hume, the British premier claimed she was now committed to doing something about the Northern Ireland problem, within the parameters of the Chequers communiqué. Hume argued that the greatest problem was the absence of law and order in the Nationalist areas, and the problem could not be solved by inter-party talks alone. Towards the end of the meeting, she made the extraordinary confession that when she first met Hume, she had not understood how people could have different loyalties, but that she did now. 'It was obvious that she had been very concerned to be conciliatory and understanding with the SDLP leader,' commented Garret Fitzgerald.

Four days later, British officials came back with new proposals that did not envisage any change in the Irish constitution. Inevitably, this package offered less because it asked for less. However, using the opportunity allowed by the vital 'enabling' paragraph 5.10 of the Forum report, London offered a joint body to discuss legal and security issues, including policing, prisons and human rights matters. There would be a Joint Secretariat, based in Belfast, with joint ministerial chairmanship. The joint body – subsequently called the Anglo-Irish Conference – would be charged with solving problems, rather than just reporting them back to respective governments.

This was the embryo of the mould-breaking Anglo-Irish Agreement. It was a far cry from the unitary state 'preferred' by the Forum, but it was also the first time a British government had committed itself to a 'regular, continuing, constitutionalised role' for Dublin in the affairs of the North. And the British might be open to further negotiation, especially on the issue of an International Fund for Ireland, first mooted in the late 1970s after Hume's conversion of the Carter administration. Thatcher had told Hume and President Reagan she did not 'stand pat' on the January package. Months of intensive negotiation ensued, including frequent contacts with the Reagan administration. Hume's old friend Sean Donlon, despatched by Fitzgerald to brief State Department officials, consulted the SDLP leader before leaving for Washington. Hume authorized Donlon to tell his US contacts that his party would support an agreement which 'if implemented fairly quickly might contribute to the emergence of a power-sharing administration in the North later in the year'.[14] Hume's undue optimism may have had something to do with approaches from Ian Paisley's DUP. The Unionist hardliners, immensely cheered by Thatcher's 'Out! Out! Out!', offered talks to the SDLP, but subsequently withdrew the offer within forty-eight hours.

Another electoral test supervened in May 1985: the district council polls in which Sinn Fein was fighting for the first time. In the event, Hume's party held Sinn Fein at bay, taking almost 18 per cent of first-preference votes against SF's figure of 11.8 per cent. The SDLP lost two seats, however, taking its total down to 101. In its first electoral excursion for local power, Sinn Fein overtook the moderate Unionist Alliance Party to take fourth place, picking up fifty-nine seats, many more than its deliberately understated target of around forty. The SDLP and Sinn Fein came to a working arrangement on some councils.

It was the secret diplomacy between London and Dublin that was uppermost in Hume's mind. He had, by now, brought his deputy, Seamus Mallon, into his tightly-knit circle. Mallon had given his tacit backing to the general thrust of the negotiations, while reserving his position. The talks moved into a higher gear from July onwards, at which point Hume also brought in his other Westminster colleagues, Dr Joe Hendron and Eddie McGrady. The Unionists, who were not involved to anything like the same degree, naturally became agitated, and took their protest to Downing Street in late August. A few days later, Douglas Hurd relinquished the Northern Ireland secretaryship to Tom King, the Employment Secretary. King was more of a Unionist than Hurd, and had reservations about where the Anglo-Irish initiative was taking his government; but the process was too far advanced, the draft Agreement too close to a deal for his misgivings to have any serious impact.

On the eve of publication of the Anglo-Irish Agreement, Hume and his fellow-SDLP MPs met Fitzgerald, Dick Spring and Foreign Secretary Barry for dinner at Iveagh House, Dublin. Hume reported that he had outlined the Agreement to a long meeting of his party the previous week, 'one of the most successful for a long time'. The SDLP leadership had decided to take a measured view, clearly designed to obviate Unionist fears. Hume would ask the people of Northern Ireland to study the Agreement in detail, and not react impetuously. There could be no repetition of the disastrous triumphalism that followed Sunningdale a decade previously. At the Dublin dinner, Mallon confessed that he had endured 'six months of hell' on the issue, but he would put aside his objections and make every effort to make the Agreement work. There was a deeply emotional moment as Hume and Mallon thanked the Irish politicians for taking the SDLP into their confidence.

The next day, 15 November 1985, in the largest hall afforded by Hillsborough Castle in County Down, Margaret Thatcher and Garret Fitzgerald signed the Anglo-Irish Agreement in front of the television cameras. It has been described as 'arguably the most far-reaching development since 1920 and the creation of Northern Ireland'.[15] Hume himself wrote: 'Though no one among us felt it was the final solution, the Agreement was a major achievement of democratic politics, and was a significant step forward on the road to lasting peace and stability . . . Everything that has happened in the past few years stems from the Agreement.'[16]

The Agreement tackled the problem of alienation among the minority community head on and sought to secure, in line with the central requirement of the New Ireland Forum report, equal recognition and respect for Nationalist and Unionist traditions. 'Nationalists could now finally raise their heads knowing their position was, and was seen to be, on an equal footing with that of Unionists,' Hume argued.

By establishing an Anglo-Irish Conference, the Agreement reflected the unique situation in Northern Ireland. The British government had agreed, in the interests of promoting peace and stability, to make 'determined efforts' to resolve any differences through the conference, whose field of activity comprised most of the matters in which the public authorities of a state exercise responsibility, including political, legal, economic, social and cultural affairs. These provisions went beyond a purely consultative role, but fell short of an executive role for the Irish government and therefore took nothing away from the legitimate rights of Unionists: 'Northern Ireland continues to be governed, as Unionists still wish, by the British government.'

However, the reaction of Unionists was even more hostile than expected. They were enraged at the idea of even a limited role in the affairs of the province being conceded to Dublin, and incensed at the setting up of the Joint Secretariat at a government building in Maryfield, County Down. The day after the historic signing, the Unionist-dominated Northern Ireland Assembly voted to demand a referendum. There were mass demonstrations, protests at the 'Maryfield Bunker', and fifteen Unionist Westminster MPs resigned to fight on an anti-Agreement platform. Tom King was attacked by a crowd in the centre of Belfast, and Unionists launched an unsuccessful High Court bid to invalidate the Agreement. When the Commons debated the issue on 22 November, UUP leader James Molyneaux said the Agreement 'will not bring peace, but a sword'.

Hume tried to bring some realism and sanity into the debate, arguing: 'This is the first time we have had a real framework in which to address the problem . . . the framework of the problem can only be the framework of the solution, and that is the British–Irish framework. There is no road towards a solution to this problem that does not contain risks. The road that has been chosen by both governments is the road of maximum consensus and is therefore the road of minimum risk ... The Agreement gives us no more than an opportunity to begin the process of reconciliation.'[17] It was regarded as a masterful speech, earning congratulations even from Mrs Thatcher.

The Commons voted to endorse the Agreement by 473 to 47, but there were ominous signs for Margaret Thatcher. Twenty-one of her own back-benchers voted against the government, and Treasury Minister Ian Gow resigned in protest. Gow, a personal friend of the Prime Minister and prominent Friend of the Union, was subsequently murdered by the IRA. Thatcher confessed she had been wrong about the scale of Unionist hostility, which continued to build towards the end of the year.

Central to the argument was the degree to which the Agreement guaranteed the Union. Its very first item, Article 1(a), laid down that the two governments 'affirm that any change in the status of Northern Ireland would only come about with the consent of a majority of the people of Northern Ireland'. Unionist semanticists pointed out that this formula did not spell out exactly what was the current status of Northern Ireland. The deal also accepted that the British government would support a united Ireland if majority consent for it emerged in the North, but even this was not new. Sunningdale had said the same thing.

Hume was caustic. The Agreement, he said, stated the clear fact that Northern Ireland would remain in the UK for as long as a majority of its citizens so wish. ('That was hardly a threat to the rights of Unionists.') It specifically recognized the particular identity and aspirations of the Unionist community. ('That was hardly "stealing their birthright".')[18] Unionists' wrath was not to be contained. The Assembly, still bereft of a minority voice, suspended its normal workings to become a focus for a concerted Unionist assault on the Anglo-Irish Agreement.

At a meeting with the Irish Prime Minister in early December on the fringe of the European Council in Brussels, Margaret Thatcher once again paid tribute to Hume's 'excellent' Commons speech, but said what was needed was action. He had said that the SDLP would sit down and talk about devolution. 'Could anything happen there?' she asked Fitzgerald, who promised to raise the issue discreetly with Hume before the year was out. Events, however, were beginning to move another way.

ELEVEN

TALKING TO GERRY

MORE THAN A DECADE before the signing of the Anglo-Irish Agreement, the British government had shown itself willing to hold direct bilateral talks with the IRA. Hume had been the midwife for these contacts, picking up and developing the Provisionals' fairly crude peace signals at a press conference in Derry, even chauffeuring Army Council men over the border under a British Army safe conduct pass. However, after the collapse of the ill-starred negotiations with William Whitelaw in the summer of 1972, such contacts ceased. In public, at least. Could they ever be resuscitated?

At his party conference in Belfast in late January 1985, Hume stuck to his unbending hostility towards the IRA. In the aftermath of the Brighton bomb, the Provisionals had confessed that their aim had been to kill half the British Cabinet. As a result, they expected widespread repression against the Nationalist community, including the reintroduction of internment, said Hume. Such casual acceptance of the suppression of their own, he argued, showed that the IRA looked on the people as 'simply tools in a bid for political power'. Hume blasted the comment by Republican strategist Danny Morrison that their objective may now take fifty years to achieve. 'How many lives do they think their objective is worth?' he asked in his leader's address. 'Is human life to be totally subjected to ideological and territorial imperatives . . . Is Ireland without its people worth more than any other piece of earth?'

Hume was nevertheless still willing to risk his political credibility by 'talking to the enemy', even if his actions risked upsetting his closest associates in Dublin. At the time of the conference, while appearing on a BBC Radio Ulster programme, he was challenged by Gerry Adams to hold talks with Sinn Fein. Adams was more interested in presenting his party as a genuine Nationalist alternative to the SDLP in the run-up to the local elections in May than in launching a new peace initiative. Hume was well aware of this, and responded sharply. 'I can't remember the language. It was very strong,' he said years later.[1] 'I didn't say I would talk to his masters, but it was something like that.' Then, searching his memory: 'I said I would talk to the organ-grinder, not the monkey.' His honesty may have been brusque, but he was only echoing what Adams has said himself: 'Sinn Fein was by and large perceived as, and was in reality, a poor second cousin to the IRA. This was not only how we were seen by our supporters and opponents; in many ways it was also how we viewed ourselves.'[2]

Hume's tactic worked. Back through the usual clandestine channels came an invitation from the IRA on 1 February for talks. Hume knew that his acceptance of the offer would infuriate his friend Garret Fitzgerald, whose refusal to treat with the IRA or Sinn Fein was absolute. The Taoiseach condemned the IRA as murderers bent on overthrowing Irish democracy and replacing it with a military dictatorship. 'We in this state will have no truck with them,' he insisted. In the words of one observer, Hume's democratic credentials were not in doubt, but his political judgement was. Douglas Hurd, the urbane ex-diplomat, was more circumspect. In the Commons on 6 February, the Northern Ireland Secretary appealed to Hume – whose commitment to non-violence he praised – not to attend any meeting with the IRA Army Council. For good measure, he warned the SDLP leader that contacts with the Provisionals could put him at risk of proceedings under the Emergency Provisions Act.

Hume refused to retreat, though the trail swiftly went cold as hordes of reporters followed him everywhere for the next fortnight. Then, one evening in late February, the go-between turned up at his house. 'He said he had a message. He told me about the arrangements for the meeting. I had to turn up at a certain friend's. I was put in the back of a van. I couldn't see where we were going. After driving around for a long time, we stopped. It was in the middle of the countryside.'[3] He was taken to a safe house, where events took a fresh turn. 'They wanted to video the meeting. I didn't know how they would use it, so I said "No". So I didn't actually get to meet them.' Contemporary newspaper accounts suggest that the failed confrontation took place in Buncrana, a well-known Provo bolt-hole just over the border in County Donegal. The IRA contact man was named as Brendan McFarlane, a convicted bomber and IRA leader in the Maze who master-minded a prison breakout in 1983 and was on the run until rearrested in the Netherlands in January 1986.

A journalist with strong Republican contacts later argued that in February 1985 the IRA was not interested in lowering its sights. A huge arms shipment was on its way from Libya. 'Their [the IRA] objective was to persuade Hume of the correctness of their analysis: that Britain had interests in Ireland, and would have to be forced out.' The meeting ended before it began because of Hume's objection to being video-taped. 'It was a measure of how treacherous the task was. It would be a full three years before a similar attempt was made.'[4]

In the interim, Hume's party and Sinn Fein were forced into a political accommodation. In Fermanagh, a Sinn Fein councillor was elected chairman of the district council with SDLP support. On Magherafelt council, the roles were reversed. As an electoral presence, Sinn Fein was here to stay. The SDLP could no longer claim to be the sole voice of the Nationalist minority, particularly among working-class voters from whom 'the Shinners' drew most of their supporters and indeed their political leaders. Hume's party was essentially made up of people like himself: middle-class beneficiaries of the 1947 Education Act that gave Catholics the entrée to a decent education. Sinn Fein leaders like Gerry Adams learned their politics in the streets, and in prison. They were self-educated, and they prided themselves on a certain hardness of spirit. If anything, they looked down on what they once described as the 'slobbering moderates' of the SDLP – an aspersion furiously repudiated by Hume.

One outcome of their harsher view of the world was Sinn Fein's substantially different assessment of the Anglo-Irish Agreement, which Adams and his colleagues usually refer to as the Hillsborough Treaty. Hume regards the Agreement as the first major step in the current peace process. The British had agreed that those who wanted Irish unity had an obligation to persuade those who did not. If the majority of people in Northern Ireland wanted Irish unity, they would have it. This 'declaration of British neutrality on the question of Irish unity', Hume reasoned, removed the traditional justification for the use of force in Irish Nationalism.

Gerry Adams and his cohorts utterly rejected Hume's analysis. They saw the Hillsborough Treaty as yet another partitionist arrangement, a natural successor to Sunningdale, the Constitutional Convention, round table talks, talks about talks and proposals for rolling devolution. In fact, it was worse, Republicans argued, because it drew Dublin into Britain's masterplan for Ireland. The objective of this strategy, claimed Adams, was 'marrying sections of "pragmatic" unionists and the SDLP with some Dublin involvement in an arrangement to govern a "reformed" Six County state. Part of this strategy was aimed at institutionalizing an anti-republican axis of Dublin/Belfast or Dublin/SDLP/unionist.'[5] In short, said the Sinn Fein president, the Agreement was 'an historic effort by the Irish and British governments to defeat Irish republicanism'.

Yet Sinn Fein did want to break out of the political and military stalemate, if Adams is to be believed. Republicans could prevent Britain making a settlement on its terms, but they could not win a political struggle on their own, much less win a war against the British Army. Therefore, they needed Nationalist allies of their own. What better than to subvert the existing, perceived 'axis' and forge a new, Nationalist political axis with John Hume?

The abject failure of the IRA's first move in February 1985, and the 'extremely polarized' relationships between the SDLP and Sinn Fein suggested that the prospects of building such an alliance were very poor. Yet there were straws in the wind. In the years following the Pope's fierce condemnation of violence in 1979, but particularly after the hunger strikes, Adams had been in private dialogue with Dr Cathal Daly, Bishop of Down and Connor, about the morality of violence. There were also secret contacts with Fr Alec Reid, a priest of the Redemptorist Order at Clonard monastery on Falls Road, the heart of Catholic Belfast. Fr Reid, born in Tipperary in the Republic, had been on the Catholic front line in Belfast since the start of the troubles. His aim was to persuade Sinn Fein leaders to reorientate the Republican movement away from 'the long war' to a political campaign. This would, of course, entail an IRA cessation of violence. On the back of this ambitious plan, Fr Reid argued, they could put together an alliance between the Irish government, the SDLP and Sinn Fein. It would be, in the horrified language of the Unionists, a 'pan-Nationalist front'.

With Adams, Fr Reid was pushing on a door already ajar. With Hume, the difficulties were greater, though even here there were encouraging signs. Having told Republicans that, with the signing of the Anglo-Irish Agreement, they no longer had any justification for violence, the SDLP leader found himself under fire. 'Sinn Fein were quick to criticize me, demanding that I prove British neutrality,' he wrote later. But megaphone diplomacy was better than nothing, and 'so began a public debate between Sinn Fein and the SDLP'.[6]

In a sense, the slow accommodation with Adams was inevitable. Not only was the Sinn Fein president discreetly seeking it, but the Unionists were driving him towards it. An offer of talks from Unionist leaders had been taken seriously by Hume in January 1985, but it came to nothing amid the hue and cry over the Anglo-Irish Agreement. Hume was still far from finding common ground with Republicans, however. Taunting the Provos for their banner of 'Principled Leadership', he excoriated the IRA at his party's fifteenth birthday conference in Belfast later that year: 'They bomb factories and shout about unemployment, they shoot a teacher in a classroom, kill school bus drivers, kill people on campuses and then lecture us about education. They kill, maim and injure and they carry out attacks in hospital, and then they tell us about protecting the National Health Service. They rob post offices, leaving people without benefit payments and then they preach to us about defending the poor . . . The real strategy and objectives are clear. Have the military wing create as much discontent and deprivation as possible. The more unemployment the better. Then have your political wing feed off the people's discontent. One of these days, Sinn Fein will disappear up their own contradiction.'[7]

Hume's personal, and genuine, loathing for the IRA could not however halt the steady momentum towards talking to Gerry. Mounting hostility to the Anglo-Irish Agreement made progress in a Unionist direction impossible, and in his own party Hume found increasing political tension. On 3 January 1986, Pascal O'Hare, a solicitor and founder-member of the SDLP, resigned from the party on the grounds that the Agreement had 'copper-fastened' the union with Britain. He went on to call for talks with the men of violence, both Republican and Loyalist, whereas Hume's recently restated public position insisted that the SDLP would enter dialogue only with 'democratic parties'.

Accordingly, Hume rejected overtures from Adams for an election pact in the Westminster mini-general election of 23 January 1986, called by the resignation of fifteen Unionist MPs. Fighting on a slogan of 'Ulster Says No', the Unionists improved their vote on the 1983 poll by almost 10 per cent. The SDLP, choosing to play neither the Republicans' nor the Unionists' game, fought only four marginal seats, and won one. Seamus Mallon, Hume's deputy, a veteran civil rights campaigner and former head teacher, took the Newry and Armagh seat at his fourth attempt to get into Westminster. Tom King, Mrs Thatcher's fifth Northern Ireland Secretary, had already rejected the outcome of the poll, saying it would not change the government's commitment to the Agreement. In fact, he drew some comfort from seeing Hume's party improve its ratings by 6 per cent, almost entirely at the expense of Sinn Fein. Both London and Dublin put the SDLP improvement down to the signing of the Agreement.

Mrs Thatcher refused to consider even the temporary suspension of the Agreement, and was determined to face down a one-day general strike called in Northern Ireland by Loyalists for 3 March. Paisley and James Molyneaux backed the walkout, and the Prime Minister summoned Hume to her room at the Commons on 27 February to gauge what she might expect from his two-man party. She was disappointed. 'I urged that the SDLP should give more open support to the security forces, to no avail,' she recollected. 'He seemed more interested to score points at the expense of the Unionists.'[8] Mrs Thatcher wrote to Garret Fitzgerald, urging him to get Hume and his colleagues to adopt a 'more sensible and statesman-like approach'. Thatcher and Hume never saw eye to eye. She was a natural Unionist, and could not understand why Hume was unable to support the RUC which had hosed him with dye from a water-cannon and harassed his community for decades.

In no small part due to intimidation by Loyalist gangs, the 3 March Unionist 'Day of Action' brought much of Northern Ireland to a standstill, and that night sniper fire was aimed at the RUC in Protestant areas of Belfast. Nearly fifty policemen were injured during the protests, and as attacks by hardline Unionists on the RUC increased in the ensuing weeks, an extra battalion of troops was flown in. Hume finally felt obliged to come to the aid of the forces of law and order.

Efforts by the Redemptorist priest to win Hume's support for a pan-Nationalist front produced thin results at first. As the historian Tim Pat Coogan observed, neither Dublin nor Hume's party had, by 1986, proved fruitful as sources of potential support: 'Fr Reid had been disappointed in his efforts to involve the SDLP in talks with its arch-rival, Sinn Fein.'[9] Indeed, Hume once again appeared to be looking towards his traditional enemies, the Unionists, predicting in the *Observer* on 27 April that the Ulster crisis would be resolved by the end of the summer when Unionists would agree to talks with the SDLP. He had always expected a furious Unionist reaction to the Agreement, but the 'Protestant' boil had to be lanced. He coupled this alarming optimism with unusual personal praise for the Prime Minister: 'Mrs Thatcher is the right person in the right place at the right time and they are recognizing that she will not be broken.'

Hume was wrong about the options for political accommodation, but right about the Prime Minister. Rather than allow the Northern Ireland Assembly to be used, as it had been for six months, as a Unionist theatre orchestrating opposition to the Agreement, Thatcher closed it down on 23 June. Twenty or more protesting Unionist Assemblymen had to be physically thrown out, Paisley snarling at the two policemen who carried him bodily from the Chamber: 'Don't come crying to me if your homes are attacked.' More pertinently, James Molyneaux said the Agreement nullified hopes of achieving democracy in Northern Ireland.

Hume's great expectations of a summer breakthrough had proved false, but as the first fruits of the Agreement began to appear – a joint British–Irish international aid fund of £35 million to finance social and economic development in Northern Ireland and the Republic's border counties – he refused to abandon his dream. With Provo bombs costing more than 40,000 jobs and unemployment edging up to 23 per cent, he could not afford to. At his party's conference in Newcastle, County Down in November 1986, he argued that the Agreement had achieved more in its first year than had been accomplished in the previous sixty. The SDLP rejected Unionist pressure for suspension or abrogation of the new deal, and on a Christmas visit to Northern Ireland soon afterwards, Mrs Thatcher made plain her refusal to back down in the face of Loyalist hostility. That same month, Tom King announced changes in the law on incitement, and the repeal of the Flags and Emblems Act: more evidence that the Agreement was working.

In early 1987, two events restarted the stalled initiative with Sinn Fein. As a result of Dick Spring's Labour Party withdrawing its support, Garret Fitzgerald's Fine Gael government fell and Charles Haughey became Taoiseach for the third time on 10 March. He had initially opposed the Anglo-Irish Agreement, but now said he was prepared to make it work. This was some comfort to Hume. The second, more discreet, development also came that spring. Fr Alec Reid, who had been in personal contact with Haughey while he was still Leader of the Opposition, wrote to Hume proposing a new round of talks with Gerry Adams. Hume consulted Mark Durkan, a quietly spoken former student leader who was now his right-hand man in Derry (and, in the eyes of some, his heir-apparent as SDLP leader). Durkan counselled caution. A Westminster election was due to be called at any time, and if news of contacts with Sinn Fein leaked out, it could damage the SDLP's electoral chances. Durkan was despatched to talk to Fr Reid, whose message was that Hume should begin a serious dialogue with Adams.

On 1 May 1987, Sinn Fein published a discussion paper, *A Scenario for Peace*, which was designed to be the launch of Adams's 'developing peace strategy'. This document called for an end to British rule in Northern Ireland, the disbandment of local security forces, and an amnesty for Republican prisoners. Adams argued that an enduring peace could be secured only as a result of a process that had the support of a wide representation of Irish, British and international

The tears of a peacemaker: weeping at
the funeral of the victims of the Greysteel
massacre, summer 1994. His wife Pat
comforts him.

John Hume greeting Willy Brandt.

In conference with Hannan Ashrawi, Palestinian leader.

John Hume with President Bush, and with President Clinton.

Bienvienu à Derry: John Hume welcomes Jacques Delors, President of the European Commission on a visit to Londonderry in 1992.

Ceasefire at last! Gerry Adams of Sinn Fein, Albert Reynolds, Prime Minister of the Irish Republic, and John Hume on the steps of Government Buildings in Dublin, 6 September 1994.

Business investment in Londonderry: John Hume and Northern Ireland Secretary Sir Patrick Mayhew greet American managers of Seagate, the US information technology firm opening a new factory in Derry.

'Go the extra mile for peace': Hume addressing the Labour Party Conference in Blackpool, October 1994.

opinion. This process, said Adams, would have to contain the frame-work, the timescale and the dynamic necessary to bring about an 'inclusive, negotiated and democratic settlement'. In simple terms, there could be no peace without direct talks with Sinn Fein. Adams promised that the rights of Unionists would be safeguarded in a new Ireland, but they could not have been encouraged by his pledge to give 'resettlement grants' to those who wished to escape to England or Scotland.

Hume was fully *au fait* with these developments when the general election of 11 June supervened. His manifesto, *Keep Building*, praised the Anglo-Irish Agreement as a step of major significance, a necessary framework within which to develop the healing process that alone could lead to final peace and stability. Hume called for more dialogue within Northern Ireland, while criticizing Sinn Fein for the 'nonsen-sical contradiction' of its politics of abstentionism. This was aimed at Adams, defending the West Belfast constituency which he refused to represent in person at Westminster, even though his party had renounced abstentionism in the Irish Republic and on local councils in the North.

Yet Hume seemed to invite Sinn Fein to put more of its cards on the table. He said, again in his manifesto: 'The path to the future that the SDLP spells out is clear. It is a peaceful and political path, and a path on which there will be many setbacks and difficulties. But we do not see any other road, and our challenge to our opponents is to spell out their alternative.' Given that the Unionists had only a few months earlier presented a 400,000-signature petition to the Queen calling for a referendum on the Agreement, he could not seriously have expected a sudden change of heart in the Loyalist camp. He was, however, well aware that Sinn Fein was looking for dialogue. Indeed, Adams was already thinking of an Irish Peace Initiative, in which a new axis – a Hume–Adams axis – would emerge. The Sinn Fein president had been in contact with leading Catholic bishops, but efforts to get the SDLP involved had thus far failed.

Lord Fitt, Hume's one-time ally, sniped from the sidelines throughout the campaign, saying the SDLP was not a socialist party and it never really had been. When they came, the results of the general election were a quiet triumph for Hume. His party's share of the vote rose more than 3 per cent to 21.1 per cent, and Eddie McGrady, the SDLP's Chief Whip, succeeded at his fourth attempt in unseating Enoch Powell in South Down. Sinn Fein's share of the poll fell by 2 per cent, but was still 35 per cent of the Nationalist vote. Adams fought off a strong SDLP challenge from Dr Joe Hendron to retain his seat with his majority more than halved to a precarious 2,200. Mrs Thatcher was returned with a reduced parliamentary majority, and, many thought, a diminished interest in Northern Ireland. Tom King remained Secretary of State, but it was autumn before he met Unionist leaders for 'talks about talks'.

By this time, Hume was already engaged in similar moves with Sinn Fein's intermediary, Fr Alec Reid. The two met several times in the second half of 1987, and despite the Poppy Day bombing by the IRA in Enniskillen on 8 November which claimed eleven lives, Hume agreed to meet Adams face to face. The Remembrance Day outrage was condemned at Westminster in the most heartfelt manner by the SDLP leader. The appalling atrocity was 'an act of sheer savagery', he said, calculated to stir the deepest emotions of the Unionist and British people. 'It was the deepest act of provocation against the Unionist people that has taken place in my lifetime,' Hume told MPs. 'I sincerely hope that no one will fall into the trap that has been laid by retaliating, because the doctrine of an eye for any eye leaves everybody blind.'[10] He pleaded for a re-examination of past attitudes, insisting: 'If we are to live together, the first lesson that we must learn is that we need each other.' Under pressure from the Catholic community, the SDLP pulled the rug from under Sinn Fein's leadership of Fermanagh council, and backed the Unionists instead.

Against this background of revulsion against militant Republicanism, Hume gave the go-ahead for initial contacts with Adams. It was a deadly serious political gamble. While Hume had always dismissed criticism of his policy of being willing to talk to anyone in the cause of peace (typically insisting he did not give 'two balls of roasted snow' for such opinions), he ran great risks in consenting to dialogue: personal, physical risk, from attack by Loyalist hardliners, and political risks not just in the predictable backlash from Unionists and the Conservative government, but from discontent within his own party.

He was also risking his dominant role in the national community, where the much younger Adams (aged thirty-nine) was battling for the same votes against Hume, now fifty years old.

Hume's closest allies in the SDLP first knew about the impending peace moves in December 1987. At a pre-Christmas function at party headquarters in Belfast, Hume disclosed to Sean Farren that he had been approached by a third party 'and was responding positively to the approaches to enter into a dialogue with Adams'.[11] Farren, a lecturer in Education at the University of Ulster, Coleraine, had been a member of the SDLP almost since its inception. He was regarded as the party's foremost intellectual, often being called on to draft policy documents and write speeches or statements for the leader. Hume trusted him. He confided that the one-to-one with Adams could broaden out into something bigger, and appointed Farren as the go-between with Sinn Fein's Mitchel McLaughlin, a senior Republican figure from Derry. The talks eventually extended to four a side: Hume, his deputy Seamus Mallon, Farren and Austin Currie on the SDLP side; on the Sinn Fein side, Adams, McLaughlin, Danny Morrison, a driving force in the party's electoral strategy, and Tom Hartley.

Despite the material improvements gained from the Anglo-Irish Agreement, 1987 had been a particularly murderous year. Deaths arising from the Troubles were up by more than half, at ninety-three. There were almost 700 shootings, and more than 200 bombings. Four hundred and sixty-eight people had been charged with terrorist offences. The year ended with vicious killings of Loyalist hardline leaders, and the disclosure that Libya had sent hundreds of tons of arms to the IRA.

Against this background, Hume had his first meeting of the Irish Peace Initiative with Gerry Adams on 11 January 1988. The meeting, just eight months after publication of Sinn Fein's policy document *A Scenario for Peace*, was initiated by Fr Alec Reid. He had written to Hume and Adams formally asking if they would engage in formal talks. The letter asked both parties 'to explore whether there could be agreement on an overall nationalist political strategy for peace'. Sinn Fein leaders welcomed the opportunity to talk to the SDLP, and instructed Adams to 'explore the possibility of finding agreement on a wide range of issues'.

Hume was more circumspect. 'Before this time, I had only known Gerry Adams slightly,' he later recalled. But he liked what he found, and evidently it was mutual. 'When I first started talking to Adams, I found him to be totally straightforward in what he said to me, and we built a strong personal trust in one another, even though we had different opinions on many matters. It was this mutual regard and trust that was crucial to our success. Neither of us was playing party politics – we were both trying to solve a very grave problem.'[12]

The first meeting lasted several hours. The prospect of an IRA ceasefire was not discussed, though it was uppermost in Hume's mind. The two emphasized after their talks that there had been 'no military agenda'. Hume's first priority was to get Sinn Fein to accept that, by signing the Anglo-Irish Agreement, Britain had declared its neutrality on the future of Northern Ireland. He reiterated that 'Britain is now saying that she has no interest of her own in being here, and that her only interest is to see agreement among the people who share the island of Ireland'. Adams was unconvinced by this optimistic analysis. Sinn Fein still regarded the 'Hillsborough Treaty' as a London–Dublin–SDLP plot. Nevertheless, he subsequently conceded that the talks 'marked the beginning of the most significant discussions in formulating a new peace initiative in the North of Ireland'.

Needless to say, others did not share this view. An alarmed Ian Paisley called for Unionist unity in the face of this 'new alliance', and James Molyneaux described the initiative as 'a fatal step for democracy'. Northern Ireland Secretary Tom King condemned the talks, and questioned Hume's judgement. The Unionist press followed suit, and even the Nationalist newspapers were nervous. The *Irish News* complained that Hume should be able to talk to Adams 'without having his principles called into question'. Two weeks later, Hume secured the backing of his constituency activists to continue the talks, and in mid-February, Sinn Fein's executive gave their approval. Tom King, anxious not to be sidelined by these unexpected moves, invited Hume to Stormont for talks on progress with the

Agreement, which, he was later to reassure Unionists, was 'an end in itself' not 'part of a process sliding to something else'.

Symbolically, the next moves in the Hume–Adams process (which *was* designed to 'slide into something else') took place on St Patrick's Day, 17 March 1988. By now a routine was established. The two sides usually met at St Gerard's Retreat House on the Antrim Road, Belfast. Occasionally, they also used the Redemptorist monastery in Clonard. At these locations, recollected Farren, 'we were reasonably assured of protection from prying eyes. We weren't security conscious, but Sinn Fein were. One meeting had to take place at Clonard because there was a security clampdown in the city, and they didn't want to be seen moving around.' Fr Reid opened the proceedings with a prayer, and the two sides sitting at opposite sides of the table would talk from mid-morning to mid-afternoon. Lunch and coffee were provided, and each side had a retiring-room. Hartley, Sinn Fein's quiet man, said little and took notes. Hume and Adams did most of the talking.

Sinn Fein had obviously prepared very well for the meetings, Farren recorded,

> to the point where I would imagine they had maybe role-played the situation, or had people who played devil's advocate to them as to what they might anticipate from the SDLP. We were very familiar with the kind of arguments we were going to put, because we had been putting them for a long time. In a sense they were better documented as a result of preparation. They had more on paper. They were always able to produce documentation to substantiate what they said, whereas we didn't consider that necessary.

There was no table-thumping. The atmosphere was 'almost academic'.

At the St Patrick's Day meeting, Hume and Adams exchanged personal letters and position papers that were to form the basis of six months of in-depth debate and argument about the scope for joint action. Adams sent a four-page proposal for 'an overall political strategy' and wrote that despite the awful realities confronting Irish society, 'I remain convinced and confident that we can overcome all of these obstacles to achieving justice and peace in our country'.

Hume's long letter to Adams incorporated his proposals, including an insistence that the objective of the talks was to bring an end to all military and violent activity in the North of Ireland. He did not mince his words. The people who had suffered most and the areas that had suffered most 'are the very people that are represented by either Sinn Fein or the SDLP'. They were also the people who suffered harassment by the security forces, house searches, a heavy military presence on the streets – a constant strain and tension in the daily lives of those who had enough problems, given the economic circumstances in which most of them lived. The authorities justified this show of force as a reaction to the IRA's campaign of violence. 'A great deal of relief could therefore be brought to ordinary people by ending the campaign and removing the stated justification for security force actions.'[13]

The old answer that the British presence was the cause of all the violence simply would not do, Hume went on. The IRA must take responsibility for their methods and the suffering they had caused. 'It is clear to us that there is little chance of those methods succeeding in the foreseeable future in achieving the stated objectives of the IRA.' The methods had become more sacred than the cause, he argued: 'And, as has already been admitted on all sides, there can be no military solution.'

Outlining the SDLP alternative, Hume went over the familiar ground that Ireland was first and foremost its people: 'The territory is secondary since without people the territory isn't much different from any other piece of earth.' The Irish people, he continued, had rights to sovereignty and self-determination, but they were divided on how to exercise those rights. The search for agreement on this subject was 'the real search for peace'. It was a search that had never been seriously undertaken by the Nationalist/Republican tradition, and one that could not be conducted by force. If such an agreement could be reached, he asked, would anyone seriously believe that the British government could refuse to endorse it?

By signing an internationally binding agreement (the Anglo-Irish Agreement), the British government had shown that if such an agreement on the exercise of self-determination took the form of Irish unity, they would endorse it. 'Is that not the clearest possible challenge to the Nationalist/Republican in Ireland?' he asked. With remorseless logic, he continued: 'And does that challenge not also remove all justification for the use of violence, because does not the British declaration on endorsing and accepting agreement among the people of Ireland on Irish unity not make clear that Britain is now saying that she has no interest of her own in being here and that her only interest is to see agreement among the people who share the island of Ireland?'

Hume concluded by posing five questions to Sinn Fein, 'with a view to creating the conditions in which all military and violent activity will come to an end'. The first two were uncontroversial. Do you, he asked, accept the right of the Irish people to self-determination? This was an article of Republican faith. The second was: Do you accept that the Irish people are deeply divided on how to exercise self-determination? This was an incontrovertible statement of fact. Third: Do you accept that in practice agreement on exercising that right requires the agreement of both Unionist and Nationalist traditions in Ireland? This, too, was unarguable.

If Sinn Fein accepted these three propositions, Hume argued, then they should also agree that the best way forward would be to create a conference table, convened by the Irish government 'at which all parties in the North with an electoral mandate would attend'. Since Sinn Fein regularly commanded 11 to 13 per cent of the popular vote in Northern Ireland, and at least one-third of the Nationalist vote, this was a clear invitation to Gerry Adams to engage in direct negotiations. The function of the conference would be to reach agreement on self-determination and living together in peace.

There was, however, one over-riding pre-condition, Hume added: 'It would be understood that if this conference were to happen that the IRA would have ceased its campaign.' It would also be understood in advance that if such a conference were to reach agreement, the British government would endorse it. Sinn Fein could reasonably be expected to deliver an IRA ceasefire, but it is difficult to see how an advance commitment by the British could be guaranteed.

Fifth, and finally, Hume asked whether, in the event of the Unionists refusing to participate in such a peace conference, Sinn Fein

would join with the Irish government 'and other Nationalist participants' in preparing a peaceful and comprehensive approach to achieving self-determination. This was a more nebulous objective, but
Hume was adamant that 'if we were to proceed successfully down
such a road, the atmosphere throughout Ireland would be transformed'. International goodwill (he had in mind the USA and
Europe) would be overwhelming, so much so that 'many things which
seem either difficult or even impossible now would become attain-
able'. Promising a 'genuine dialogue', Hume ended by expressing his
hope of an end to military and violent activity.

Sinn Fein immediately complained that Hume had 'subtly shifted
ground' on the objective of the talks by proposing an end to the IRA
campaign. Adams's document trod much familiar historical ground,
and accused Hume's party of creating the dangerous political illusion
that the Anglo-Irish Agreement had ended Unionist power and the
Unionist veto on Irish self-determination. It accused the SDLP of
accepting 'the legitimacy of the British connection'. Adams posed
his own seven questions that exhibited some common ground on
the issue of self-determination, however. He called for 'a common
platform of political activity'. In particular, Sinn Fein looked for
SDLP backing for 'a common solution' to the political situation, and
joint action to impress on the Dublin government the need to launch
an international and diplomatic offensive to secure national self-
determination. These were the makings of a new political axis – the
'pan-Nationalist front' so feared by the Unionists.

Hume was convinced that he was on to a winning formula. The
Unionists had played the Orange card, hoping to bring down the
Agreement, 'and this time it hadn't worked. Mrs Thatcher stood up
to them.' He accepted that the Agreement was not a solution to the
Northern Ireland problem, only a framework within which to create
a solution. Article 1(c) guaranteed to the Unionists that there would
be no change in the state of the province without the consent of its
people. Equally, the Agreement conceded that if a majority agreed
to change, the British government would legislate for it. 'I used that
to say the government had declared their neutrality on the future of
Northern Ireland, and Irish unity was a matter for those who want

it to persuade those who didn't, and that could not be achieved by guns or bullets. That was the beginning of the peace debate.'[14]

The two sides met again at Clonard monastery on 19 May, only weeks after the shooting of three unarmed members of the IRA on a murder mission in Gibraltar, the killing of three mourners at their funeral in Belfast by a Loyalist terrorist and the deaths of two Signals Regiment corporals at the hands of a Republican mob when their car strayed into the path of an IRA funeral. Fr Reid condemned the execution of the corporals, to whom he gave the last rites: 'Our parish is seen as dripping in the blood of the murders.' Hume had been equally shocked, telling the Commons: 'The dictionary is no longer full enough of words to express proper condemnation and the revulsion that people feel.'[15]

Sinn Fein brought to the third round of talks a second paper answering Hume's questions about national self-determination and the way forward for Ireland. Naturally, Adams and his colleagues agreed that the Irish people had a right to self-determination. They cited international law and the United Nations in support, and argued that exercising that right was 'a primary political objective'. However, they quarrelled with the SDLP's second question concerning the deep divisions among Irish people on how to choose their own future. The people of Ireland had never been permitted to exercise self-determination, Sinn Fein argued, except in the 1918 Westminster elections seventy years previously.

There was 'no basis of practical experience' to support the SDLP line of argument, therefore. It was all the fault of the British, and, answering the third question on Unionist/Nationalist agreement on self-determination, SF insisted that only an end to current British policy and a removal of the Unionist veto on ending partition could produce a consensus between the two traditions. Naïvely, Sinn Fein demanded that 'as a first step, both governments must establish Irish reunification as a policy objective'. This was at a time when Mrs Thatcher was considering banning Sinn Fein, sending in more troops, bringing back 'selective' internment and compelling the people of Northern Ireland to carry identity cards.

Gerry Adams accepted that this was a qualified response, but Sinn Fein did respond 'positively' (as he put it) to Hume's proposal of a round table conference of all Irish parties. However, he did not think it 'the best way forward', and he rejected any suggestion of pre-conditions (i.e. an IRA ceasefire). There was one pre-condition for London, none the less. A conference would have to be 'prefaced' by an indication from the British government that it would relinquish sovereignty over the Six Counties. A stated policy objective of Irish reunification would be 'the minimum requirement'. Without it, the Unionists, secure behind their veto, would simply ignore such a conference. In this, at least, Adams was right. He closed with some encouraging words about the value of a 'pan-national consensus' and asked how Hume foresaw the possibilities of consent for change.

The four-man negotiating teams met again on 13 June, when Sinn Fein challenged the political viability of Hume's assertion that Britain no longer had any interest in being in Ireland, except to see agreement among its people. In its third position paper, Sinn Fein said it was unconvinced by this argument, but offered to put it to the familiar test: will Britain join the 'persuaders' for an end to the Union? Adams and his colleagues conceded that such a scenario appeared 'improbable', but they invited the SDLP to join them in an appeal to London and Dublin to begin talking about Irish reunification, leading to 'a peaceful and orderly British political and military withdrawal'. No mention of a ceasefire, much less an end to the war.

Hume would not let Sinn Fein off the hook. His comment on Sinn Fein's earlier proposals emphatically repudiated the 'armed struggle', which Adams had not addressed. He accused the Republicans of being obsessed with abstract principles, such as whether the British had a legitimate right in Ireland. 'The Irish will always argue that they haven't, and the British will always argue that they have.' These arguments stemmed from different historical perspectives, and went nowhere. Why not deal with reality – the British are here – rather than debate ideological rectitude endlessly – should they be here? The real question, Hume insisted, was: 'How do we end the British presence in Ireland in a manner that leaves behind a stable and peaceful Ireland?' This was unusually close to Republicanism for the SDLP. Had the Unionists (and the British government for that matter) appreciated how much common ground was emerging, the alarm would have been raised loudly at this stage. Hume's answer to his own rhetorical question was: 'Unite the people of Ireland first.'

Not, however, at the point of a gun. The SDLP accepted that the IRA 'may be politically motivated', but no legitimacy could be conferred on its actions. To do so would be to sign away the rights of the Irish majority to an unelected, unrepresentative and unaccountable paramilitary organization. 'Violence only produces further violence,' Hume reiterated. 'The most effective response to violence in Northern Ireland is non-violence, despite the temptation to do otherwise. Condemning the violence perpetrated by British forces cannot excuse paramilitary violence as a legitimate response.' The speediest way to be rid of armed police and the military was still the political way. He challenged Sinn Fein and the IRA to end the campaign of violence. If that happened, the SDLP and Sinn Fein could co-operate.

In a further paper, the SDLP's third, Hume returned to his gospel of British neutrality, claiming: 'There is nothing to stop British governments becoming pro-Irish unity in their policies.' It was 'our task' to persuade them in that direction, and to take the Unionists with them, into a 'New Ireland' in which Unionist interests were accommodated. The SDLP stood ready to engage in concerted political action to achieve this objective, and he quoted Parnell: 'Ireland can never be united and can never have its freedom until the prejudices of the Protestant people are conciliated.'

There the issue lay for three more weeks. Hume and Adams met again in private on 11 July. Hume tabled his fourth position paper, in which he said: 'we accept Sinn Fein's statement that the Irish people as a whole should exercise the right to self-determination.' Adams was encouraged by this form of words, but not by the rest of the document, which was an unwavering insistence that the IRA cease its campaign before Sinn Fein could attend a conference of all Irish parties convened by Dublin. Citing Article 1 of the Anglo-Irish Agreement, Hume used for the first time his formula that Britain had 'no strategic, military or economic interests' in remaining in Ireland. This political definition was to inform the entire peace process.

Hume expressed the view that, politically, the positions of Sinn Fein and the SDLP were 'not unduly removed from one another and not unbridgeable'. He recognized that Adams and his colleagues were still not convinced of 'British neutrality', but he appealed to them to 'formally ask' the IRA to lay down its arms and use their considerable influence to persuade it to do so.

The talks adjourned to 14 August, when Gerry Adams presented a 'letter of review' (addressed directly to 'John') on seven months of dialogue. He was disappointed that they had not made more progress, but he felt the talks had been worthwhile. They had closed a gap between the parties, and were good for the morale of a hard-pressed Nationalist community. However, there were some hard words. He accused Hume and the SDLP of trying to engineer a public percep-tion that the 'Hillsborough Treaty' was an end to Loyalist power and the Loyalist veto, and that the British government had become neutral. 'We believe that your analysis helps the British to internalise the conflict. In fact, you accept the union with Britain.'

Adams had exposed the contradiction at the heart of SDLP think-ing. On the one hand, its Nationalist objective was an Ireland united by the force of argument rather than by the argument of force. On the other, its social democrat programme, stemming from the early civil rights days, was for parity of esteem as citizens: that is, votes, and equal opportunity for Catholics on housing and jobs. But parity with whom? Other citizens of the UK, presumably. Implicit in this strategy was an acceptance of remaining part of the nation – the United Kingdom – that could grant these reforms. The government had just introduced a new White Paper on fair employment, designed to strengthen the existing legislation introduced in 1976. As recently as 1 July, Labour's Northern Ireland spokesman Kevin McNamara (a staunch ally of Hume) had declared in the Commons that while inequality of job opportunity still remained, the greatest disparities in housing had disappeared and political gerrymandering had been 'brought under control'. These changes were won within the Union, indeed through the Union.

Hume's assessment, Adams charged, 'lacked real political depth and analysis'. It relied on emotional rhetoric camouflaged in Nationalist language. He accused Hume of being drawn into ambiva-lence over Unionist plans for devolution in the province, which would cement the Union. The British intended to build on this equivocation, he warned. Hume's claims for British 'neutrality' flew in the face of all the facts.

Nor, Adams suggested, had the SDLP taken the whole process seriously enough. The response to Sinn Fein's first document was disappointing: 'Sean Farren delivered a verbal reply lasting just over ten minutes, which was completely negative.' Adams accused Hume of failing to provide responses that had been promised, and, worse, of amending the written version of his contributions to the talks 'as if you had more of an eye to future publication'. The Sinn Fein president added: 'We felt at times that the talks were not being taken seriously, since our analysis was taken lightly . . . we often found the SDLP evasive.' Adams even accused the Hume delegation of damaging breaches of confidentiality, leading to newspaper stories that Sinn Fein was divided.

However, after this catalogue of criticism, Adams said: 'We do not regard our dialogue as being concluded. We should remain in regular contact. Given past opposition to face-to-face talks, the laying aside of that prejudice, I am sure you will agree, was a breakthrough in itself.'

On 5 September, Hume and Adams issued statements on the end 'of the present round of talks'. Each restated his position, and blamed the other for the failure to agree. The SDLP offered hope that the debate would continue 'in the public and private arena', particularly among Republicans, and that it would lead to an end to the agony of the people of the North sooner rather than later. Adams scorned Hume's claim that Britain was now neutral and charged the SDLP with 'recognition and acceptance of the loyalist veto'. Yet he too confirmed Sinn Fein's commitment to dialogue and looked forward to more debate and discussion.

Hume's considered verdict was that the talks had failed. However, the statements promising to continue the debate in public and private contained the grains of success. He recorded later: 'That private contact subsequently developed into the peace talks and the so-called Hume–Adams Initiative.'[16]

Adams moved more quickly, delivering his verdict in the magazine *Fortnight* in January 1989, when the Sinn Fein leader defended himself and Hume from the 'cliché-ridden hostility from political opponents and detractors'. Hume had entered into dialogue to achieve an end to violence. He had done so to examine the ways of establishing conditions for peace. 'My meeting with John Hume may also fail to find a solution, but it has proved that there can be life after dialogue. Neither John Hume nor I has been contaminated by our contact with each other. Dialogue for consenting adults may actually be good for us.'

Adams put his own interpretation on the likely outcome. Sinn Fein had a duty to listen to others. 'That is what I did with Mr Hume.' They were not negotiating a ceasefire. John Hume did not represent the British government, and Adams did not represent the IRA. Hume denounced IRA actions in a forthright manner, while Sinn Fein 'explained' the weakness of the SDLP position: its gradualist approach made it subservient to British interests. His duty was to win support for Sinn Fein's policy that the Loyalists should not have a veto over change. Hume's duty was to persuade Sinn Fein of the merits of the SDLP approach. 'That is what Mr Hume and I were doing.'

Austin Currie, another SDLP member of the talks, declared that 'we were almost logjammed from the start'.[17] However, he identified one ideological seed among the rhetorical chaff: the future of Ireland had to be decided by the wishes of people indigenous to, or domiciled in, the whole island. 'That in a sense was the embryo from which the thinking on self-determination would evolve in the future.' Currie felt at the close of the talks that Adams and McLaughlin wanted to pursue a political solution rather than continue the violence. Sean Farren, the SDLP's thinker, found the Sinn Fein delegation blinkered about the true nature of Unionism. They imagined that if the British announced a withdrawal in, say, five years, the Unionists would reach an accommodation. 'They had a blind faith that the Unionists might put up a token resistance, and that could be dealt with by the British Army, the RUC and the UDR. But following token opposition, the unionists – hard-headed people and realists – would sit down and negotiate a new arrangement for the whole of Ireland, themselves included. We never believed that. And still don't believe it.'[18]

In retrospect, it was never likely that one series of encounters, however well-intentioned, would produce sufficient common ground for Hume and Adams to make substantial steps towards a peaceful settlement. Adams did not have enough from Hume to go to the IRA and plead for a cessation of the 'armed struggle'. Hume did not have enough from Adams to persuade his party or his allies in the South that Sinn Fein should be brought in from the cold. The ice, though, had been broken. In Adams's view, 'the republican peace strategy was already in gestation'.

TWELVE

BREAKTHROUGH

THE ABRUPT END to Hume's peace moves in public concealed the fact that he was continuing to talk privately to Adams. Officials of Charles Haughey's Dublin government also held secret discussions with the Sinn Fein president, coming to the same conclusion as Hume: that fanciful talk of a pan-Nationalist front would remain exactly that until the violence ceased.

More remarkably, Hume opened up a dialogue of sorts with the Unionists, whose condemnation of his Sinn Fein initiative could not have been more comprehensive. Once again, Fr Alec Reid was instrumental. The talks took place in a hotel in Duisburg, West Germany, in mid-October 1988. Inevitably, because of the para-mount need for secrecy, it was a second-eleven affair. Austin Currie represented the SDLP. Officially, the SDLP, the two main Unionist parties and the Alliance Party discussed a formula for inter-party talks in the province. It was a laudable, home-grown initiative, not a creature of London, and it deserved to succeed. But the effort foundered on the old rock of the Anglo-Irish Agreement. Hume refused to concede the Unionists' central demand of suspension of the Agreement, knowing that, once suspended, it would prove impossible to revive it. Instead, he proposed talks outside the AIA to reach 'an agreement that will transcend any previous agreement ever made'. This ingenious proposal was rejected, but Hume made an appeal: 'Let's keep the informal contact and let's keep working at it.'[1]

In the wake of the failed peace initiative with Gerry Adams, Hume's contempt for IRA/Sinn Fein was never more eloquent than at that year's annual conference of the SDLP in Belfast. 'They are more Irish than the rest of us, they believe. They are the pure master race of Irish. They are the keepers of the holy grail of the nation. That deep-seated attitude, married to their method, has all the hallmarks of undiluted fascism,' he said in his leader's speech on 26 November 1988.

He told delegates in the Europa Hotel: 'I had discussions with them recently. The talks were designed to explore whether they were willing to lay down their arms and join the rest of the people in this island in the lengthy and difficult search for peace ... I put some questions to them about the price of their means and method, about the consequence of victory for their viewpoint, about peaceful alternatives. They replied with sheaves of paper reiterating well-worn declarations.' He accused Republicans of 'extreme moral cowardice' and claimed: 'There is not a single injustice in Northern Ireland today that justifies the taking of a single human life. If I were to lead a civil rights campaign in Northern Ireland today, the major target of that campaign would be the IRA.'

The facts supported Hume. In the twenty years of the Troubles, 2,705 people had died. Less than a third of these were members of the security forces. More than half were ordinary men and women, and of these 69 per cent were Catholics. Who killed them? Almost half (44 per cent) had died at the hands of the IRA and splinter Republican groups. Only one in ten had been killed by the British Army, and one in fifty by the RUC. 'Some defenders!' he spat out. 'Was it O'Casey [the Irish playwright] who said: "The gunmen are not dying for the people, the people are dying for the gunmen".'

Hume made a direct invitation to the men of violence: 'My challenge to any of those people in Ireland, North and South, today who regard themselves as republicans is to accept the straightforward offer made to them in our talks. Lay down your arms once and for all.' If they did so, they could come to the conference table.

The political tide in London was running the other way. Home Secretary Douglas Hurd had just banned Sinn Fein spokesmen from the airwaves. Tom King, the Northern Ireland Secretary, curtailed a defendant's right to silence in court in a move to make the conviction of terrorists easier, and on the eve of the SDLP conference Mrs Thatcher had slashed remission for prisoners in the province's gaols from half to a third of their sentences. This package was the Iron Lady's response to Enniskillen and the IRA's summer offensive.

The government also brought in a new law requiring candidates for district councils – Northern Ireland's last remaining instrument of democracy – to sign a declaration that they did not support terrorism. Anyone gaoled for more than three months was disqualified from politics for five years. These measures, clearly directed against Sinn Fein, became law in March 1989, just in time to take effect before the May elections. Sinn Fein's electoral performance worried both London and Dublin, as well as Hume's party.

In the 1989 poll, the SDLP recaptured some of the ground it had lost in the early and mid-1980s to Sinn Fein. Hume's people took 21 per cent of the first-preference vote, up more than 3 per cent on 1985, while Sinn Fein lost ground marginally, down just over half a per cent to 11.2 per cent. The SDLP gained twenty seats, taking its total to 121. Sinn Fein saw its tally fall by sixteen to forty-three. Hume's party now controlled two district councils, and shared power in five others. It was their best performance so far, consolidating the SDLP's position as the main representative of Nationalist opinion.

The European Parliament election a month later confirmed the trend. Hume's popular vote fell slightly – fewer than half the electorate bothered to turn out – but his share of the poll rose from 22 per cent in 1985 to 25.5 per cent. Sinn Fein's Danny Morrison mustered just over 9 per cent, a drop of 4 per cent but 40,000 in number. Ian Paisley topped the poll yet again, but his share fell to below 30 per cent, finishing only five points ahead of Hume.

In his leader's address later that year, Hume allowed himself some self-congratulation: 'Both elections are the clearest possible evidence of the steadily growing public support for the steadiness of the SDLP approach summarised by our slogan "Keep Building". We have never offered short cuts or instant answers to complex problems of human relations.' He told delegates at the Slieve Donard Hotel, Newcastle: 'We have never promised years of victory. We do not spill blood, we do not ask others to spill blood. We spill sweat, we ask others to do the same.'[2]

As Parliament went into recess in late July 1989, Thatcher reconstructed her government. She made a virtual clean sweep at the Northern Ireland Office, bringing in former Conservative Party chairman Peter Brooke as Secretary of State with three new ministers under him. Brooke was an interesting figure, the descendant of a Speaker of the House of Commons in the sixteenth century and a famous cricket buff. He was a courteous charmer, but a critical one, too. He would initiate the next stage of the stalled peace process. A distant relative of Lord Brookeborough, a hard-line Unionist premier in the old Stormont who once described Cardinal O'Fiaich as 'an evil prelate', Brooke none the less took an impish delight in reminding people that another ancestor, Charlotte, was a poet who first used the word 'Fenian' in the English language.

Brooke inherited Tom King's slow-moving efforts to get all-party talks going on some form of devolution. King, irate about the SDLP/Sinn Fein discussions, had been somewhat mollified by Hume in a private briefing. London was still deeply suspicious, but Brooke went out of his way to consult Hume while making his analysis of the political state of the province. Brooke maintained the polite fiction of talks with the Unionist parties, while also sanctioning secret contacts with Sinn Fein. Hume urged him to take seriously the new readiness to contemplate a non-military strategy evident in Gerry Adams's recent speeches and in some of the contributions to the 1988 initiative. Hume, who met Adams four times privately in 1989, ensured that Brooke was kept fully informed.

The new Northern Ireland Secretary used the opportunity of a Press Association interview on his hundredth day in office, 3 November 1989, to make a major pronouncement on the future of the province. Brooke conceded that 'it is difficult to envisage a military defeat' of the IRA, though they could be contained by the security forces. He went on to say that a debate might start within the terrorist community, and if that proceeded to a point where they 'wished to withdraw from their activities', then the British government 'would need to be imaginative in those circumstances'. He spoke further of being 'flexible' and used Cyprus as an example – as had Hume, on numerous occasions – arguing that he would not say 'never' to talks with Sinn Fein should violence be repudiated. A political storm immediately broke over the hapless Brooke's head, and he had to moderate his stance, withdrawing the Cyprus analogy which gave the impression that 'terrorism works'.

Brooke kept his head down until the new year, and on 9 January 1990 he suggested to a group of businessmen in Bangor, County Down, that he had found sufficient ground to make inter-party talks on devolution worthwhile. But he did not concede the 'natural break' in the operation of the Anglo-Irish Agreement that alone would have brought the Unionists to the conference table. Six months later he reported failure in his efforts to the Commons. It was not until October that the SDLP's hand in this initiative was disclosed. Hume's party had 'stymied' Brooke's prepared speech, which was to have ruled out substantive talks between Dublin and Northern Ireland until real progress had been made on the internal government of the province.[3]

Hume had consistently set his foot against any internal settlement, and on 7 October he proposed that Brooke should wipe the slate clean and start again. He noted that previous attempts to engineer devolution had failed, and revived his suggestion of a process that could 'transcend' the Anglo-Irish Agreement, thereby resolving Unionist hostility to any talks while the Agreement was still operating. One month later, in the celebrated Whitbread Speech delivered in his City of London and Westminster constituency, Brooke took his cue from Hume's oft-stated 'neutrality' argument and declared that the British government had 'no selfish strategic or economic interest in Northern Ireland'.

The Northern Ireland Secretary had not chanced upon this expression. With the addition of the word 'selfish', this was exactly the formula used by Hume in his August 1988 summing-up review of the failed talks with Sinn Fein. Gerry Adams would not believe Hume then, not least because the message did not come from British lips. He was hearing it now. Hume had visited Brooke in the preceding weeks and pressed him to include this formula in his 9 November address on 'The British Presence'.

Brooke took the risk, and presented Hume with a political coup. The SDLP leader could now say to Gerry Adams that his interpretation of British government intentions was correct, and should be put to the test by ending IRA violence. Brooke went further, insisting:

'Our role is to help, enable and encourage. Britain's purpose, as I have sought to describe it, is not to occupy, oppress or exploit, but to ensure democratic debate and free democratic choice. That is our way.' On the day, Brooke's dramatic intervention was eclipsed on the front pages by the election of Mary Robinson, a forty-six-year-old lawyer, as the first woman President of Ireland. Her victory was seen as a sign that the Republic might be breaking out of the 'old politics' of the civil war. In the long run, Brooke's courage may be seen as the greater watershed.

Sinn Fein – 'Ourselves Alone' – might still be a seductive identity in Ireland, but in the wider world events were rapidly favouring Hume. In 1988, he had argued that Britain no longer had the same strategic interest in Northern Ireland. Sinn Fein disagreed, but manifestly this was so. Defence establishments, including the naval base in Derry, had closed down. In the early summer of 1989, the Berlin Wall was torn down. Hume was in Berlin a week after the wall fell, 'a moment of great hope right across Europe', he recalled later. 'But I was conscious that, as the Berlin Wall was falling, the Belfast walls were rising.' Hume made a speech in the Reichstag, presenting Willy Brandt with a piece of the Belfast wall he had brought with him.

The Warsaw Pact disintegrated soon after, and with it the Soviet threat that compelled British reliance on the Atlantic sea routes on Ireland's flank. It was time for Irish politics to come to terms with these changes and with the move in Europe towards 'pooled sovereignty', said Hume in his leader's speech on 4 November. 'It is sometimes forgotten that the battle at the origin of our quarrel, the Boyne, was fought not just by Protestant and Catholic Irish but by French, Germans and Walloons fighting English, Dutch, Danes and other Germans. They have long since settled that quarrel and many others . . . Only in Ireland does the integrity of the ancient quarrel remain.' Hume asked: 'Is it not about time we followed the example of those with whom we now share sovereignty throughout Europe?'

Yet in his next paragraph Hume could not resist a jibe at the Unionists, which suggests that he was still in thrall to the past. He recalled that the Unionists now described themselves as the party of the '90s: 'They may forgive me for reminding them that they have always been a party of the '90s – the 1690s!' The crack drew laughter, but it could not have helped his appeal, a few sentences later, for all-party talks 'without prejudice' to solve the Northern Ireland problem.

Hume wanted the Unionists to sit down with the Dublin government and other parties in the Dail 'to discuss how we share this island to our mutual satisfaction'. Any agreement reached would have to be endorsed by a majority on both sides of the border in referenda held on the same day. The strength of his proposal, he added, was the assurance it gave that 'we mean what we say when we talk of an Agreed Ireland'.

His appeal fell, as usual, on deaf ears. Then, unexpectedly, things changed. Margaret Thatcher had been experiencing problems for some months. In the weeks after the Tory Party conference that October, Michael Heseltine challenged her for the party leadership and the occupancy of Downing Street. Thatcher, determined to remain above the fray, fulfilled an engagement to visit Ulster as the shades drew close about her premiership. Her aloof campaign was a disaster, and on 27 November, John Major became party leader and Prime Minister. Peter Brooke, who had supported the former Northern Ireland Secretary, Douglas Hurd, in the contest, nevertheless kept his job. Having never been a minister either in the NIO or the Home Office, Major was not on sure ground in Northern Ireland. He needed stability, for the time being at least. His first act in the affairs of the province was to send 500 extra troops to cope with an expected IRA bombing campaign. The IRA promptly wrong-footed him by calling a three-day Christmas truce, the first for fifteen years. One Republican source claimed this was a signal to Major that 'there is a willingness to examine possibilities which Brooke is exploring'.[4]

In case the new Prime Minister got the wrong message, however, the IRA took their 'long war' into Downing Street six weeks later. On the morning of 7 February 1991, as the Cabinet met to discuss the Gulf War, three mortar bombs were fired at Downing Street from a van parked in nearby Horseguards Avenue. One of the bombs exploded in the garden of No. 10. Only the blast curtains and toughened windows saved ministers – some of them visibly shaken – from a potentially lethal shower of glass.

The government refused to be distracted. Aside from holding out an olive branch to the IRA, Peter Brooke continued his year-long efforts to coax the constitutional parties (not Sinn Fein, while there was no ceasefire) round the negotiating table. In an end-of-year interview with the *Belfast Telegraph*, he talked up his ploy, saying there had been 'new thinking about difficult issues'. In truth, neither Hume's party nor the Unionists wanted to be seen as the ones standing in the way of progress.

Hume played his part in what became known as 'the Brooke talks', but he was concentrating on getting the IRA to lay down their arms. His continuing private diplomacy with Gerry Adams convinced him there was a genuine possibility of achieving a cessation of violence. His European aide, Denis Haughey, noticed him on a flight to Berlin about this time reading the Sinn Fein papers from the abortive talks. He was concentrating so hard he looked 'as if he was trying to inhale them'.[5] Hume was searching for any point of contact that might help restart talks with Sinn Fein.

As he did so, the Brooke talks halted in the face of Unionist intransigence. The Northern Ireland Secretary officially closed his peace bid on 3 July, leaving the province in a political impasse. The Anglo-Irish Agreement was still operational, but it could not progress. The only way forward, it seemed, was a direct approach to those who were doing the fighting. The British government was in regular, clandestine contact with Sinn Fein, though only John Major and two other Cabinet ministers (Hurd and Brooke) were aware of the exchanges.

In the autumn of 1991, after Brooke had failed to restart his own talks, Hume turned his mind to the prospect of a more formal attempt to engage Sinn Fein in the drive for peace. What had he and Adams both accepted in 1988? That there should be some kind of joint approach, with the Dublin government, by all Nationalist parties with a view to reaching agreement on the exercise of national self-determination. The objective thereafter would be to convince the British government to become a 'persuader' for this strategy.

Hume's shorthand for this whole process was 'a joint declaration': a statement from both governments designed to achieve a peaceful settlement in Northern Ireland. One night in October 1991, Hume sat down and wrote his own version. It would form the basis of the

Downing Street Declaration a little over two years later. In Hume's neat, copperplate handwriting, the two-page joint declaration by both British and Irish prime ministers ran to seven sections. The first set aside the past, while regretting the pain caused by failures to settle relationships on the island satisfactorily, and the second sought recognition that the advent of the European Union and the Single Market would intensify the need for maximum co-operation. The third pointed out the legacy of 'a deeply divided people', and the fourth called for recognition that these divisions could be ended only with the agreement of the people, North and South.

Section 5 committed both governments to promoting intensive co-operation to strengthen the process of agreement, and the sixth restated that the British government had no selfish strategic interest in remaining in Ireland, but substituted 'political' for 'economic' in the original formula. It then invited both governments to say that their sole interest was to see peace and agreement among the people who inhabit the island.

Section 7 was directed solely at Dublin. It required recognition that the traditional objective of Irish Nationalism – the exercise of self-determination by the people of Ireland as a whole – could not be achieved without the agreement of the people of Northern Ireland. It therefore committed itself to building the necessary trust for the future by working for institutions North and South that would respect diversity but encourage the people 'to work their substantial common ground'.

The Irish government would set up a permanent Irish Convention to plan and implement policies required to break down the barriers that prevented the exercise of agreed self-determination. Importantly, if the British government refused to go down the road of a joint declaration, Dublin would go ahead with an elected all-Ireland Convention open to parties 'who share the objective of a united self-determined Ireland'.

Hume's blueprint drew heavily on his previous peace initiatives, but particularly on the inconclusive talks with Sinn Fein in 1988. The Dublin-convened conference, which pre-supposed an IRA ceasefire, was in there, as were the European context and the attempt to find a formula on self-determination that satisfied Nationalist aspirations while reassuring Unionists that the status quo would not be changed except by the wish of the majority. At the risk of appearing to be all things to all men, the Hume programme did offer a diplomatic framework in which the two governments could seek to reach a settlement with the warring traditions of Northern Ireland.

Charles Haughey, presented with Hume's handwritten blueprint, was impressed. He called in his closest advisers on Northern Ireland, and they worked on a more formal presentation. Hume took this document back to Belfast, and delivered it personally to Gerry Adams. The Sinn Fein president consulted his tightly-knit leadership collective, most of whom had been involved in the 1988 talks, and Hume's ideas began to gain ground. John Major was privately alerted to what was going on in talks with Haughey in Dublin in December. He was deeply sceptical, but willing to 'wait and see', agreeing to meet the Taoiseach every six months.

Despite a further upsurge in IRA violence, Peter Brooke then called in the Northern Ireland party leaders with a new proposal for talks. It was a course of action that Hume had been urging for some time. At the SDLP conference in November 1991, he appealed directly to the Unionists, arguing that their security rested in their strength and numbers, rather than in Acts of Parliament. 'We are inviting you to join us in a genuine and lasting peace process,' he declared. Only such a process could yield 'a settlement of all relationships', because it would be aimed at giving security to all. 'It would remove the objections to such talks that are based on the existence of other agreements whether of 1920 or 1985. That is why we have called, and call on Mr Brooke again, to convene such talks without delay.' He begged the Unionist leaders to respond in the same spirit.

His peace bid was stillborn. Brooke met Hume and the other constitutional party leaders at Westminster, and then announced 'with regret' on 27 January 1992 that it was not possible to take his talks proposal further. He had routinely ruled out Sinn Fein's bid to enter the process, on the grounds that they could become involved only after 'a cessation of violence', rather than a temporary ceasefire like the three-day pause in operations over Christmas. Only a handful of ministers knew that Sinn Fein's Martin McGuinness had already opened a secret line of communication with Downing Street, having first met British government officials in October 1990. These contacts continued throughout the ensuing years.

Outwardly, John Major was more concerned with addressing the security situation in Northern Ireland, not least because a general election was looming. Surprisingly, however, he met Hume and the other Northern Ireland party leaders on 11 February 1992. At the Prime Minister's request, they agreed to meet again to discuss obstacles to further political dialogue.

Major may have been responding to the sudden political change in Dublin, where Charles Haughey had bowed to the inevitable and resigned over a series of phone-tapping and business scandals that tainted his time in office. His successor as Prime Minister in February 1992, Albert Reynolds, promised to open the windows of Irish politics and let in some fresh air, a promise he kept. Within two weeks of becoming Taoiseach, he met Hume and other SDLP leaders, and pledged that the Irish territorial claim to the North enshrined in Articles 2 and 3 of the constitution would not be up for discussion unless the Government of Ireland Act that formalized partition was too. Two days later, on 26 February, Reynolds, a self-made businessman with a brisk, no-nonsense style, made clear at his first meeting with Major that Northern Ireland would be high on his political agenda.

The Anglo-Irish Agreement was set to one side for the duration of the Westminster general election, called for 9 April 1992 by John Major amid much false expectation that the Conservatives might be ousted after thirteen years in power. Neil Kinnock's Labour Party was tipped, if not to win outright, at least to emerge as the largest party in the Commons. Despite the SDLP's superficially close political consanguinity with the Labour Party – and Hume's close personal links with Kinnock – Hume had his doubts about the prospects for progress in the event of a Labour victory. In the first place, in recent years it had been the Conservatives who had shown the political confidence to throw off the imperial yoke from Britain's colonies, and while Northern Ireland was certainly no colony, there were similarities. Hume's favourite prime minister of his generation was Ted Heath, who had had the nerve to negotiate the power-sharing agreement at Sunningdale.

In the run-up to the election, Kinnock had even played down his party's long-term commitment to a united Ireland, insisting that reconvened talks under a Labour government would not be designed to advance the cause of Irish unity. For his part, Hume courted criticism by sending Richard Needham, the engaging Northern Ireland Tory Commerce Minister, a message of support, praising him as 'a truly outstanding minister' to his electorate in North Wiltshire – a constituency which contained many British defence establishments.

As it turned out, a combination of John Major's meet-the-people soapbox campaigning, doubts about Labour's tax plans and Kinnock's own fitness for the highest office combined to secure an unprecedented fourth term for the Tories, with an overall majority of twenty in the Commons. Patrick Mayhew, a former Attorney General who had often clashed with the Irish government over the extradition of suspects to the UK, was appointed Northern Ireland Secretary. He took with him a new ministerial team including Michael Mates, a former British Army officer and defence expert.

Hume's party increased its share of the popular vote, from 21 per cent to 23.5, while Sinn Fein's declined marginally, to only 10 per cent. More significantly, the SDLP gained a fourth seat at Westminster, as Dr Joe Hendron, a popular local general practitioner, ousted Gerry Adams in West Belfast. His victory was only slightly clouded by Sinn Fein allegations of collusion with hard-line Protestants to drive out the only Republican MP. The IRA chose to celebrate the election by blowing up the City of London financial district, causing £800 million pounds-worth of damage – more than all the compensation paid in Northern Ireland for damage since the Troubles restarted in 1969. This bomb, more than any other single explosion, intensified behind-the-scenes pressure on Major's government. It exposed the vulnerability of Britain's commercial heart, which had become the IRA's primary target.

In fact, London and Dublin were still trying to re-establish all-party talks (excluding Sinn Fein) through the complex three-strand approach initiated by Peter Brooke. One month after the election, Hume submitted a proposal to 'Strand One' of the talks, which concerned itself with the governance of Northern Ireland, arguing that the province should be ruled by a six-member Executive Commission. Power would be shared among three members directly elected in the province under a proportional representation system, together with one each nominated by the British and Irish governments and the European Community.

As is virtually inevitable in Irish politics, the proposal was leaked to the press, allowing the Unionist parties and Mayhew to undermine it before realistic negotiations could begin. The 'moderate Unionist' Alliance Party condemned the Hume idea as 'unrealistic and impractical'. The Unionists' bid was for a devolved assembly, with key posts going to parties according to their performance at the polls, an arrangement specifically excluding Dublin and the EC. Hume's idea remained in abeyance when Sir Ninian Stephen, a prominent retired Australian diplomat brought in by London to act as independent chairman of the talks, opened 'Strand Two' and 'Strand Three', covering North–South relationships in late June 1992.

While not involved in the Brooke talks, Sinn Fein, through its secret contacts with the Major administration, knew what was going on, and Sir Ninian's move coincided with a new expression appearing on the face of Republicanism. Giving the annual address over Wolfe Tone's grave in Bodenstown, County Kildare, on 21 June, Jim Gibney, a leading Sinn Fein figure, asked if Republicans were deafened by 'the deadly sound of their own gunfire'. He added that the most pressing issue was 'the need for peace in our country', acknowledging: 'We know and accept that the British government's departure must be preceded by a sustained period of peace and will arise out of negotiations.' Sinn Fein denied any change of policy, but Hume and the British government discerned a shift in emphasis. Could the Republican movement be preparing the ground for a ceasefire?

Encouraged by Mayhew's private rejection of the Hume formula in a letter to James Molyneaux, the Unionists agreed to talks with the Irish government; but a series of deliberately damaging leaks from these meetings at Stormont and then Dublin Castle made it impossible to reach even the foothills of an agreement on devolved government. Exasperated, Hume went public with his proposal for a six-member Executive Commission in a Radio Ulster interview on 26 September. He argued that Northern Ireland 'is not a political identity, and therefore you cannot have a normal democracy'.[6]

Ian Paisley's DUP seized on Hume's comments as proof that the

SDLP had hardened its attitude, 'making it impossible to reach agreement'. Six weeks later, the Brooke–Mayhew talks collapsed, taking with them Hume's hopes of building on the Anglo-Irish Agreement. The latest in a long line of failed initiatives, which had cost £5 million to stage, starkly illustrated the unbridgeable gap between Northern Ireland's two traditions. In retrospect, it is not hard to see why. The two sides had mutually contradictory aims: the Nationalists to enhance the Irish dimension in the province's governance, the Unionists to diminish the scope of the Anglo-Irish Agreement and preserve the Union in perpetuity. Neither side trusted the other, but intelligent observers noted 'a new subtlety in political discourse'. This finesse was not much in evidence amid the welter of political recriminations that followed the breakdown. The Alliance Party even complained that there was little chance of agreement on the future of the province while John Hume remained leader of the SDLP.

The situation appeared bleak. However, contacts between London and Sinn Fein were continuing, and bore fruit in a speech by Mayhew on 16 December 1992 when he reaffirmed Brooke's promise that an IRA cessation of violence would lead to British troops being taken off the streets and possibly to the involvement of Sinn Fein in future talks. Mayhew rejected a return to the old Stormont, and explicitly recognized the need for a new North–South arrangement that would 'cater for and express both traditions'. In a symbolic act, he announced the removal of the ban on Irish street names in the province. The Unionists were incensed, but at the close of the year Michael Lillis, who as a senior Irish civil servant had a key role in negotiating the Anglo-Irish Agreement, wrote in the *Irish Times*: 'I have been deeply convinced by John Hume's argument that, while dialogue should continue without interruption, this is the right time for a concentrated negotiation of a definitive solution in which the inequalities and wrongs which burden the minority (so usefully accepted by the Secretary of State) are manifestly on the way to correction.'[7] So, despite Unionist criticism, the year closed with Hume's pivotal role undiminished.

The new year found Hume and his SDLP colleagues included in a threat by Loyalist paramilitaries to 'target' what they characterized as the 'pan-national front' of Sinn Fein, the SDLP, the Irish government and sporting bodies such as the Gaelic Athletic Association. This was no idle threat. In the five years to mid-1993, eighteen Sinn Fein councillors and party workers were assassinated, and the outlawed UDA had vowed to intensify its campaign of violence 'to a ferocity never imagined'. SDLP councillors' homes were firebombed, and armed Loyalists were intercepted on their way to murder an SDLP politician.

Hume continued to press his own agenda, securing from John Major in January 1993 a partial apologia for the murderous actions of British paratroopers in Derry on Bloody Sunday. Hume was still demanding an independent inquiry into the deaths two decades previously, and the Prime Minister, while refusing his demand, subtly changed the government attitude to the fourteen men killed in January 1972. Instead of being 'not guilty' of allegations that they were shot handling weapons or explosives, the victims were now 'innocent' of these charges.

By the spring of 1993, the secret contacts between the British government and Sinn Fein reached such a promising stage that John Major envisaged direct talks at a neutral venue. The IRA would call a two-week ceasefire to permit discussions. These hopes were destined to fail, a victim of IRA bombings in Warrington and London, and the realpolitik of a government facing a huge internal revolt over the Maastricht Treaty on European integration. Major could not contemplate opening a second front, and any disclosure of talks with Sinn Fein would have triggered a potentially fatal rebellion by the sizeable, and influential, Unionist wing of his party on the backbenches. The Prime Minister had to settle for a two-day visit to the province in which he called for a resumption of the all-party talks. 'There are grounds for hope,' he mused.

John Hume suffered no such inhibitions, shrugging off Unionist bile that 'it seems to Unionists that John Hume has an absolute veto over any progress in the province'. While London drew back from the natural progression of contacts with Sinn Fein, Hume reopened discussions with Gerry Adams. On Saturday 10 April, they met secretly in Derry for the first time in two years. A fortnight later, Adams was spotted slipping into Hume's house in West End Park, above the Catholic Bogside. If they were seeking privacy, the choice of venue is inexplicable. Gerry Adams is as instantly identifiable in Derry as Hume himself, and he was promptly recognized by a neighbour, who in turn gave the hot news to Eamonn McCann, Hume's long-standing political adversary. McCann is also an astute freelance journalist, and he quickly called the broadsheet *Sunday Tribune* in Dublin with the story. Hume later regretted the premature publicity. 'In my opinion, had we maintained secrecy, we would have made progress much more quickly.' Once the talks became known, 'the resultant pressures and vilification were awful, making life extremely difficult for both of us'.[8]

Unionists were predictably outraged, and though some British politicians praised Hume's courage, others were perplexed by his timing and by his motives. Hume was unmoved. 'Look,' he said, 'it's a highly sensitive process. I am working for a lasting peace. There are only two possible outcomes: one is that it will fail, and the other is that it will succeed. If it fails, nothing has changed, but if it succeeds, the whole atmosphere has changed. I am prepared to explore that possibility with Mr Adams, and I think it my duty to do so.'[9] After this first stage of the Hume–Adams initiative (it was always that way round, never Adams–Hume), the two political leaders issued a statement. They said: 'Everyone has a solemn duty to change the political climate away from conflict and towards a process of national reconciliation which sees the peaceful accommodation of differences between the people of Britain and Ireland and the people of Ireland themselves.'

Hume and Adams rejected the idea of an internal settlement, engaging only the parties in Northern Ireland, 'because it obviously does not deal with all the relationships at the heart of the problem'. Their statement publicly reflected the private language of the 1988 exchanges, arguing that 'the Irish people as a whole' had a right to self-determination, but it also tied the Republican side to seeking 'a peaceful and democratic accord for all on this island' that would enjoy the allegiance of differing traditions – i.e. the Unionists – by accommodating diversity and providing for national reconciliation. Behind these bland, well-meaning expressions lay an unspoken, but implicit, assumption that the fighting would have to stop. How else could the 'solemn duty' to move away from violence be read? Indeed, Hume subsequently wrote: 'We decided that our dialogue would concentrate on the search for agreement and the means of reaching agreement. Since an agreement by coercion is a clear contradiction in terms, it was implicit that agreement had to be made freely and without the use of force.'[10]

Hume and Adams concluded their statement: 'As leaders of our respective parties, we have told each other that we see the task of reaching agreement on a peaceful and democratic accord for all on this island as our primary challenge.'[11] Their message of hope was blunted by another IRA bomb in the City of London that weekend. A ton of home-made explosives devastated the area round the NatWest Tower, killing a press photographer and injuring thirty other people. Damage was put at more than £1 billion, the costliest evidence to date that the IRA could not be beaten militarily.

However, the ice was breaking. In the *Independent on Sunday*, the well-respected Ireland correspondent David McKittrick noted that the Provos were thinking more in terms of agreement and diversity than they once did. 'At least some of this may be due to the influence of John Hume,' he remarked. If the Republicans could not be defeated militarily, it made logical sense to tackle them not just by military means but by force of reason as well. 'This appears to be the tortuous and hazardous process in which John Hume is engaged, in the belief that it might inch Ireland along the road to peace.'[12]

If the Hume–Adams talks had dismayed Hume's natural constituency in Northern Ireland, it certainly did not show in the results of district council elections the following month. In this poll, the only yardstick of active democracy for elected bodies within the province, the SDLP vote went up. Hume's party captured 22 per cent of the vote, up 1 per cent, winning 127 seats, up six. Sinn Fein also improved its performance, increasing vote share by 1 per cent to 12.5 per cent, taking fifty-one seats against forty-three in 1989.

The silence south of the border was about to be broken. True to his word, the Taoiseach, Albert Reynolds, was opening the windows. After discreet feelers put out to the Republican movement, he put together his own draft document on Northern Ireland, telling his press officer Sean Duignan: 'This is about the IRA being persuaded to lay down their arms.'[13] Duignan admitted later that the document, which Reynolds believed he could sell both to John Major and the IRA Army Council, 'scared the bejasus' out of him. Duignan, a veteran of the 1973 Sunningdale talks and the Anglo-Irish Agreement diplomacy, admired Hume's courage in entering talks with Sinn Fein, though he was justifiably nervous about the Irish Prime Minister following suit. Reynolds welcomed the Hume–Adams talks (he was the only senior politician in the South to do so) and invited the SDLP leader to Dublin to bring him up to date.

Duignan recorded in his diary on 4 May 1993: 'He [Hume] looked dreadful when he came in to see Albert. Tells me he's got hypertension. He's a hypochondriac. He'll bury us all. Albert says John blew it by letting it out that he talked to Adams, but he may not have been responsible for [the] leak.'[14] Not directly responsible but, as has been observed, at least careless. It was as if Hume and Adams wanted the world to know that their joint initiative had regained its momentum. Otherwise, 'Diggy' Duignan paints an accurate picture of the politician he had known and come to admire down the years.

Hume often 'privately' told friends and contacts that he was suffering from hypertension. His eighty-a-day Dunhill habit (which he overcame in July 1996), and his fondness for a gin and tonic or red wine (similarly abandoned in the spring of the same year), bore testament to the props he sought under stress. During this period, he later recalled, many of the homes of individual members of the SDLP were attacked, 'but my party maintained total solidarity with me and continued commitment to the talks between Adams and myself. There were enormous stresses and strains on all of us and, without the total solidarity of my colleagues, I could not have continued.'[15] His chief support throughout this difficult time, however, was, as it always has been, the unstinting affection and strength of his wife Pat.

The Republican movement gave Hume the credit for coming to the conclusion that the 'marginalization and attempted exclusion' of Sinn Fein had proved futile. Adams wrote: 'During our discussions, he [Hume] had also formed the opinion that republicans were serious and sincere in trying to create the conditions for peace.'[16] Hume's talks with Adams had breached the wall of Republican opinion, and 'for daring to talk to us' he had been subjected to the kind of vilification usually exclusively reserved for Sinn Fein leaders.

Hume's political goal was a joint declaration by the British and Irish governments, which included the Brooke formula of 'no selfish economic or strategic interest in Northern Ireland' and a recognition that the Irish people as a whole have a right to self-determination. He and Adams produced several drafts of what this might look like, which Hume still keeps filed in his Derry home.

The first draft is dated 6 October 1991. 'We maintained contact and began a private dialogue in 1991,' he disclosed later.[17] 'I put the proposed joint declaration to Gerry Adams. That was the beginning of the exchanges. They [Sinn Fein] would come back to me with their version of a joint declaration of the two governments that Britain had no interest of her own and that it was for the people of Ireland to sort out their differences by agreement. They came back with their version and I came back with mine, and we kept exchanging documents until we got agreement. I kept the British and Irish governments fully informed. And that is what led to the Downing Street Declaration of December 1993. You can see how similar the wording is.'

The ninth, and final, draft declaration drawn up by Hume in June 1993 contained seven sections. It was the product not just of lengthy exchanges with Sinn Fein, but with senior civil servants of the Dublin government also, who had been involved in the process almost from the beginning. These three typewritten foolscap pages make up the 'Hume–Adams Document', the very existence of which was initially denied. It was shown to me by Hume in the front room of his Derry home. The first paragraph committed the Taoiseach and the British Prime Minister to acknowledge that 'the most urgent issue is to remove the causes of the conflict, overcome the legacy of history and heal divisions.'

The second paragraph argued that the development of the European Union fundamentally changed the nature and context of British–Irish relationships, 'and will progressively remove the basis of the conflict still taking place in Northern Ireland'. Paragraph 3 stated that the Taoiseach and the Prime Minister were convinced of 'the inestimable value of healing divisions and ending the conflict which has been so manifestly to the detriment of all'. It went on to lay down that 'both recognise' that the ending of divisions could come about only through agreement and co-operation. They therefore 'make a solemn commitment to promote co-operation at all levels' with the aim of reaching agreement and reconciliation leading to a new political framework 'founded on consent and encompassing the whole island' of Ireland.

The fourth paragraph required the Prime Minister to reiterate the Brooke formula, stating that the British government has no selfish strategic, political or economic interest in Northern Ireland, and its sole interest was to see peace, stability and reconciliation established 'by agreement among the people who inhabit the island'.

Critically, the document went on to affirm:

The British government accept the principle that the Irish people have the right collectively to self-determination, and the exercise of this right could take the form of agreed independent structures for the island as a whole. They confirm their readiness to introduce measures to give legislative effect on their side to this right over a period agreed by both governments, and allowing sufficient time for the building of consent and the beginning of a process of national reconciliation.

The British and Irish governments will use all their influence and energy to win the consent of a majority in Northern Ireland for these measures. They acknowledge that it is the wish of the people of Britain to see the people of Ireland live together in unity and harmony, with respect for their diverse traditions, independent, but with full recognition of the special links and the unique relationship which exists between the peoples of Britain and Ireland.

The final paragraphs laid a similar duty on the Irish government, in particular a commitment to setting up a New Ireland Convention, long an ambition of Hume's.

This document, absorbed and refashioned as Dublin's blueprint for peace, probably represents the high-water mark of Hume's political influence in a career spanning three decades. Had it ever been fully acted upon, the course of Irish history would have been different, arguably for the better.

The final version of the joint declaration was conveyed to John Major by Albert Reynolds amid extraordinary secrecy. It was handed over in a sealed envelope by the Taoiseach to Sir Robin Butler, the Cabinet Secretary, at Baldonnel military airport in the Republic in the first week of June 1993. Having received Dublin's imprimatur, the Hume–Adams document was now Albert Reynolds's 'formula for peace'. Coming from the Irish government, it stood a much greater chance of being accepted by Major, or at least of being used as a basis for serious negotiations about the future of Northern Ireland. Hume was on tenterhooks that summer, as Downing Street temporized. Duignan recorded that the Reynolds's 'formula for peace' was being minutely examined in London 'practically as if it were booby-trapped'. Adams said the Irish peace initiative contained the political dynamic for demilitarization and a lasting peace, but everything depended on the British response.

John Major discerned only too clearly the handiwork of John Hume and Gerry Adams, and did not like it. The draft showed some new thinking among Nationalists and Republicans, but not enough. London would talk about it, but not negotiate on it. Hume's patience – never his strongest suit – was wearing thin. Unable to contain his restiveness, he went to Downing Street on 17 September to press John Major for a positive response. He did not get it, and a week later he and Adams raised their game by publicly announcing that they had made 'considerable progress' in their talks and had submit-ted their proposals to Dublin. They added in a joint statement: 'We are convinced from our discussions that a process can be designed to lead to agreement among the divided people of this island which will provide a solid basis for peace.'

Hume and Adams had not disclosed that their blueprint had already gone to London, with Dublin's blessing, and in public they remained 'infuriatingly delphic',[18] refusing to be drawn by inter-viewers on the nature of their peace proposals. Hume then left the country for a two-week mission to the USA, drumming up business and jobs for Derry. He promised to get in touch with Dublin on his return. Reynolds was incensed. Duignan wrote in his diary: 'What's Hume up to? ... Either he's lost the head or he is crafty as a fox – or both? – because we're getting conflicting reports from the US ...

still, nobody here wants a public row with John.'[19] Another 'Dublin source', according to Eamonn Mallie and David McKittrick in their illuminating book *The Fight for Peace*, was quoted as saying that Reynolds and his key advisers were 'totally devastated' by what Hume had done: 'He had blown up the Hume–Adams process to a point where it was almost impossible now to deal with the British about it ... you could only negotiate with the British about the basic propositions that were already in existence provided they had no fingerprints on them – and suddenly there was Adams–Hume fingerprints all over them.'[20]

This was a serious point. The more Hume talked up his role, and referred to the peace plan as a Hume–Adams document, the quicker the British Cabinet would run away from the initiative. Reynolds and Dick Spring, his Foreign Minister, carpeted Hume on his return from the USA, criticizing him for going public on the formula for peace. A reticent statement from the Taoiseach's office simply stated that John Hume had given a written and verbal report to the Irish government. Political correspondents were briefed that it had 'significant potential' and would be part of the peace process. There was no disguising Dublin's fury. Hume was excluded from the inner circle, and by mid-October John Major was privately telling Reynolds that the Hume–Adams initiative was impractical. There would be no joint declaration of the kind Hume and Adams had laboured over for two years. Not, at any rate, for the foreseeable future.

Even for a man of Hume's long-distance stamina, this was a cruel blow. The elation of midsummer had turned sour, and his risky diplomacy with Sinn Fein appeared to have taken him down yet another of Northern Ireland's cul de sacs. Then the IRA took a hand in events. Around mid-day on 23 October, Shankhill Road, the heart of Loyalist Belfast, was devastated by a huge bomb. It went off without warning in a crowded fish shop, whose upstairs room housed the outlawed paramilitary UDA. Ten died, nine innocent Protestants and the IRA bomber, Thomas 'Bootsie' Begley. The terrorists' plan had been to assassinate the UDA leadership. But the upstairs room was empty, and the bomb went off prematurely.

The IRA observed clinically: 'There is a thin line between disaster and success in any military operation.' British security sources conceded this intellectual point, but the IRA had also crossed a different line: the one between occasional tit-for-tat killings and the sectarian savagery that now followed as Loyalist gangs exacted their revenge, first at Greysteel in Hume's County Londonderry where eight died in a Halloween attack on a Catholic bar. Hume wept openly at the funeral of the victims, after the family of one of the dead said they had prayed for him 'for what you're trying to do to bring peace'.

However, John Major, revolted at the sight of Gerry Adams helping to carry the IRA bomber's coffin, distanced himself even further from the fledgling peace process. It seemed as though everything Hume had fought for was falling about his ears. He complained he was being 'hung out to dry', and he was. Albert Reynolds and Major met on the fringe of a European summit on 29 October, and issued a joint statement that effectively dumped the Hume–Adams initiative. It insisted that only the two governments could negotiate on the future of Northern Ireland. There could be no question of adopting or endorsing 'the report of the dialogue which was recently given to the Taoiseach and which had not been passed on to the British government'. This last point, as subsequent events showed, was patently untrue.

Major kept up the fiction in the Commons on 1 November, reporting his bilateral talks with Albert Reynolds on the fringe of the European Council a few days previously. Reynolds had given him 'an account' of the Hume–Adams report, together with the Irish government's assessment. 'He did not pass the report itself to me,' he told MPs. Major added that he and the Taoiseach acknowledged Hume's 'courageous efforts' but agreed that 'the report could not in itself be a basis for action'.

The Prime Minister went on to condemn the Loyalist gunmen of the Ulster Freedom Fighters who had a few days previously opened fire in Greysteel. Hume joined in the condemnation, but added bitterly: 'It is the responsibility of all people – especially governments – to do everything in their power to try to resolve the conflict and bring the violence to an end.' Why, then, had John Major rejected his peace proposals, Hume asked, 'before he has even talked to me about them?' Major repeated his admiration for Hume's courage and persistence over the years, and offered to meet him again.

In fact, Major's apparent hard line was strictly for Tory back-bench and public consumption. So soon after the Shankhill outrage, he could not be seen to be engaged in any form of dialogue that derived, however indirectly, from the Republican movement. Reynolds had reluctantly acceded to the joint statement formally abandoning Hume, just as (so the reasoning went) Adams had shouldered 'Bootsie' Begley's coffin because failure to do so would have destroyed his credibility with the IRA. Much later, Reynolds confessed to his advisers: 'Hume–Adams was being declared dead, in order to keep it alive.'

Hume, unaware of this secret agenda, saw it as his duty, his mission almost, to rescue the formula for peace from the mire of governmental indifference and media hostility. Despite being reviled on all sides, he went on a barnstorming tour of radio and television studios, and on 4 November he took his message of hope to Downing Street. After his meeting with Major, Hume astounded waiting journalists by predicting that peace could come 'within a week' through his initiative. He later vouchsafed that he had told the Prime Minister: '"Let me tell you something. Gladstone failed. Loyd George failed. Churchill failed. The PM that brings peace to Ireland will go down in history more than a PM who puts Value Added Tax on fuel." He laughed, and said, "You are right." Privately, I think that had a big impact on him.'[21] Hume also put aside his anger at Dublin's apparent volte-face on his agreement with Adams, and privately pressed his case with Reynolds and Dick Spring.

It helped that Hume had his party right behind him, though not without some misgivings among the faithful. When the news of his 'secret' agreement with Adams leaked out, Hume had something of a revolt on his hands. What, his party executive wanted to know, was he doing? The SDLP was the party of peace. Had Hume not rejected bilateral talks of this nature on many occasions, unless the IRA agreed to lay down their arms? Hume had already felt obliged to give profuse thanks to the SDLP rank and file for their patience and trust in the Brooke–Mayhew talks, arguing in his leader's speech to the annual conference in Newcastle, County Down, in November

1992, that the talks had taken place on the basis of confidentiality. 'We have been unable because of that to keep you regularly informed of the nature of the talks process,' he admitted. Indeed, the most consistent criticism made of Hume by once-close confreres who have gone their separate ways is that he plays his cards too close to his chest, and operates too much, to quote Paddy Devlin, as 'a one-man band'.

On this occasion, Hume decided to come clean. At a hastily arranged meeting of his party executive in O'Neill's Hotel, Toome, he sought to reassure his closest colleagues. He told them he was 'not departing one iota from our declared position'. He explained the nature of the exchanges, and then read out the draft declaration, entitled *Strategy for Peace and Justice in Ireland*. 'They couldn't believe it,' he recalled wryly. 'They were very positive in their response.'

Alex Attwood, a senior SDLP member of Belfast City Council who had earlier broken with Hume over the talks with Adams in 1988, remembers:

> Hume decided he had to bring people into his confidence. He did so by reading them the document. It was a very clever move – and the right thing to do. His judgement was proved absolutely correct. My view was that considering what was going on, the minimum we knew the better – and rely on his judgement. Who else could have got us there? And somehow we were surviving, and sustaining, and growing.[22]

The hostility elsewhere grew in a crescendo, particularly in the Republic where political writers took their cue from Reynolds's declared position and repudiated Hume as a dupe of the Provos or, even worse, a willing tool. He was portayed as 'the problem, not the solution'. Some politicians in Dublin argued that he had gone too far in his 'deals with terrorists' and should step down in favour of his deputy, Seamus Mallon. Newspapers in the South were largely critical, though one astute columnist observed: 'We should be grateful to Hume for at least trying. If he succeeds, who will cry Judas?'

Few politicians could take this kind of punishment, and for Hume, who had lived on his nerves for a quarter of a century, the pressure finally proved too much. He collapsed and was taken to Altnagelvin Hospital in Derry, where so many of the casualties of the Troubles had been treated before him. It seemed as though the hopes of peace had collapsed with him. But Hume's breakdown prompted an enormous upswell of support from ordinary people – chiefly Catholic and Nationalist, but from the Republic as well as the North, and some, remarkably, from Protestants. Letters even arrived from the towns and cities of England. In all, 1,169 messages of goodwill and support deluged his sickbed, thanking him for what he had done, and urging him to keep going in his search for peace. Fifteen Catholic families in West Belfast joined in a plea: 'We all want peace . . . don't give up on us, you've given us hope.' An eighty-four-year-old woman in County Dublin wrote to him: 'the self-seekers jockeying for power and the limelight are not fit to polish your shoes. May God reward your efforts.'

His reward was about to come on earth. In mid-November, John Major told the Lord Mayor's Banquet in London that 'there may now be a better opportunity for peace in Northern Ireland than for many years'. Even more than John Hume, he was in a position to know. In the face of repeated denials, the British government had been in regular contact with the Republican movement. News of the secret discussions had filtered through to the Rev. William McCrea, hardline DUP MP, who confirmed rumours being picked up by Eamonn Mallie, the well-informed Belfast journalist. Mallie went public on Ulster Television, and the Northern Ireland Office issued a scornful denial, dismissing his story as belonging 'more properly in the fantasy spy thrillers'. Within four days of this stinging repudiation, Mallie was in possession of an official British government set of instructions to its representative who was delivering a document to Martin McGuinness, Sinn Fein leader in Derry. The instructions spoke of 'a potentially historic opportunity' and uncannily echoed Hume's consistent argument: 'We agree on the need for a healing process.'

Mallie revealed his explosive findings in the *Observer* on 28 November 1993. Hume was attending his party's annual conference (the twenty-third) in the Glenavon House Hotel, Cookstown, County Tyrone. In his leader's address, he held out the prospect of a new kind of society that harnessed all Ireland's talents and capitalized on all its friendships across the world. 'The key to opening the doors, the key of peace, that will lead to all of this now exists,' urged Hume. 'John Major is in possession of that key. It will require no great effort from him to turn that key and open the door to our new future, based on agreement and respect for diversity.'

Ironically, that very same day, Major had written privately to Reynolds, complaining about the leak of a draft Dublin document on the future of Northern Ireland, and about a new joint statement from Hume and Adams calling on London to respond to their initiative. Major wrote: 'Association with Hume–Adams is a kiss of death for any text intended to secure acceptance on both sides of the community.'[23] The Prime Minister proposed abandoning Dublin's proposals, derived substantially from Hume's painstaking negotiations with Adams, and starting again with all-party talks that would exclude Sinn Fein. But the *Observer*'s disclosure of Major's behind-the-scenes talks with Republican leaders destroyed at once this discredited route, and restored Hume's ideas to prominence. His plan for a joint declaration by Dublin and London was back on the agenda. This time, it would stay there.

THIRTEEN

CEASEFIRE

ON THE EVENING BEFORE the guns fell silent, John Hume escaped from the glare of media attention to the suburban Derry home of former Bishop Edward Daly, with its matchless view of the Donegal hills. 'He was very taut and tense,' recalled Daly. 'It was all still hanging in the air. He was smoking non-stop, and making telephone calls every twenty minutes. There was no definite answer.'[1]

Hume knew it was coming but, it seemed, not precisely how or when. Gerry Adams had secretly tipped him off a few days earlier. The IRA had also signalled its intention to Albert Reynolds, and informed John Major and President Clinton. News of the ceasefire was first given on Irish radio shortly before noon on 31 August 1994. There would be a 'complete cessation' of military operations from midnight. Hume was in the studio of BBC Radio Foyle in Derry when the story broke. He gave the thumbs-up sign, his trademark of approval. Twenty-five years after he began his mission for peace, the violence was over.

Events had moved rapidly in the closing weeks of 1993, when the Irish government persuaded London that the principles of the Hume–Adams peace initiative could be a basis on which to end the 'long war'. Perhaps not quickly enough for Hume, who is often swift to show his impatience, but much quicker than most observers expected. Hume wrote privately to the Prime Minister on 29 November, expressing his concern 'lest a major opportunity for lasting peace in Ireland will be lost ... As you are aware, at our meetings in Downing Street I made clear that I was certain that the proposed joint declaration presented to you in June by Albert Reynolds would lead to a total cessation of its campaign by the IRA. Given my experience of the past twenty-five years, I do not make such state-ments lightly.'[2]

Major was moving his way, but could not admit it. After the disclos-ure of long-term contacts between the IRA and the British govern-ment, the Prime Minister agreed to a summit with Reynolds in Dublin on 3 December 1993. In the days preceding the meeting, the British side tried to draw back from its earlier acceptance of a joint declaration based in substantial measure on the Hume–Adams formula of self-determination on an all-Ireland basis. But faced with Reynolds's refusal to budge, Major withdrew his counter-proposals and the summit went ahead on the original basis. Sean Duignan told Downing Street press secretary Gus O'Donnell: 'We resented you guys telling us we had to keep a million miles away from Hume–Adams when you were inviting the IRA to have three of their boys meet three of yours – tea on the verandah, etc.'[3]

The Dublin summit was a tense and at times unpleasant affair – Major snapped a pencil in frustrated rage – and a meeting a week later on the fringes of an EU summit in Brussels failed to break the deadlock. But some frantic diplomacy cleared the way for a signing in Downing Street of the Joint Declaration on 15 December. The two prime minister described the historic document as 'an agreed framework for peace'. It was not that, yet, but it was the culmination of Hume's breakthrough with Adams.

For the first time, a British government had not only declared that Britain had no selfish, strategic or economic interest in Northern Ireland, but that it would encourage, facilitate and enable the achieve-ment of agreement among all the people of Ireland. That agreement 'may, as of right, take the form of agreed structures for the island as a whole, including a united Ireland achieved by peaceful means'. Moreover, the Declaration laid down that the people of Ireland had a right to self-determination on the subject of Irish unity, based on consent 'freely and concurrently given' in Northern Ireland and in the Republic.

In other words, the majority in the North still retained a veto over a united Ireland. Inevitably, the declaration was a compromise. Britain had retreated to neutral ground, rather than moving forward into the ranks of persuaders for eventual Irish unity. Indeed, when the two prime ministers were about to stage a joint press conference in Downing Street that morning, Major asked Reynolds if the Taoiseach minded him saying that he was a Unionist. This idea was considered unduly provocative and was rejected out of hand.

Understandably, Hume regarded the outcome of the months of tortuous negotiations as 'a major step on the road to peace'. He asked all the parties to consider it in detail before responding, and appealed for 'an absence of knee-jerk reaction'. He rightly considered the Anglo-Irish commitment to 'see peace, stability and reconciliation established by agreement among all the people' of Ireland, an agreement that would have to address all the relationships that go to the heart of the Irish problem, as delivering a political context for peace. Furthermore, the promise on self-determination showed that the British government had accepted a key principle put forward by Nationalists and the IRA.

The IRA Army Council took an unpublicized decision not to reject the Downing Street Declaration, even though reliable sources reported a wave of rejectionist sentiment among their ranks. Sinn Fein responded by asking for 'clarification', and set in train a 'peace commission' – a lengthy process of consultation with the Republican movement on both sides of the border. Major angrily rejected any suggestion of clarifying his 'peace gauntlet', but Dublin and the SDLP were willing to allow time for the Republicans to come to terms with the declaration. Reynolds's advisers let it be known that John Hume would act as a 'conduit for clarification'.

In further private talks (described by an insider as 'fairly tense') on 14 January 1994, Hume pressed the Prime Minister to disarm Sinn Fein's objections to the declaration by answering any genuine requests to spell out the meaning of the text. He had already gone to some lengths himself to convince a doubting IRA Army Council and Gerry Adams that the declaration was a genuine opportunity to make political progress, and was unquestionably the alternative to the armed struggle that violent Republicans insisted they wanted. In a letter to Adams, he argued that the Downing Street formula contained 'the substance' of the proposed declaration that had come out of their dialogue. 'Is whatever differences there are between our June document and the joint declaration – and I see no difference in substance – worth the cost of a single human life?' The IRA gave its answer in the way it knew best: more bombing, more shooting. In the six weeks following the declaration, twenty people were injured and a British Army soldier was shot dead by a sniper in Crossmaglen. Stores in Belfast were attacked by incendiary bombs, frightening shoppers away from the New Year sales.

As the sense of urgency began to drain away, the Irish government embarked on a series of steps to commit the IRA to a peace process. Reynolds lifted the twenty-two-year-old ban on Sinn Fein representatives appearing on Irish state media, and worked behind the scenes to win a United States visa for Gerry Adams. Hume was also instrumental in this diplomatic breakthrough, working with Senator Edward Kennedy. Major was infuriated by the coup, which took Adams into the White House and boosted Sinn Fein's standing at home and abroad enormously. It was a calculated risk, designed to draw the Republicans ineluctably into a one-way route to ceasefire.

Then, suddenly, it was John Hume's own future, rather than that of the peace process, that dominated the headlines. On 6 March 1994, the *Sunday Times* published an in-depth magazine profile of the SDLP leader, describing him as 'Iron John' and predicting that he might withdraw from Westminster. He had told his wife Pat he would not stand at the next election for the seat he first won in 1983. The *Sunday Times* reported:

> Pat knows he is working too hard, and knows better than to try to stop him even when she would like to herself. That day may not be too far distant. Pat Hume talks increasingly of a time to pull back, a time to enjoy the grandchildren. John has told her that, although he is currently preparing for the European elections this summer, he will not stand again for Westminster.

The inevitable publicity storm broke next day, with the *Belfast Telegraph* splashing the story. The paper quoted unnamed sources, one saying it was 'an open secret' that Hume preferred the European Parliament to Westminster. Another said: 'I doubt if the party would be happy about him standing down as MP if it diminished his position as leader in any way.'

Hume himself was in Strasbourg, insisting on the record that no decision had been made. 'I have made no such decision. If I were to make such a decision, the first people I would tell would be my party colleagues,' he told the *Irish News*. However, when pressed, 'he said he was thinking about it in addition to many other things'. He was concerned about the effect that such speculation could have on the peace process. The general reaction of SDLP colleagues was: 'I'll believe it when I see it.' Hume told the *Derry Journal* later that week: 'I have no intention of quitting politics. There is too much work to be done.' This could have been an indication that he would stay in politics, but not at Westminster. Pat Hume confirmed to the *Journal* that she was doing her best to get him to do less. 'He is an unbeliev-able workhorse. He has an absolutely incredible workload and I would like to see him reduce it. How he does it is up to him.'

The story was short-lived, but it set Ulster's politicians – not just those of the SDLP – thinking. As Hume jetted off to the USA for yet another business tour and a live-television address of the National Press Club of America, the Republican movement continued its 'con-sultations'. The IRA kept up its barrage, targeting London's main airport, Heathrow, with rocket attacks on six nights during mid-March. The mortars failed to explode, prompting suspicions that they were intended to 'remind' rather than maim. Hume, in Wash-ington for a spectacular St Patrick's Day bash in the White House, could not understand what the Provos were playing at.

Ten days later, the IRA announced a seventy-two-hour 'suspen-sion' of operations over the Easter holiday, and were taken aback when this token show of non-violence was received with widespread derision. John Hume immediately went back on the propaganda offensive. In a speech on 12 April, entitled 'Peace Through the Joint Declaration: a Challenge to All, a Threat to None', he challenged the Republicans directly. Sinn Fein and the IRA may be 'a product of our history,' he admitted, 'as is their philosophy.' However, the major responsibility now rested on them alone 'to recognize that their philosophy is out of date, and that there is no justification of any description for their methods'.

The Downing Street Declaration committed the British govern-ment not only to promoting agreement between North and South, but legislating for whatever its outcome, he pointed out. To Hume, this was 'Clear self-determination'. In the new Europe of the Single Market, borders were going down everywhere. Even in Ireland, all that remained were the British Army checkpoints. 'The IRA could remove those tomorrow by laying down their arms . . . The challenge to the IRA and Sinn Fein is clear. There is no justification of any description for the taking of a single human life. Let them lay down their arms and join everyone else in the real task of breaking down the barriers in our hearts and minds and in tackling the real human problems of economic deprivation which is what politics is really about – the right to a decent existence for all our people in their own land. They cannot be unaware of the mass movement and the strength of the Irish at home and abroad that the peace process has created, and that strength will achieve more than any guns or bombs, without any human tragedies. Given the personal commitment that I have given to that process, I think I am entitled to ask them to do that now.'

Hume kept up the pressure on both sides. In early April, on the eve of a brief three-day IRA ceasefire, he called on the British government to break the deadlock by sending a minister to meet Sinn Fein and give the party written clarification. The Republicans, he argued, should now be taken at their word. John Major should send a member of the government or a senior back-bencher to meet representatives of the party and ask them to put what they want clarified in writing. He could then return with the government's response. That way there could be no allegations that secret deals were being done and Sinn Fein's request would have been met. There was no question of negotiations and Sinn Fein would have made clear they accepted that negotiations must involve all the political parties. His appeal, however, went unheeded.

In the European elections of 9 June, Hume scored another personal triumph, lifting his own vote by 25,000 and taking 28.9 per cent of the overall poll, a record for his party. Even more remarkable, his tally of 161,992 votes was not much more than a thousand fewer than the votes for the Rev. Ian Paisley, who had campaigned on the Downing Street Declaration, seeking to turn the poll into a hostile referendum. Hume's achievement in almost driving Paisley into second place reflected a vote of confidence in him and his peace initiative.

Yet the killings mounted inexorably, developing into a horrendous tit-for-tat rivalry between the IRA and Loyalist terrorists. Its culmination was the massacre by the UVF of six people watching the Republic of Ireland football team play Italy in the World Cup on television in a Catholic bar in Loughinisland, County Down. Loyalist paramilitary indications that they would match any IRA ceasefire were ignored. However, just as hope appeared to be dying, Major relented and gave a detailed list of answers to questions on Sinn Fein's 'clarification' list.

This gesture, argued Dublin, removed a serious obstacle. In late July, seven months after the historic declaration in London, Sinn Fein finally called a special conference in Letterkenny, just over the border from John Hume's Derry in County Donegal, to give their formal verdict. It was a confusing affair. Delegates backed policy resolutions deeply critical of the declaration, but also made some positive noises. Adams made a reasonably favourable, if ambiguous, speech, which was lost in the hardline posturing. Sinn Fein officials, fearful of newsmen getting the wrong impression, cautioned them to 'look for the silver lining'. Hume could see it and so could Albert Reynolds.

The Irish press interpreted the Letterkenny conference as 'Shinners say NO!' Hume was on holiday in his beloved France, in Bordeaux with family friends. He was out of reach, but not out of touch. He put out a statement enjoining optimism, though his fellow-negotiator with Sinn Fein, Sean Farren, who visited him a few days later, found Hume 'on edge'. He was also in constant contact with Dublin, where Albert Reynolds shared his guarded confidence that all was not lost. His press secretary thought the Taoiseach behaved 'like someone who knows the day and the hour'.

The delay and uncertainty strengthened the hands of the hawks in Major's Cabinet, particularly Mayhew, who had serious reservations about the 'peace formula'. Put frankly, they did not trust John Hume and resented his power among moderate Nationalists. The Northern Ireland Office briefed journalists that Hume was 'an unreasonable leader', pursuing a wrong policy: accommodation with Sinn Fein rather than the Unionists. At one point, an official complained bitterly: 'He runs his party like Mussolini.'[4] He might more accurately have observed that political parties in Northern Ireland have never been obsessively democratic, much like the province into which they are born. And the SDLP's record is a great deal better than most.

Hume's strategy was working. During the summer of 1994, alongside the Letterkenny conference, the Republican movement was considering an internal IRA–Sinn Fein policy paper which became known as the TUAS, said to mean 'Totally Unarmed Strategy', Document. 'Totally unarmed' was the spin put upon the document by Republican spokesmen. This version was never accepted by the Unionists, who later claimed it signified 'Tactical Use of Armed Struggle', indicating that the ceasefire was only tactical, and could be called on and off at will to suit the prevailing political and military context. TUAS laid down that the Republicans' goal – a united thirty-two-county democratic Republic – had not changed. However, the method of achieving that objective had shifted from 'the long war' to a political solution. The aim now was 'to construct an Irish Nationalist consensus with international support on the basis of the dynamic contained in the Irish peace initiative' – i.e. the Hume–Adams–Reynolds formula. That international support had to come from Dublin and Washington.

The SDLP, and its leader in particular, had a critical role to play in this new direction. 'Hume is the only SDLP person on the horizon strong enough to face the challenge,' the document insisted. This fresh approach made Sinn Fein/IRA to a degree dependent on Hume, because he brought access. 'Hume's role was pivotal,' said one of their leading figures. 'We couldn't get the Dublin government without Hume and we recognise we couldn't get the American government without Dublin.'[5]

The violence continued until the eleventh hour, with an IRA attack on the Springfield Road army base on 30 August 1994. Three days earlier, according to Brendan O'Brien, Adams had privately informed Hume of the IRA Army Council's decision to announce a 'complete cessation' of military operations from midnight on 31 August. Adams and Hume certainly met on 28 August, and told the world that 'significant progress' had been made. They added: 'It is our informed opinion that the peace process remains firmly on course. We are, indeed, optimistic that the situation can be tangibly moved forward.' Reynolds also had prior notice of the historic announcement. He telephoned the news to John Major, who only half-believed it, and to President Clinton.

The news finally broke in an RTE announcement at 11 a.m. on the day the ceasefire took effect. Hume, its principal architect, heard it in the studios of BBC Radio Foyle in Derry. He gave a thumbs-up sign of approval. Later that day, he talked to Reynolds on the telephone. Sean Duignan recalled the two were 'curiously cool and careful with each other' and asked another press officer: 'Is it vanity, rivalry, jealousy?' His colleague replied: 'Posterity. They're already jostling for their place in the history books.' Duignan confided to his diary: 'I hope Albert and Hume stick together. Hume is my hero, the man who started the movement, but Albert took the ball and ran with it.'[6]

Hume's considered view came later. With the ceasefire still holding, he wrote that Sinn Fein had committed itself to a peaceful and democratic means of reaching an agreement between the people of Ireland that could 'earn the allegiance of all our traditions'.[7] He explained: 'That was the clearly stated objective of my dialogue with Gerry Adams. Since five British governments and twenty thousand troops had failed to stop the violence, I took the view that, if the killing of human beings on our streets could be ended by direct dialogue, then it was my duty to attempt to do just that. I am naturally pleased that we were able to achieve this first step to lasting stability.'

How much *had* actually been achieved? The guns had been put away, but there was still no political settlement with the men who possessed them. The Loyalist terror gangs had not yet laid down their arms, and the British government was once again dragging its feet, complaining that the ceasefire declaration did not contain the word 'permanent'.

In the week after the ceasefire announcement, Hume travelled to Dublin for a private meeting with Reynolds. Staff later described the atmosphere as 'awkward'. Hume was still tetchy with Reynolds, and was having what was described as 'one of his periodic disagreements' with his deputy, Seamus Mallon. Reynolds wanted Hume to join him in his first meeting with Adams, which would be the first formal meeting between an Irish government and Sinn Fein for twenty-five years. Hume demurred, saying he had to be in Vienna on the date set: 6 September. It was difficult to plead pressing continental business at such a watershed in history. Hume relented, and the tripartite meeting went ahead in the Taoiseach's office in government buildings in Dublin. Unusually, it was a tea and buns affair. Hume allowed that it was 'a great day for Ireland'. The three then went out to face the cameras, and photographers persuaded them to join hands in an image of reconciliation that flashed round the world. They then issued a statement, crafted in large part by Hume, which put forth an olive branch to the majority in the North: 'We reiterate that we cannot resolve this problem without the participation and agreement of the Unionist People.' The establishment in Dublin of a Forum for Peace and Reconciliation, foreshadowed in the Hume–Adams document, was announced along with other measures designed to bring Sinn Fein into the political mainstream. Had not the IRA ceasefire declaration promised 'a definitive commitment to the democratic process', after all?

Six week of phoney peace ensued, as the Loyalist gangs considered their position. Then, on 13 October, the Combined Loyalist Military Command announced its own ceasefire, and Ulster's guns finally fell silent. However, the Loyalists warned that any resumption of military operations would meet with counter-measures. The violence did not stop: the IRA stepped up punishment beatings meted out to petty criminals in 'their' areas. Nevertheless, a new language began to emerge from the new breed of working-class Loyalist politicians who, like their Sinn Fein counterparts, had learned their politics on the streets and in gaol. David Ervine, an ex-UVF prisoner, argued: 'The politics of division see thousands of people dead, most of them working class, and the headstones on the graves of young men. We've been fools; let's not be fools any longer. All elements must be comfortable within Northern Ireland ... You can't eat a flag.'[8] The sentiments are pure Hume, the last five words are those of his father. Not everyone agreed. The recidivist Rev. Ian Paisley denounced Hume as 'an inveterate hater of the union'.

Hume grew impatient as the British government's days of inactivity lengthened into weeks. John Major stalled, demanding that the Republicans concede the word 'permanent' in their ceasefire, ignoring the fact that the IRA had not done this even when calling off the Irish Civil War in 1923. The peace process (as it was now widely known) was established, even if its destination was not yet clear. It was a sturdy enough plant to withstand several blows, including the murder of a postal worker by an IRA gang during an armed robbery in Newry, and, much more critically, the ousting of Albert Reynolds only three months into the ceasefire. Reynolds had been a pivotal figure in propelling the Hume–Adams initiative to the centre of the political stage, and putting the weight of the Irish government behind it. Now, he was forced to resign when Dick Spring's Labour Party pulled out of the ruling coalition in protest at the government's apparent reluctance to extradite from the Republic to the north a Catholic priest accused of molesting children in Northern Ireland. John Bruton, his successor from the Fine Gael party (traditionally more hostile towards Republicanism) insisted that the peace process was safe in his hands. Some doubted that.

On the ground, civilian life gradually became more tolerable as the Army lowered its profile in the province. Street patrols were much less frequent. Tourists began to return to Northern Ireland. Business improved. The peace was a godsend, and it was bearing fruit, just as Hume had hoped and promised. In December 1994, the European Commission announced a £231 million package of aid, and Major set up an investment conference to be held in Belfast in mid-December. Initially, the British government excluded Sinn Fein from the conference, arguing that it was too soon to invite those whose friends had spent most of the last quarter-century destroying Northern Ireland's biggest city.

Hume realized the danger of this decision, and intervened quickly, telephoning his contacts in Washington to request that American pressure be applied to the Major administration. Dublin did the same. It worked, and Sinn Fein was invited, though as representatives of district councils where they had many seats rather than as a fully fledged social partner. Through the Dublin Forum for Peace and Reconciliation, operating regularly since late October, Adams was in close touch with politicians in the new Dublin government. The crowning point of the year for Republicans came on 9 December when Martin McGuinness, Hume's political rival in Derry, led a Sinn Fein delegation to talks with Northern Ireland officials at Stormont, scene of so many failed initiatives.

The meeting was more symbolic than real. Only three days earlier, the Ulster Unionists had flexed their parliamentary muscles, helping the Labour Party to defeat the government at Westminster on an important part of its annual budget: doubling the rate of tax on fuel. While there were no doubt sound political grounds for siding with the opposition – VAT on home heating and lighting was as unpopular in Northern Ireland as elsewhere – the alliance with 'New Labour' was a clear shot across John Major's bows, a signal that the votes of the nine Unionist MPs could not be taken for granted. In fact, to Hume's considerable chagrin, Labour was now making discreet overtures to the Unionists.

Nineteen ninety-four closed in uneasy calm. Summing up the year that saw the silencing of the guns, David McKittrick wrote in the *Independent* that each passing week without killings made the full-scale resumption of conflict more difficult to imagine. The people of Northern Ireland had tasted peace, relished it and would not treat kindly anyone who placed it in jeopardy. With awful prescience, he also said: 'It is impossible to be entirely confident that the campaigns of violence are over for ever. It is a fair bet, in fact, that if the government were to simply ride roughshod over the republicans, the campaign would start again.'

With a new coalition in power in Dublin, negotiations between the Irish and British governments resumed with a Framework Document to further the peace process. The document would be 'a shared understanding between the two governments in order to bring the parties back round a table to negotiate a political settlement,' Northern Ireland Political Affairs Minister Michael Ancram told the Commons on 19 January 1995. A few days later, giving the annual Bloody Sunday memorial lecture in Derry's Guildhall, Hume said: 'At last, we have got the British government to agree there will be no internal solution here.' He also called for Nationalists to rethink their old territorial mentality: 'If we are going to solve our problem – and there is a real opportunity now to get a settlement and end forever the conflict – then we've got to look at our own past attitudes and see how they brought us to where we are.' An agreement to end the conflict, he warned, 'mightn't be exactly what we all want', but it would mean everyone could start working for the goal of 'a new Ireland'.

The next step in the peace process, publication of the Framework Document, did not happen until February. While Hume champed at the bit – almost six months had elapsed since the ceasefire – there was little he could go but make encouraging noises from the sidelines. His initiative with Adams was now in the hands of Dublin and London. A few days before publication on 22 February, a highly partial version of the document was leaked to *The Times*, whose front page trumpeted that it brought a united Ireland closer than at any time since 1920.

It was clearly a leak designed to undermine the process then gaining ground. Hume was angry. 'At this very sensitive period, speculation is not only wrong, it's utterly irresponsible. Let's stop,' he said.[9] The Unionists' rejection was instantaneous. They had not even seen the Document, but they declared they would not talk to the government on the basis of such proposals. Paisley described them as 'a declaration of war on the Union and the Unionist people', while the mainstream Ulster Unionists predicted ten more years of violence. Hume dismissed the Unionist objections, and forecast that their attitude would soften. He offered to listen to what they had to say, and ignored suggestions that they would destroy the peace process.

When it was finally unveiled by Major and Bruton in Belfast, the fifteen-page Framework Document enshrined much of Hume's thinking. It proposed a new, ninety-member Assembly for Northern Ireland, restoring a measure of home rule for the first time in twenty-three years. The Assembly would be elected on proportional representation with weighted majorities, together with further checks and balances to ensure that minorities – i.e. Catholics – were not consistently outvoted. This had been a core SDLP demand. A panel of three, elected within Ulster, would oversee the work of the Assembly – another idea popularized by Hume. Committees of Assembly members would monitor the work of government departments, and heads of those departments would sit on a new North–South body with their Dublin equivalents.

This body, a Council of Ireland in all but name, would have executive powers over European Union programmes, marketing Ireland abroad as a business investment centre and tourist destination. It would also have responsibilities for culture, heritage and what were described as 'sectors involving a natural physical all-Ireland framework'. It would have harmonizing and consultative functions in wide-ranging policy areas, including agriculture, industrial development, education and the economy. These reforms went a long way towards Hume's goal of a 'new Ireland'.

In return, the Republic agreed to abandon its territorial claim to Ulster by amending its constitution – if the Irish people agreed in a referendum. By the same token, Britain would amend or replace the Government of Ireland Act which gave Westminster hegemony over the North. The whole package was contingent on agreement between the political parties, the people of Ulster (again in a referendum) and Parliament. Finally, Britain once again reiterated that it had no 'selfish strategic or economic interest' in Northern Ireland, would pay 'parity of esteem' to Nationalist and Unionist traditions and would not prejudice an eventual move towards a united Ireland.

In the teeth of bitter objections from Unionist politicians, but significantly in the absence of Loyalist rioting on the streets, Major was bullish about the prospects for a settlement. Republicans cautiously welcomed the document. Hume simply pleaded: 'Dialogue has brought us to where we are and dialogue is the only way to get us to an agreement – so let's all keep very cool and calm heads today.'

Experienced commentators saw the Framework Document as a modified form of the Sunningdale Agreement negotiated by John Hume, the Unionists and the two governments two decades previously. The key difference was that consent was at the heart of the new initiative, whereas Sunningdale had been imposed on an unwilling majority. Most agreed that London and Dublin had travelled a long way towards Nationalist aspirations, David McKittrick arguing in the *Independent* that John Major had 'blasted Unionist political theories out of the water' by opting for an all-Ireland approach. A Gallup Poll of British voters in the *Daily Telegraph* yielded 92 per cent approval for the Document, and almost seven out of ten said the Unionists should negotiate on it. Hume scored well in the poll: 59 per cent said they 'liked and respected him', well ahead of the ageing Unionist leader James Molyneaux.

The euphoria did not last long. The negotiations everyone expected did not take place. British ministers did not talk to Sinn Fein. The Unionists did not talk to the Irish government. In fact, nobody really talked to anybody who mattered. The British government lobbied Washington, but only to prevent Gerry Adams from being received at the White House, which proved unsuccessful. Hume suffered another setback in March when Labour's new, pragmatic leader Tony Blair sacked his Northern Ireland spokesman, Kevin McNamara, and gave the job to one of his 'modernizers', Marjorie Mowlam. McNamara, a Catholic and long-time ally of Hume, was described as 'a de facto member of the SDLP' in the *New Statesman*, which observed: 'His removal and replacement by Mowlam was met by scarcely concealed glee in Unionist circles.'[10] Mowlam agreed that her appointment meant a change of policy. 'I accept that a Labour government, when in office, would not act as a persuader to a united Ireland . . . we would instead act as a persuader to a balanced political settlement,' she told the magazine.

Was this the same Labour Party that, only six months previously, gave John Hume a standing ovation at its conference in Blackpool, when he begged Major to 'go the extra mile' in search of a lasting peace in Northern Ireland? Hume openly expressed his support for McNamara, and delegates unanimously backed a resolution calling on the government to do as the SDLP leader bid and 'go the extra mile for peace by responding positively' to the IRA ceasefire. Ominously, however, the conference also approved a National Executive statement that foreshadowed Labour's shift away from being a 'persuader' for a united Ireland.

The importance of these moves lay in the strengthening of the bipartisan political pact on Ulster between government and opposition at Westminster, which correspondingly weakened the voice of Hume's four-strong parliamentary party. There was a further consideration. As one by-election defeat followed another, John Major's reliance on the Ulster Unionist MPs increased, and his inclination to put pressure on the Unionists to engage in talks with Dublin (if it ever existed) diminished.

In the way of progress stood the British government's insistence that the IRA should give up some of its arms before ministers would deal with its political wing, Sinn Fein. The Republican line was that 'decommissioning' of arms was contingent on a satisfactory negotiated settlement. This, it was repeatedly asserted, was the tradition in Ireland. Neither had the advance surrender of arms ever been a condition of negotiations with other 'terrorist' Nationalist movements in Britain's long colonial withdrawal. Dick Spring, Irish Foreign Minister, even warned that the British demand for prior decommissioning was 'a formula for disaster'.

President Clinton sought to break the deadlock by linking permission for Sinn Fein to raise funds in the United States to a more flexible Republican attitude on decommissioning. In the run-up to the 17 March St Patrick's Day celebration, a formula along these lines was agreed through intermediaries. Sinn Fein would discuss the arms issue in parallel with meaningful talks with ministers. It looked as though the great Hume–Adams gamble was about to pay off.

Tim Pat Coogan recalled that St Patrick's Day in the White House that year was a night to remember: 'The roof almost lifted off to the sound of the cheers that greeted John Hume, when he broke off singing "The Town I Love So Well' to say: "Come up here, Gerry, and join in".' The crowds cheered. 'It was truly a night in which Irish eyes were smiling. Nuns and priests, Loyalist paramilitary leaders, Cardinals and diplomats, the great and the good of America seemed to be saying that peace in Ireland was assured.'[11] The party was only a prelude to more to come: an international economic summit on Northern Ireland in Washington in late May; and a visit by President Clinton later that year to Belfast and Dublin to give his weight to the peace momentum.

It was too soon to rejoice. John Major, slighted by Clinton's approval of fund-raising opportunities for Sinn Fein, went into high prime ministerial dudgeon. In Parliament on 27 April, Seamus Mallon accused the government of vacillation, clumsiness and a lack of any defined strategy. Sir Patrick Mayhew clarified the official line: there would be no talks with any save those who had 'set aside any connection with the use of violence'. Hume, exasperated with Tory MPs who praised the government's temporizing, asked: 'Does he now agree that the past eight months have given the greatest hope that our people have ever had? Would the Secretary of State please advise his back-benchers to keep their negative mouths shut, because all they are doing is undermining that great new atmosphere among the people? May I appeal to his government, whom I consistently praise for putting this problem at the top of their agenda, where it belongs – I thank him totally for that – to move swiftly now to get all parties to that table to create the basis for order and stability: agreement on how we are governed?'[12]

Sir Patrick responded with platitudes. It was another month before talks took place between Political Affairs Minister Michael Ancram and Sinn Fein's Martin McGuinness, the first for two decades. Even then they were merely 'exploratory'. Hume was deeply dismayed at the slow pace of progress. On 4 July, he told a BBC Radio 4 'World at One' interviewer that 'this decommissioning nonsense' showed insensitivity and misunderstanding of the situation among the people of Northern Ireland. 'The real question is: have the guns stopped being used?'

As the July marching season came to a close, Hume and Adams met the Taoiseach John Bruton and his Foreign Minister Dick Spring in Dublin. The four issued a call for all-party talks to begin as soon as possible, amid Sinn Fein warnings that the peace process was 'falling asunder'. Hume went on Ulster Radio on 15 July to renew his appeal to the Unionists to join all-party talks. 'I am not saying that nobody can persuade the IRA to give up their arms. I am saying they have stopped using them, and that they will get rid of them . . . I believe that can be settled in the process of the dialogue. I have no doubt about that.'

The Unionists, scenting an opportunity for delay, rejected the invitation out of hand. David Trimble, legal spokesman for the UUP who was positioning himself for a bid for the leadership of main-stream Unionism, accused Hume, Adams and the Irish government of trying to duck the issue of decommissioning. Paisley's DUP went further, naturally, accusing the SDLP and Dublin of needing the IRA at talks with their guns intact because that was their main negotiating strength: 'Adams, Hume and Bruton can call for talks until the cows come home. But they cannot force Unionists to talk with Sinn Fein terrorists.'

It was an impasse. Jack O'Sullivan, interviewing Hume for the *Independent* soon after this failed initiative, found him exhausted, chain-smoking his favourite Dunhills and battle-fatigued. On the eve of his annual fortnight in Provence, he appeared to hold himself personally responsible for the crisis. 'Some people do not realize that politicians are human beings,' he complained. 'We and our families have been placed under enormous strain and stress.' Yet there were manifest consolations – not least that there were 150 people walking the streets of Northern Ireland that day who would have been dead without the painstakingly negotiated ceasefire.

'It has been a major relief to all sections of the community that the killings have stopped. Young people under thirty years of age had known nothing else in their lives other than violence, soldiers on the streets, perpetual searches. Now their lives are more tranquil, and they are seeing normality. That has created enormous benefits.' Not quite normality. There were riots in West Belfast that summer when the government freed Private Lee Clegg, a British Army soldier gaoled for life for killing a Catholic girl passenger in a joyrider's car. The punishment beatings and kneecappings, often but not always of petty criminals and drug dealers, continued in Republican areas, and intelligence reports suggested that the IRA was continuing to build up men and material even though its guns were silent.

Hume insisted the cessation was permanent, a claim that seemed to spring from an inner conviction that it would remain true only if he kept on saying it. 'I now think the violence is over, because not only have I lived with it for twenty-five years, but I have also experienced it directly, with major attacks on my home and being perpetually warned that I was on the top of an assassination hit-list. Worse, people you have known personally were killed.'

He blamed weak government at Westminster for the failure to exploit the ceasefire: 'Tragically and unfortunately for us, this breakthrough coincided with squabbling in the Conservative Party. Had there been a strong government in London, peace would have moved on faster.' John Major had put peace in Ireland at the top of his agenda. 'The problem is that certain people do not want him to succeed at anything.' By introducing an extra condition – decommissioning – for Sinn Fein's entry to all-party talks, the British had shown that they did not understand 'the psyche of the situation', he added. 'No one is going to be seen surrendering in that way.'

Hume reserved his strongest criticism for the Unionist politicians. The goodwill shown by Protestants, he argued, should have been translated into political leadership by the Ulster Unionist Party. That it had not might have had something to do with the struggle to succeed James Molyneaux. 'We need a Unionist de Clerk, who can get over the siege mentality. The question the Unionists must ask themselves is: do they want agreement, or do they want victory?' It was an extraordinary question for Hume to ask. The history of Unionism demonstrated beyond a doubt that the Unionists wanted victory. They feel they were chosen to rule Ulster and they feel that way because they actually *were* chosen to rule Ulster by their English and Scottish ancestors who shipped them over to Northern Ireland to become the new colonial masters in a 'plantation province'. The argument that they needed a Unionist de Clerk missed the point: more likely, they felt they needed a Pik Botha to hold on to what they had.

While Hume was in France, the Dublin *Sunday Tribune* leaked the news of fresh secret meetings between Sinn Fein and government ministers. Michael Ancram was forced to admit that he had met McGuinness twice, and Sir Patrick Mayhew that he had held talks with Gerry Adams in Londonderry. Unionist outrage was as loud as it was instantaneous, but the government was doing no more than Hume had been urging them privately to do for months: talk to Sinn Fein and remove the obstacles to all-party talks. Ancram said the meeting had taken place 'to see if we could find a way forward in terms of the peace process'. As the first anniversary of the ceasefire approached, and Sinn Fein was no nearer the negotiating table, the risk of breakdown was increasing.

Returning from holiday, Hume was faced with a familiar problem: the Apprentice Boys' march round the city walls of his native Derry. This provocative march had been banned for many years, but in 1995, the twenty-fifth anniversary of the Bogside, the authorities allowed the Apprentice Boys to march, and not just in Derry but in Belfast's strongly Nationalist Ormeau Road as well. Hume appealed on television and radio on 13 August for all-party talks to begin within a month. Commentators noticed his voice was 'charged with emotion'. Some leading Sinn Feiners were now privately warning of a breakdown in the ceasefire if Republicans continued to be excluded from all-party talks, and Hume was clearly conscious of these discreet threats.

Seven days later, he reiterated his plea on the Sunday morning BBC programme *Breakfast with Frost*. He was still convinced that the parties were on the real road to peace, but he warned: 'I'm quite disturbed at the slowness of the government to move ... I find increasing concern among ordinary people. They don't understand why the government will not bring people to the table.'

He voiced his anger that the talks were being stalled by the one issue of decommissioning arms: 'a pre-condition that was never mentioned at any stage when I was engaged in the dialogue [with Gerry Adams] and keeping governments informed.' Decommissioning, he argued, could be dealt with in the course of the talks process, and anyone who knew anything about Irish history would know that most major political parties were founded with the gun. 'Did they ever hand their guns over to British governments? No, they didn't. But where are they now? They're gone.'

Hume also had to explain the off-the-cuff remark by Gerry Adams at a rally in Belfast a few days earlier that the IRA 'haven't gone away'. Hume's Jesuitical training was stretched. 'When he [Adams] said the IRA's not gone away, he was saying that the members of the IRA have not emigrated. Other people interpreted that to suit themselves, but I sat and watched it and my immediate interpretation was that he was simply telling the truth.' More to the point: 'they have stopped [their campaign], and that's what matters.' Citing the RUC Chief Constable's intelligence that the IRA wanted the peace to continue, Hume insisted: 'I believe that it's totally finished.'[13] On the same programme, Michael Ancram naturally did not share Hume's sentiments, but he left the door open for further discussions with Sinn Fein.

As the ceasefire anniversary approached, the British government held to its line that 'substantive political dialogue' could not begin until Republicans had shown their commitment to exclusively peaceful methods, by 'beginning the process of decommissioning of illegally-held arms'. Then came a change of mood. Britain would agree to a Dublin proposal for an international commission to supervise the handover of IRA weaponry. Political talks could take place in parallel with arms decommissioning. Receiving a glazed-plate award for his role in resolving the conflict at a peace ceremony in County Mayo, in the west of Ireland, on 27 August, Hume welcomed the possible breakthrough. He said it would be unrealistic to expect Republicans to hand over their guns before talks started 'as that would amount to a symbolic surrender'.

In a message to mark the ceasefire anniversary, Hume tried to reassure the Unionists: 'My appeal to the Unionists is very simple. You have always relied on guarantees from British governments which you have never trusted because you have always feared that a deal is going to be done behind your back. Now, in my opinion, you are getting the clearest and best offer you have ever got, which is to come to the table and negotiate your own agreement with the people with whom you share a peace in Ireland. I presume the agreement you reach will protect your heritage for ever.'

All eyes were now fixed on a projected summit between John Major and John Bruton due to take place on 6 September. The two governments appeared to be on the brink of a deal. Then, at the last minute, the summit was called off amid bitter mutual recriminations. At this point, the Unionists changed their leader. James Molyneaux quit on his seventy-fifth birthday, plunging the province into fresh uncertainty. Seemingly out of nowhere came David Trimble as Unionism's new standard-bearer, described in the *Independent* as having a reputation as 'an ill-tempered, unalloyed hardliner'.

For Hume, it was a disastrous choice. Trimble was a product of the ultra-Loyalist Vanguard Party, an intransigent opponent of the Anglo-Irish Agreement that first gave the Republic a say in Ulster affairs, and a headstrong Orange populist, particularly when there was political advantage at stake. Was he, some wondered, the Unionist de Klerk of Hume's wistful hopes? After all, de Klerk did not look like a reformer until he took over the reins of power. David McKittrick cautioned against such expectations. Trimble's record in politics suggested he had 'no vision beyond Unionism and Orangeism'.[14] He was none the less the clear choice of his party. Hume met Trimble only three days after his election, and agreed to seek joint talks with Major on shared economic objectives.

Amid all the high-level politicking, a tiny paragraph in the *Irish Times* that month demonstrated what Humeism was all about. It said the International Fund for Ireland had committed support of £310,000 to the fishing village of Greencastle, County Donegal, for local development. The money would be spent on measures to alleviate the decline of the fishing industry. Without Hume there would almost certainly have been no International Fund for Ireland. (Greencastle is where Hume has his home in the Republic, a single-storey, modern, stone and glass building on the shores of Lough Foyle, with a panoramic view across the water to Magilligan strand, where Hume's supporters were attacked by paratroopers in a protest over internment.)

Hume met John Major in Downing Street once again on 26 September, and emerged after more than an hour of talks in optimistic mood. Some new ideas and proposals had emerged. All sides would go away and consider them. 'We have no doubt of the Prime Minister's continued commitment to the peace process,' he added. His view was not shared by Gerry Adams, who argued that the British government was 'interested only in destroying the peace process'. In fact, there was a real danger of the so-called pan-Nationalist consensus disintegrating. John Bruton refused to meet Hume and Adams in October 1995, clearly seeking to portray himself as a Taoiseach with more room for manoeuvre than his predecessor, Albert Reynolds. John Major proved more receptive, meeting Hume again in mid-October to discuss proposals that had 'the full backing' of Sinn Fein.

It was not until the end of the following month – Budget Day, 28 November – at a late-night summit in Downing Street, that Major and Bruton agreed to a three-man international body charged with drawing up a blueprint for arms decommissioning and the holding of all-party talks. Hume welcomed the agreement – drawn up under intense pressure from Washington on the eve of President Clinton's historic visit to Britain and Ireland – as a 'positive breakthrough' towards inclusive dialogue. 'Seamus Mallon and myself proposed to John Major that they fix a date [for all-party talks] and set up a commission on arms. It appears to me that's the direction they are moving in.'[15] The Nationalist *Irish News* agreed with him, headlining that the deal 'opens the way for talks'. Appearances sometimes lie, as Hume was to discover yet again. Former US Senator George Mitchell was appointed chairman of the Commission, with a Canadian, General Jean de Chastelain and Harri Holkerri, ex-premier of Finland, assisting him. They were asked to report by the end of January 1996.

The morning after this bizarre instant treaty-making, President Clinton's plane touched down. His visit to Northern Ireland (the first by an American president) and the Republic prompted the greatest upsurge of hope and expectation on both sides of the border in living memory. It was a brilliant public relations coup, but it also genuinely touched the hearts and minds of all parts of every community. Clinton attracted large crowds in Belfast, but his reception there was as nothing compared to the tumult in Derry. Addressing several thousand people crammed into Guildhall Square, the President was fulsome in his praise for the SDLP leader. He and his wife Hillary were 'proud to be here in the home of Ireland's most tireless champion for civil rights, and its most eloquent voice for non-violence, John Hume'.

He recalled the historic links between Derry and Philadelphia, capital of a stage based on the principles of religious tolerance expounded by William Penn, also an Irishman. As Hume had recorded many years earlier in his master's thesis on Irish emigration, Philadelphia was the main port of entry for migrants from the North of Ireland. 'Today,' continued the President, 'when he travels to the States, John Hume is fond of reminding us that the phrase Americans established in Philadelphia is the motto of the nation, "E Pluribus Unum" – out of many, one . . . We are struggling to live out William Penn's vision and we pray that you will be able to live out that vision as well.' Hume thanked Clinton for putting 'our problems at the top of his agenda'. Everyone noticed that Clinton said Derry, not Londonderry. His reception was equally warm in Dublin, and in forty-eight hours the US President appeared to have single-handedly changed the course of Irish history.

The euphoria did not last long, unfortunately. A few days later, sharing BBC's *Breakfast with Frost* with David Trimble, Hume said: 'I think we are on the way forward ... I'm satisfied that the arms are out of commission.' Trimble pointed out that the IRA guns were not silent. Three drug dealers had been shot dead in Belfast. The IRA, he claimed, was starting to move weapons around, and he cited reports alleged to come from MI5 that the ceasefire was about to break down. In the heated altercation that followed, Hume struggled to regain the initiative, asking Trimble to break out of the Unionists' 'no surrender psychology' and come forward with completely new ideas and new structures that could command the loyalty of both traditions. The UUP leader changed tack, arguing for elections in Northern Ireland to a body from which negotiations could develop. It was a cunning ploy, hinting retrogressively at the old 'internal settlement' for Ulster, and it dismayed Hume. He insisted that the mandates in Northern Ireland were very clear; another ninety-member assembly would 'just be a shouting match'.

Possibly so, given Ulster's track record; but it was also an option finding favour with John Major. The very same day, 3 December 1995, Downing Street sources were guiding political journalists towards the idea that the government would back the Unionists' proposal for a new elected assembly in the province – not to govern, but from which the delegations to all-party peace talks would be drawn. In a rare public statement, the IRA said a week later there was no question of meeting the 'ludicrous demand' for the surrender of its weapons, and accused the government of caving in to Unionist demands for 'a return to Stormont'. The year ended as it had started, with the arms issue unresolved and all-party talks on a new Ireland no nearer.

FOURTEEN

WAR ONCE MORE

DELAY BRED DEEP SUSPICION on the Republican side. Leading Sinn Fein activists began talking openly once again of their fear of a collapse of the IRA ceasefire. A senior Republican involved in the peace-brokering process privately told veteran observer Tim Pat Coogan that Adams and McGuinness would be inviting political assassination if they argued in favour of continued cessation of violence. 'A grim prophecy,' Coogan recorded, but every sounding he took indicated that it could be an accurate one. The RUC continued to talk up peace, but MI5 warned Major that the IRA was continuing to stockpile arms and material, and to stage dummy attacks on targets. The war was suspended, rather than at an end.

The new year of 1996 opened with an extraordinary personal accusation against Hume by David Trimble. The UUP leader first attacked Nationalists for suggesting that John Major was committed to arms decommissioning solely because he was likely to lose his Commons majority, and therefore would have to rely on the nine Unionist MPs to stay in power. 'There are other parties he could deal with,' Trimble claimed. 'If Major really wanted to drop the insistence on decommissioning and was being held back from doing so by Unionists, I am sure that John Hume would then solve that problem by offering the support of the four SDLP MPs.'[1]

This was most unlikely. True, John Hume has consistently believed that the Tories are more likely to deliver a Northern Ireland settlement than Labour: partly because of the Conservatives' strong links with Ulster, and partly because Labour's record in conflict resolution in the province had been so lamentable. But the idea of a Nationalist Social Democratic party being able to form a stable coalition with the Tories was risible, not simply because of their differing ideologies, but because such a shameless marriage of convenience would have triggered an open revolt among pro-Union back-bench Conservatives whose numbers were much greater than John Hume's faithful band of Commons warriors.

If this was straying into the borderlands of political insanity, much more encouraging was a Sinn Fein statement on 10 January, in the form of a submission to the Mitchell Commission. The Republican movement held out the prospect of an independent third party verifying the disposal of paramilitary weapons, including those held by the IRA. The SDLP also gave evidence to the arms commission, but Hume joined with Sinn Fein in rejecting the government's plans for an elected assembly for the province. 'There is no way we would consider an elected body as a means of starting the dialogue, because it will only make the dialogue much more difficult and make it virtually impossible to reach agreement,' he said. Here, Hume was on less certain ground. A *Sunday Tribune* poll found that 68 per cent of Nationalists agreed with an elected assembly, despite their leaders' well-advertised reluctance.

The Mitchell Report finally appeared on 24 January. It laid down six principles for the ending of violence in Irish politics, the key ones being 'total and verifiable' disarmament and the renunciation of force and the threat of force by parties wishing to take part in all-party talks. It accepted that disarmament would not come before talks, but proposed means by which guns could be given up during talks. In the Commons, John Major endorsed the six principles, and called on all other parties to do so, 'speedily and unequivocally'. He then astounded Hume and his SDLP colleagues by seizing on a minor aspect of the report – conceding that elections reflect the popular will – and making that the keynote of his response. Tony Blair, the Labour leader, rallied to his support, agreeing that it deserved consideration. A delighted Trimble suggested an election in April or May – effectively putting off all-party talks for another six months.

Hume was beside himself. In the Chamber he agreed that people's lives were at stake, but he clearly believed that the parliamentary votes of the Unionists were too. He virtually accused the government of playing politics with the lives of people in Northern Ireland. 'It would be particularly irresponsible for a government to try to buy votes to keep themselves in power,' he said. Mitchell had not recommended an election, but had simply reported what had been said to the Commission.

There remained, Hume continued, a need for urgency. 'Will he [Major] accept that advice and now fix a date for all-party talks,' he asked, 'rather than waste time as he has for the past seventeen months?' At this point, Tory MPs shouted: 'Disgraceful!' Hume rounded on them angrily: 'I live with it – you don't!' He accepted the six Mitchell principles on behalf of the SDLP, and again asked the Prime Minister to fix a date for talks. Major was flattering about John Hume's leading role, saying it would be 'a tragedy of enormous proportions' for him to now become a barrier to peace, but declined to take up his urgent pleadings. It was, one commentator noted, a graceful crushing.

Hume was not easily mollified but, after private talks lasting ninety minutes with Major a week later, he drew back from an outright confrontation. He appeared satisfied with Downing Street's assurance that the election plan was not designed to lead to an internal settlement from which Dublin would be excluded. There was, said Hume, 'a process under way which we will pursue with the Prime Minister'. By contrast, he walked out of a private meeting with Tony Blair, threatening a rupture in relations between the once-close parties.

Dublin was furious with the 'fixing' of Mitchell. A flurry of diplomatic notes ensued. Alarm bells rang in Washington. The Anglo-Irish Inter-Governmental Council was called into session. A Major–Bruton summit was provisionally arranged. The Irish Foreign Minister put forward the idea of an intensive peace conference on the lines of the Dayton, Ohio, 'proximity talks' that ended the war in Bosnia. Hume said yes, Mayhew said no. While they havered, the IRA prepared its response. All Hume's worst fears were about to be realized.

In the evening rush hour of Friday 9 February, the IRA struck at the showcase of British capitalism – London's Docklands, where billions of pounds have been spent on urban regeneration. A 500lb bomb on a flat-top lorry detonated at 6.57 p.m. The device laid waste to a large area of South Quay, just across the harbour from Canary Wharf, the prestigious tower block that had been the object of an earlier, abortive raid. There was panic in the streets. Dozens were injured, and the bodies of two men were found in a wrecked news-agent's shop. Damage to property, particularly new office blocks, was put at £100 million. On the night of the bomb, Hume was in Dublin attending seventieth birthday celebrations for his old friend Garret Fitzgerald. Fellow partygoers said Hume was 'devastated' by the news.

Nationalist reaction was initially divided. Gerry Adams blamed 'the refusal of the British government and the Unionist leaders to enter into dialogue' for the breakdown of the ceasefire. Hume con-demned 'this terrible atrocity' unreservedly, but added: 'I was worried all along that slowing up the dialogue was a risk ... I have been asking the British government publicly and privately for the last eighteen months to move to the next stage, which is all-party talks. If we had done that, we would have been in a much stronger position today.'

The day after the blast, Hume was at his granddaughter's confir-mation in Derry. His considered response in an article in the *Indepen-dent* was: 'This is no time to despair. The ill-conceived gloating of the I told you so sceptics is distasteful.' Indeed, surveying the field of options, he thought it possible to 'distil the essence of a successful peace process'. First, the Republicans must accept, *pace* Mitchell, once and for all, that violence is not acceptable. Second, 'peace means all-party talks'. He conceded the 'rational kernel' in the Unionist case that Sinn Fein must gain a popular mandate before entering all-party talks. So, Hume argued, let us have a referendum on both sides of the border, asking if voters want an end to violence and all-party talks. Instead of a parade of parties, there would be a poll for peace. 'It is time to let the people speak,' he wrote. Hume raised his referendum proposal in the Commons on 12 February. Major politely promised to take it into account, and then quietly forgot about the idea.

The Docklands bomb revived the controversy over Hume's role in the peace process. Trimble lost no time in taking advantage of his discomfiture. 'John Hume's proposition was and is false,' he wrote. 'There can be no illusion about the nature of Sinn Fein/IRA. It is not about to become a democratic party. It remains locked in the culture of Irish republicanism.' Northern Nationalists, he argued, must be given an alternative to the existing strategy. 'Here the duty of the SDLP is inescapable. John Hume cannot continue his relationship with Sinn Fein.'[2] Yet even the Northern Ireland Secretary recognized that an 'official link' had to be kept open with Sinn Fein. Hume's dogged adherence to dialogue with Republicanism was now official policy for all except the Unionists. The British and Irish governments could not be seen talking to Republicans, but they could keep open their lines of communication.

Ten days after the South Quay explosion, a second bomb went off in London, this time prematurely, killing the IRA bomber, Edward O'Brien, aged twenty-one, as he sat on the top deck of a bus in the Aldwych. Two other, smaller devices were detonated without causing much injury or damage. A renewed sense of urgency took hold. At a summit in Downing Street on 28 February, Major and Bruton conceded the key demand consistently made by Hume and Adams: a date for the entry of Sinn Fein into all-party talks. If the IRA could deliver a renewed, credible ceasefire, Sinn Fein could sit down with the other parties for talks on the future of Northern Ireland on 10 June. Hume's deputy, Seamus Mallon, called it 'the moment of truth'.

Hume worked tirelessly to silence the guns again. He accompanied Adams to a secret meeting with the IRA to ask them why they had restarted the violence. The IRA chiefs blamed 'the consistent bad faith' of the British government and 'the absence of real negotiations', and refused to reinstate the ceasefire. Gerry Adams disclosed details of the joint meeting in the New York-based paper the *Irish Voice*, quoting the IRA as saying: 'We sued for peace. The British wanted war. If that's what they want we will give them another 25 years of war.'[3]

In its traditional Easter statement, the IRA claimed it was seeking 'a genuine and lasting peace' and stressed the paramount need for negotiations on 'core issues'. Hume said he was encouraged by the positive indications of IRA willingness to embrace a comprehensive, negotiated settlement. 'I think that that is the chink of light that I was looking for.'[4] The Unionists accused him of clutching at straws, and it was difficult to gainsay them.

Hume was left with no alternative but to take the SDLP into the Assembly elections, despite his own misgivings. May 30 was set for polling day. The election was to be held under a uniquely confusing list system, which gave every elector one opportunity to vote but produced a 110-member 'pool' of representatives, from which the teams of negotiators for the 10 June talks would be drawn. Sinn Fein followed Hume's example and agreed to participate in the poll. In a long Commons debate on the Bill authorizing the elections on 22 April, Hume confined his intervention to a demand for his party to appear on the ballot paper as the SDLP instead of its full, rather long-winded title. He got his way.

The campaign was slow to take off. The SDLP ran under the slogan 'Your Vote for Peace', and handbills featured a message from John Hume asking for 'your mandate to protect and promote this important opportunity to reach agreement'. He was described as 'our Leader' who had opposed violence and worked for peace for twenty-six years and whose steadfast efforts led directly to the paramilitary ceasefires of 1994. Voters could have been forgiven for thinking that he *was* the SDLP.

Writing in the *Belfast Telegraph*, Hume reiterated his commitment to consensus. The consent of both traditions was central to any agreement, he argued. 'For that reason we will be proposing that any agreement reached on the central relationships that go to the heart of our problem should be put to the people north and south requiring a yes from each. That in our view should reassure the Unionist people that we are serious about their agreement, and from a National point of view it would be the first time that all the institutions created would have their allegiance.'[5] There was no SDLP manifesto, simply an election statement setting out the party's aims. Hume pledged to boycott any moves by the Unionists to turn the assembly into a new Stormont.

On BBC's *Newsnight* two days before the poll, Hume was admittedly 'pessimistic'. He pleaded for a more positive attitude all round, arguing that if the two governments made clear to Sinn Fein that the talks due to begin a fortnight later were 'comprehensive, with an open agenda', then there was an opportunity to take the gun out of Irish politics altogether. Yet on the ground, the electoral picture was disheartening.

On the stump with the SDLP in Tyrone, I found rising support for both extremes – Sinn Fein and the DUP – with the more moderate parties being squeezed out. In the housing estates of Strabane, a town particularly hard-hit by unemployment, local youths stoned Hume's party workers. Gerry Adams toured the province, appealing for votes as 'the peace party' and promising: 'We will not let you down.' It was a seductive formula. Since the election was for a negotiating forum rather than a real parliament, some Nationalists opted to give Sinn Fein a stronger bargaining hand. At the other end of the spectrum, anxious Loyalists took refuge in the reassuring 'no surrender' bluster of Dr Paisley.

When the results were declared on 1 June, the performance of Gerry Adams's party was hailed, even in the most hostile press, as 'a major victory'. In Hume's own constituency of Foyle, the SDLP took three seats but Sinn Fein picked up the other two. Overall, the Ulster Unionists predictably topped the poll with thirty seats in the new Assembly. Close behind came the DUP with twenty-four. Hume's party was the most popular within the Nationalist community – but only just. The SDLP took twenty-one seats, Sinn Fein won seventeen. In West Belfast, the SDLP was humiliated, taking only half the votes given to 'the Shinners'. If Major's aim had been to marginalize Sinn Fein through the electoral process, it had backfired. The province was now even more polarized in its allegiance, and dangerously so.

In London, the *Daily Telegraph*, fast becoming Hume's chief critic, headlined its leading article 'John Hume's to Blame'. Pointing out that Sinn Fein's share of the popular vote, 15 per cent, was its highest ever, the *Telegraph* argued: 'And the biggest loser is, of course, John Hume's party ... It is not even as though Mr Hume has won his permanent ceasefire.' Hume would continue to win plaudits abroad while his colleagues lost at home. 'Mr Hume has opened the ballot box for the IRA, which has drawn the Armalite from it.'[6]

Despite optimism in some quarters, Sinn Fein's political windfall did not lead to an IRA ceasefire. Hume took his party into the new

'Talks Forum', while Sinn Fein boycotted it. Talks between the constitutional parties did begin, but they went nowhere, in large measure because Sinn Fein was excluded in the absence of a credible ceasefire. Hume renewed his call for an end to the violence, and in the Commons on 13 June put his customary question to the British government: 'Will the minister reaffirm the fact that the real challenge that faces us is that, although the talks process threatens no section of our people, it in effect challenges all of us to come up with the new thinking that will accommodate both our traditions and give us the lasting stability that all sections of our people are now screaming for?'[7] The government had no 'new thinking' to offer. Sir John Wheeler, the colourless Minister of State at the Northern Ireland Office, simply repeated that the violence had to stop.

When the Talks Forum held its first meeting in Belfast on 14 June, the feeling that the players were acting a charade was inescapable. Hume, exasperated at the weak chairmanship of war hero John Gorman (a Roman Catholic member of the UUP, who won the Military Cross for disabling a tank in Normandy), walked out at one stage. Unionist wrecking tactics made even the simplest task of drawing up guidelines for the Assembly's work virtually impossible. Hume said impatiently: 'Let's sign, set up a rules committee, and get home.'

The very next day, 15 June, the IRA made its position clear in the usual way. A massive lorry bomb, the largest ever planted in England, exploded during the Saturday shopping rush hour in the centre of Manchester, tearing the commercial heart out of the country's second city. It was a miracle that no one was killed, though more than 200 were hurt. Thousands of shoppers had been evacuated after an IRA coded warning was given. Damage once again ran to hundreds of millions of pounds.

The Docklands bomb had been a huge shock, but the political fall-out from the Manchester bomb, in a city where thousands of Irish people live and work, was even greater. Dublin turned its back on Sinn Fein, while in London the government and the opposition joined forces to isolate the IRA's political wing from the peace process. The 'all-party' talks could go ahead without them. Tony Blair warned Sinn Fein not to expect any better treatment from a Labour government, and echoed Seamus Mallon's grim assessment that the Republican movement faced 'a moment of truth'. Paul Bew, Professor of Irish History at Queen's University, Belfast, characterized the bombings in London and Manchester as 'the politics of fuck-you rage and resentment rather than political calculation'. Whatever the motive, the sound of detonating Semtex on the streets of England's major cities appeared to spell the end for John Hume's search for peace.

Hume, however, is not a quitter. On 2 July he met John Major again privately in a bid to restart the peace process. Reporting on his continuing contacts with Gerry Adams, Hume argued that a new – and permanent – ceasefire was available if the government 'clarified' its position on certain key issues: the nature of the multi-party talks at Belfast, arms decommissioning and possible future confidence-building measures. Hume gave Major the terms of a possible restatement of the government's position. Major was sceptical, but agreed to consider it. Later that month, Major sent Hume the terms of a possible restatement. Hume, after talking to Adams, came back with a different form of words, that did not satisfy Downing Street. The diplomatic traffic was put on hold.

The Unionists, aware that something was going on behind the scenes but not knowing what, were understandably nervous. Their marching season was heading for a climax on 12 July, and they decided on a show of strength in their heartland. What became known as Drumcree 2 – the second stand-off between militant Loyalists and the security forces at the same spot for the second successive year – emerged from the shadows. Members of the Orange Order gathered outside Drumcree parish church on the edge of Portadown, County Armagh, determined to stage a triumphalist march into the town along Garvaghy Road, a Catholic stronghold.

The occasion was vested with enormous symbolic significance, as though it marked a second siege of Derry. Initially, the RUC banned the march but, faced with a resurgence of Loyalist violence, widespread disruption of roads across the province and the threat of 80,000 hardliners turning up to confront the security forces, Sir Hugh Annesley, Chief Constable of the RUC, allowed the marchers to go through on 11 July. David Trimble, his Orange sash worn flamboyantly, was there to greet them with open arms.

Hume was appalled. In the Commons, barely able to conceal his anger, he asked the Northern Ireland Secretary to 'explain the disgraceful decision to surrender' to Orange violence. For four days, Catholic homes and businesses had been under sustained Loyalist attack. Had the government any role in the capitulation, he asked. Sir Patrick Mayhew denied any involvement, but few in the Nationalist camp believed him. Hume shared their disbelief. He told BBC Radio Ulster: 'I find it very hard to believe that a decision of this seriousness affecting the basic fundamental government of the community as a whole was taken without any consultation with government and that government had no role.'

The Unionists were jubilant. Direct action at Drumcree had worked. A wave of Loyalist exultation swept the province. Republican reaction on the streets was swift. That night, 11 July, Derry saw its worst rioting for many years. More than 900 petrol-bombs were thrown in city-centre clashes with police. The riots hit Belfast and many other towns. IRA gunmen reappeared on the streets. Scenes of burned-out cars, blazing properties and stone-throwing mobs once again dominated the television news. It was if the intervening twenty-eight years had never happened, and in Hume's city the cry to arms was, 'It started in Derry, and it'll end in Derry.' However, Gerry Adams and Hume appealed for calm, despite the death of a young rioter crushed by an army personnel-carrier in Derry.

Hume called his party's leadership and its members of the Forum into emergency session the next day. The outcome was an SDLP withdrawal from the talks body, though not from the talks themselves. Hume said the Assembly had 'no basis', and promised to redirect his peace efforts through Dublin and the Clinton administration. That same night, the Killyhelvin Hotel outside Enniskillen, County Fermanagh, where the SDLP was due to hold its annual conference in November, was destroyed by a bomb planted by the Continuity Army Council, an IRA splinter group. Unrest in the province subsided surprisingly quickly, and John Major vowed to 'try, try and try again' to reach a peaceful settlement. As he did so, police in London seized an arsenal of IRA bomb-making equipment destined to bring death and disruption of gas, water and electricity installations in the south-east of England that summer. Seven suspected terrorists were arrested. Clearly, despite Hume's best endeavours, the Provos were not on the brink of declaring a fresh ceasefire.

The next flashpoint was in Derry, just three weeks later, when Hume intervened to prevent more violence over a march by the Apprentice Boys on the city walls overlooking the Bogside. He brokered talks between the Loyalists and Catholic community leaders, seeking to defuse the crisis by cutting the numbers of Apprentice Boys. His attempt at agreement failed, and the authorities moved to block off the section of the walls with a commanding view of Nationalist Derry. John Lloyd, writing in the *New Statesman*, noted: 'John Hume, who chaired the talks, ended them in despair: Sinn Fein called the shots.'[8] They had also commandeered Hume's language, he argued. 'Consent', the underpinning term of Hume-speak, now meant 'what was acceptable to Sinn Fein'. Conor Cruise O'Brien, the veteran Irish politician and journalist, paid tribute to Hume's hard work in *The Times*, but observed that the Bogside Residents' Association was showing only 'a degree of outward respect' to their MP. The large gains made by Sinn Fein at the expense of the SDLP in the Assembly elections 'probably made Mr Hume seem increasingly irrelevant in the eyes of the younger Sinn Fein elements'.[9] In the event, the Apprentice Boys did march, though not where they wished, reserving that privilege to 'a time of our own choosing'.

Hume was still conducting his own private diplomatic shuttle with Gerry Adams, but struck out in an unexpected direction in early September. He led the SDLP into direct talks with the Ulster Unionists. The two parties met twice, formally, to discuss an agenda for the reconvened multi-party talks. There were reports of a special sub-committee to handle the issue of arms decommissioning, and Hume said the contacts were aimed at getting down to 'the real agenda. That means discussing relationships within Northern Ireland and how we are going to have to give institutional expression to them as well as to relationships between North and South.'[10]

The Unionists regarded this interpretation of the contacts as wishful thinking. Trimble said later:

We managed to get agreement on procedural aspects in the talks, and that helped to change the atmosphere and get a bit of progress. But they were limited to procedural matters. The discussions were cordial. The SDLP thought they were successful. From our point of view it was a pleasant chat, but when you put down in hard print what had been agreed, it was very little.[11]

The SDLP, he argued, have 'a different habit of mind, a different approach'. The Unionists' chief negotiator, Reg Empey, complained that the great difficulty in negotiating with the SDLP – and John Hume in particular – was that 'We are looking at the text, and they are looking at the context.'

Hume's latest initiative with Sinn Fein was not helped by the aggressive pessimism of his long-time political rival, Martin McGuinness, who said the current multi-party talks were doomed to failure, would not bring about a ceasefire and should be scrapped. 'They are going nowhere. They will not succeed,' he declared on 21 September. In the same breath he revealed the substance of Hume's talks with Adams. The British should draw up proposals for fresh talks that would include Sinn Fein, and drop all pre-conditions including decommissioning of IRA weapons. These words were a hardline exposition of the formula that Hume was working on. Any hope that Hume's initiative might be accompanied by a cessation of violence disappeared on 8 October, on the eve of the Conservative Party conference, when the IRA exploded two 800lb bombs at the British Army's headquarters barracks at Lisburn, outside Belfast. One officer died and scores of service personnel and civilians were injured. Sean O'Callaghan, the reformed IRA terrorist, argued that the strategy of the long war still dominated IRA thinking. His analysis was supported by RUC revelations that the IRA had started preparations for the Lisburn attack in June, just as it had done months before the Docklands bomb. The outrage prompted John Major to declare in his leader's speech to the Bournemouth conference: 'I don't believe Northern Ireland will leave the United Kingdom, nor do I wish it to.' This uncompromising stance did not augur well for peace moves based on concessions by London.

Hume was dismayed by the first British Army death in Northern

Ireland since the end of the ceasefire. The murder of Warrant Officer James Bradwell, a married man with children, was 'an unnecessary tragedy', he said, but despite this, 'I happen to believe from my experience of the last twenty-five years and my experience as a historian that we now have the best opportunity that we've ever had, not only to get a restoration of the IRA ceasefire, but to take the gun forever out of our politics.'[12] He was still talking to Adams about a restoration, 'and I'm very hopeful we will be able to achieve that', he added.

Few shared his optimism, though the multi-party talks did resume on 15 October, based on the SDLP–UUP five-point agenda negotiated between Hume and Trimble. Hume was still demanding immediate entry into the talks for Sinn Fein in the event of a cessation of violence, despite John Major's insistence in the Queen's Speech that month that the IRA would have to show that any new ceasefire was not a tactical move to be abandoned when they wanted. Major's mind was working towards a 'contamination' period in which the IRA would prove that the ceasefire was 'for real' (in the words of one senior Northern Ireland minister) before Sinn Fein could come to the negotiating table. Hume was working in the opposite direction, demanding on 29 October that the all-party talks, inclusive of Sinn Fein, should be limited to six months. 'That would concentrate our minds on the real issues,' he argued.

Hume's continuing contacts with Sinn Fein were startlingly converted into 'Major's secret link with Gerry Adams' in early November, in 'revelations' by the *Sunday Tribune* that the SDLP leader was a secret channel of communication between the Republicans and the British government. Since Hume had made no secret of his meetings with Adams, or his strategy of keeping both London and Dublin informed of progress, it was difficult to understand the excitement. But he used the publicity opportunity to best advantage, calling in his leader's address to the SDLP annual conference at Cookstown, County Tyrone, on 9 November for a fresh ceasefire and a move by Major to create the conditions to allow all sides to come to the negotiating table once violence stopped.

The Prime Minister was fully aware of the formula that Hume and Adams wished him to reiterate in public, either by way of a speech or an article. Hume now dropped heavy public hints about the contents of the formula. The British government could achieve lasting peace 'by reiterating in the strongest possible terms the nature, objectives and time-frame of the talks, together with confidence-building measures that can improve the atmosphere at the talks themselves'. Martin McGuinness described Sinn Fein's demands as 'very reasonable indeed', and if achieved there was considerable hope of a second ceasefire.

However, it was clear that a serious rebuff for Hume and his fellow-peacemongers was in preparation. Barely had Hume sat down at his conference when Andrew Hunter MP, the strongly pro-Unionist chairman of the Northern Ireland Committee of Tory back-bench MPs, accused him of selective loss of memory: 'I think John Hume is suffering from a form of amnesia because it was he a year ago who coined the phrase "you can't negotiate with people with guns on the table, guns under the table or outside the door".' Since then, he pointed out, the IRA had killed four people, injured 400 and inflicted hundreds of millions of pounds-worth of damage.

Two weeks later, Sinn Fein held a closed conference. The mood had changed. McGuinness said a cessation of violence would be 'much more difficult' a second time round, while Hume was left repeating his familiar mantra that a ceasefire was 'extremely possible'. He insisted: 'I have been involved in intensive dialogue with Gerry Adams, the objective of which has been an unequivocal restoration of the ceasefire . . . and I believe from my involvement that we now have an opportunity of removing the gun forever from Irish politics.' Dr Joe Hendron, SDLP MP for Belfast, threw caution to the winds. There would be a ceasefire before Christmas, of that he had no doubt. He was wrong.

Downing Street admitted that the government was in touch with the constitutional politicians. The position on a ceasefire was un-changed: it had to be unequivocal and believable. That weekend's papers were full of intense speculation that Major might be about to make a statement endorsing Hume's formula. Only Trimble, the UUP leader, saw through the charade. He asked the Prime Minister to put into the public domain the outcome of his exchanges with Hume, to put an end to unsettling speculation. He doubted whether

Major would change his tune, and he did not think there would be a Christmas truce. Hume refused to back down, playing up his role in brokering peace and promising: 'I will put my head on the line and take full responsibility if I'm wrong, but I know what I'm talking about.'[13] Hume was in the midst of intense diplomatic traffic with Downing Street but he was, perhaps, to regret those words.

Republicans, unhappy at the delay in a positive response from Downing Street to the new Hume–Adams package, began to make threats about a wave of violence in Northern Ireland and Britain. John Major discreetly responded to Hume with 'a further text' on 23 November. This version included the government's views on the terms and process of Sinn Fein entry into talks after any restored ceasefire. The terms were set in the context of continuing IRA attacks, particularly the bombing of Lisburn Army HQ. They did not make encouraging reading to Sinn Fein. Hume took the new text to Adams, with a view to narrowing the points of difference. In the interim, he warned against allowing the Westminster 'numbers game' to stand in the way of the peace process. The government, about to lose its parliamentary majority through the abdication of a Tory MP from the parliamentary whip and the return of another opposition MP at a by-election in the safe Labour seat of Barnsley East, would depend even more on Trimble's nine MPs to survive through to a general election on 1 May 1997. Hume asserted: 'This is an issue above party politics.'

Before Hume could return with a refined version of the government's latest text, John Major launched a pre-emptive strike. During Prime Minister's Questions in the Commons on 27 November, Major delivered a prepared statement on the Hume initiative. Opposition MPs were dumbfounded, and demanded that he make a proper parliamentary statement rather than smuggle in a policy announcement in answer to a 'planted' question from a Tory. But the deed was done. Major had announced policy, without having to endure a political grilling. Copies of his statement were immediately made available to political reporters, putting the best possible gloss on the government's position. In effect, it was the kind of statement for which Sinn Fein had asked, but couched in John Major's language. At key points, it did echo Sinn Fein. Major talked about 'the conflict being permanently ended', a form of words similar to phraseology employed by McGuinness. But it made clear that a renewal of the 1994 ceasefire would not be sufficient to allow Sinn Fein to the bargaining table, and it laid down that 'sufficient time' would have to elapse after a ceasefire to ensure that it was 'convincingly unequivocal', in other words, a contamination period would apply.

Hume was furious that he had been upstaged while still trying to finesse the document with Adams. Again, he accused Major of pandering to Trimble's parliamentary clout. 'It is quite obvious,' he declared, 'that the internal politics of Westminster are more important than getting peace on our streets.' Dublin was incensed too, openly contradicting the Prime Minister. Editorial opinion was divided. The *Independent* described the statement as an 'olive twig', and agreed that Major had 'explicable political reasons' for denying Sinn Fein immediate entry into talks. 'Gerry Adams and John Hume, who must know this perfectly well, should not give up just because Major dismissed their proposals this time.'[14]

Indeed, Hume did not give up. In spite of the Rev. Ian Paisley's wild declaration that 'Major is in the surrendering business to the IRA and its bed-fellows, John Hume, Dublin and the White House', Hume told David Frost on television that he had held a 'quite constructive' meeting with Gerry Adams. There was still 'a major opportunity to bring about a complete end to violence'. It did not seem like it on the ground. The IRA was surprised trying to plant a 2,500lb bomb near an Armagh city army base. The Sinn Fein president condemned the government's response to the new Hume–Adams as 'outright rejection' and unacceptable. A summit between Major and the Irish Prime Minister John Bruton on 9 December failed to clear the way.

FIFTEEN

WHAT FUTURE?

ONE YEAR ON from the bombs in London, it was clear that the IRA had blown the heart out of the peace process. John Hume, however, clung stubbornly to his belief that the force of argument could eventually defeat the argument of force. He hoped John Major would make a statement based on the form of words he had put to him, allowing for a pre-Christmas ceasefire, followed after a decent interval by all-party talks including Sinn Fein in mid-January 1997.

It was a vain hope. Hume put the failure down to lack of commitment in London. 'It shows us that the Westminster scene, and holding power until they decide the date of the general election, is more important than any other issues, because had they done what I asked them to do it would give no offence to anyone. There were no political concessions in it. But they [the Major government] were frightened the Unionists would reject it.'[1]

Hume refuted the Northern Ireland Office assessment that he is 'a window, not a solution', arguing: 'A solution comes within the talks. The last thing I am asking the government to do is impose a solution. I have proposals to put on the table, but I don't disclose them in advance.'[2] He did not hint at what these terms might be, relying instead on his familiar assertion that there had been a sea-change in Republican attitudes that ministers had not fully grasped. 'In their last statement, the IRA said their objective was a negotiated settlement,' he said, 'and that that is tied to joint statements that Gerry Adams has put out with me: that the objective of dialogue and negotiations would be agreement among our divided people that would have to have the allegiance of all traditions.

'That is very different from "Brits Out" and "United Ireland".

There has been a great debate in the Republican ranks. There is no doubt about that. Like any other political group they have their "wings". But the difference between theirs and others, where, if you have a difference of opinion you operate according to majority decisions, in their [the IRA] situation you have to bring everybody with them. If you are serious about trying to bring violence to an end, you do everything to help them.'[3]

If this was so – and Hume was better placed than anyone to know – the IRA showed no sign of wanting to be helped. After the arrest of eight men in London on charges of plotting to blow up the UK national electricity grid, frustrated Republicans escalated the terror campaign in Northern Ireland, mounting two dozen attacks in the province in the first two months of 1997. However, the Combined Loyalist Military Command refused to be goaded into abandoning its official ceasefire, denying the IRA a military and propaganda opportunity to restore its role as defender of the Nationalist community. RUC intelligence sources briefed journalists that informers were penetrating the IRA to a greater degree than before the cease-fire, while their foot-soldiers were declared to be 'rusty' or less motiv-ated by political ideals. 'The new breed of volunteer is less ideological and not as resilient as his predecessors,' said an RUC anti-terrorist officer. 'Today's terrorist is more selfish and corruptible.'[4]

The dangers of trying to reach a political accommodation with people of this calibre were obvious, and Hume's own position was further subverted by reports appearing in February that the IRA had planned to kill him in 1982, and that Gerry Adams had been involved in the assassination plot. Sean O'Callaghan, now the darling of Tory hardline Unionists, claimed in the Belfast magazine *Fortnight* that he had been approached by the Sinn Fein president fifteen years previously. 'Adams realised that Hume had to be dealt with. The SDLP couldn't just be dismissed. Something new was needed. I remember Gerry Adams asking me if we should kill Hume.'

O'Callaghan, who has admitted to two terrorist murders himself, said he advised Adams not to go ahead. 'It was too late by then. The SDLP had become too big and was respected by ordinary Catholics. Killing Hume would have been a major disaster for the Provos. But even if Adams would no longer contemplate such a thing, it shows their complete ruthlessness.'[5] The IRA's ruthlessness has never been in doubt, but O'Callaghan's claim was. His apostasy has made him a hated figure in Republican circles, and scorn was poured on his claims. Hume himself refused to comment. He has endured his home being picketed and daubed with paint, and his car torched by the Provos over the years, but he has never had a dedicated police body-guard and does not carry a gun as he is entitled to do, as are all Ulster politicians. He would have been an easy target for assassination, though perhaps it would have been more likely to be at the hands of a Loyalist.

Sinn Fein's official assessment had been delivered a few weeks earlier. Mitchel McLaughlin, SF chairman, told a Republican rally in Limerick on 5 January that: 'So long as Gerry Adams and John Hume continue their collective enterprise, then we have grounds for hope and reasons to weigh in behind their enterprise.' Hume and Adams continued to meet and talk privately, yet the grounds for optimism further diminished. Rumours began to circulate in the media that President Clinton's new Secretary of State, the tough-minded Madeleine Albright who had been the USA's ambassador to the United Nations, would jettison the policy of aligning America with Hume and Adams. With the departure of Nancy Soderberg and Tony Lake from Clinton's National Security Council, Hume had just lost two powerful allies in key positions. Now, there was also talk that Jean Kennedy Smith, US ambassador to Dublin and another Hume confidante, would be recalled. His influence in the USA was under threat. Clinton himself ruled out Sinn Fein participation in the peace process without a 'credible' IRA ceasefire, interpreted as a sign of Washington's growing disenchantment with Hume and Adams.

Hume decided to go on the offensive. On 21 February, he launched what the *Independent* described as 'an unusually scathing attack' on Sinn Fein, warning that a vote for them was effectively a vote for violence. In an article for the Nationalist *Irish News*, the SDLP leader rejected Adams's proposals for an electoral pact in the forthcoming Westminster general election, and accused Sinn Fein of vote-stealing and intimidating his party's workers. In West Belfast, where Adams was contesting the seat held by the SDLP's Dr Joe Hendron, there was evidence of 'packing' the electoral register, using forged medical cards and empty flats to inflate the ranks of their supporters. Observers noted sceptically that 'the Shinners' were now so convinced of the merits of democracy that they hoped to vote more than once.

Hume thundered: 'Having availed of our good faith as honest brokers, they now intend to cast us aside, using any means, fair or foul. To make an electoral pact with Sinn Fein without an IRA ceasefire would be the equivalent of asking our voters to support the killing of innocent human beings by the IRA. The electorate should be aware that in voting for Sinn Fein that is what they are voting for: Sinn Fein calls it the armed struggle.'[6]

He had used similarly strong language before – stronger, even. But Hume's intervention at this stage was not purely party political. True, the SDLP faced the loss of one or more of its four Westminster seats to Sinn Fein, newly resurgent in the polls. Sinn Fein had registered 15.5 per cent of the popular vote in the Forum elections of May 1996, uncomfortably close to the SDLP's 21 per cent. Yet the risk of losing his political leverage in Washington was uppermost in Hume's mind. He could always keep the personal dialogue with Adams going. That was seen as 'above politics' and capable of resuscitation at the right time. Mixed with the readiness to keep talking, however, there was a lingering resentment. An SDLP official was quoted as saying: 'People are very resentful of the way that Sinn Fein invoke Hume's name to justify their own actions. But Hume is not going to walk away from Adams.'[7] In his *Irish News* article, Hume had actually threatened to do just that: to 'look elsewhere' for peace partners, suggesting that the SDLP could negotiate directly with the Unionists on a constitutional settlement. The Unionists were quick to seize on this prospect. Ken Maginnis MP, the UUP's security spokesman, wrote a response in the same paper appealing to Hume to allow his party to return to 'the Northern Ireland Forum for Political Dialogue' from which the SDLP had withdrawn seven months previously. 'We have got a forum which is basically a Protestant forum because John Hume has marched his party out. We all need to be there, and no one knows better than Ulster Unionists that boycotts are self-defeating,' said Maginnis. This was remarkable coming from the Unionists, who had privately signalled to John Major their view that the talks should be suspended until after the general election – and had got their way. Others argued that Hume might be hinting at acceptance of another imposed London–Dublin settlement.

Adams had his turn in the *Irish Times*, accepting that an unequivocal restoration of the IRA ceasefire was the most important confidence-building measure the Republicans could offer. But he insisted: 'Sinn Fein can only speak for ourselves and the electorate. Sinn Fein is not the IRA.' This cut little ice in Dublin, where Prime Minister John Bruton reiterated that only when the killing stopped, and a conscious, comprehensive decision was taken by the Republican movement 'as a whole, once and for all' that violence was not the way to solve political problems, could there be a new political environment. It was the end, for now.

Hume travelled to the USA for a lecture tour in March 1997, culminating once again in a St Patrick's Day reception at the White House. This time it was a more muted affair. Gerry Adams was *persona non grata*. But the Unionists were honoured guests, and Ken Maginnis, accompanying his party leader David Trimble, seized the opportunity to repudiate a fresh peace move by Hume's closest Irish American ally, Senator Edward Kennedy. He condemned as 'arrogant and naive to the point of irrelevancy' Kennedy's proposal that Sinn Fein be allowed into all-party talks due to restart on 3 June, after the general election. Kennedy, who clearly spoke with Hume's foreknowledge, said that peace was 'tantalisingly within reach' and urged both Tony Blair and John Major to make a clear statement that if the IRA restored its ceasefire, Sinn Fein would be allowed to join peace talks 'with no further pre-conditions'. Both Major and Blair snubbed him.

The most extraordinary aspect of Hume's annual March pilgrimage was the re-emergence of the story he thought he had quashed about the presidency of the Irish Republic. On 12 March, Mary Robinson announced that she would not seek a second seven-year term as Aras an Uachtarain, or President, when her term of office expired in the autumn. Her name was linked with various United Nations posts, including director of the Geneva-based International

Labour Office and UN High Commissioner for Human Rights. Mrs Robinson, fifty-two, increased speculation when she said she wanted to 'make a contribution, probably in the area of human rights and in a wider context'.

Speculation then focused on Hume. Was his earlier disavowal final? He issued a statement in the USA saying he was 'not a candidate', but this did nothing to dampen the fires of conjecture. The Dublin *Sunday Independent* ran an opinion poll in the Republic to ask voters whom they wanted to succeed Mrs Robinson. The people's choice was John Hume. He emerged a clear front-runner in the IMS/*Independent* poll, ahead of former Irish Prime Ministers Albert Reynolds, Charles Haughey and Garret Fitzgerald – despite being a British citizen, and despite having said that the Irish presidency was 'not a subject I have ever thought about'.

Others evidently had. In a poll of more than 1,000 voters in seventy-five locations, Hume took 19 per cent of the votes, a clear five points ahead of Albert Reynolds on 14 per cent. Haughey scored 11 per cent, while Garret Fitzgerald, Hume's old ally, trailed at only 9 per cent. Hume was more popular among older age groups, and among men. Men gave him 23 per cent, women 16 per cent. Among pensioners, he also scored 23 per cent. Not surprisingly, he was twice as popular among Fine Gael voters as among Fianna Fail or Labour voters. Hume continued to insist that he was committed to his work in the North, but the *Sunday Independent* commented: 'His comments have done little to deter potential voters. The margin of support makes it clear he remains first choice for the Aras among a significant number of voters.'[8]

Hume's enduring popularity with older, middle-class and many upwardly-mobile Catholics throughout Ireland was confirmed by this poll. He is seen, rightly, as a persevering campaigner for a decent society, who does not give up when the going gets rough. Much political opinion concurs. Albert Reynolds, the Irish Prime Minister with whom he negotiated the ceasefire, calls Hume 'the most respected constitutional leader in Northern Ireland, at home and abroad, because of his courage, common sense and moderation'. Without him, the peace process would not have been possible. He took very great political risks, and put his leadership on the line in the supreme cause of peace. 'John Hume will always be remembered with gratitude by the Irish people for his courage, his vision and his single-minded determination,' maintains Reynolds.[9]

For many, Hume's admirers in particular, that is the final verdict. It is a valid tribute, but it does not tell the whole story. Only a year after it was delivered, Hume's critics felt strong enough to denounce him. Eilis O'Hanlon, a Belfast-based columnist with the *Sunday Independent* who has family links with the Republican movement, was contemptuous of the SDLP leader. Irish nationalism, she argued, was in stasis, intellectually ill-equipped to cope with the IRA's resumption of terrorism. No Nationalist leader could admit that the attempt to 'civilise the IRA' had failed. Ms O'Hanlon accused Hume's constitutional Nationalists of fooling themselves into believing that

> a little tinkering will square the circle. If only the deception with which they secured the ceasefire in the first place can be kept going a little while longer, they imagine, then the base metal of the Troubles will, by some mysterious alchemic process, transmute into the gold of a lasting peace. This is not political analysis, but wishful thinking, and it leaves Irish nationalism wide-open to the alternate hope-building, hope-dashing strategies of Sinn Fein and the IRA.[10]

Soon afterwards, Conor Cruise O'Brien, a long-standing Hume sceptic, dismissed the Anglo-Irish Division of the Irish Foreign Affairs Department as 'made up exclusively of admirers of John Hume, and committed from the beginning of Hume/Adams, to a process which became dominated by Mr Adams'. Now that Hume had publicly stated that the IRA and Sinn Fein were one and the same thing, he hoped to see the end of 'the political rot, and intellectual corruption, which the "peace process" as we have come to know it, represents'.[11]

Harsh judgements such as this cannot be cast aside simply because they disturb the cosy vision of the man of peace. Hume is too intelligent a thinker about Ireland's future to reject such criticism out of hand, however much it may hurt. Asked if he would do it all again, he replies, in somewhat delphic manner: 'The facts are: you live your life, and things happen. You do them.' Then he returns to political justification. 'I believe over the last twenty-five years there have been a number of major missed opportunities, the biggest one being the bringing down of the Sunningdale Agreement, and the government of the day not standing behind that Agreement. Brian Faulkner said to me those were the best five months of his life.'[12] And, later: 'If Ted Heath had been Prime Minister when Sunningdale had been challenged, I believe the Agreement would still have been there.'

Does he still think a new accommodation can be reached, which values Catholics as much as Protestants, and can it be accomplished by the present generation of politicians? 'Yes, I believe so,' avers Hume. 'I think the British government in particular must realize the importance of its role in promoting agreement. And the Unionist leadership whose self-confidence lies in geography and numbers must recognize that the problem cannot be solved without them. Every British government says Northern Ireland is an integral part of the UK. Yet if they allow any party in Northern Ireland to exercise a veto on dialogue, they are allowing 1 or 2 per cent of the population to dictate to the government. The only progress made to date has been because the government of the day took a strong line – for example, the progress on civil rights, housing, voting rights and fair employment. That all took place because the British government of the day insisted on it.'

Hume still insists that any agreement on the future must address three sets of relationships: relations within Northern Ireland, between the North and the Republic and between Britain and Ireland. And he emphasizes the European dimension. 'The Unionists do not seem to have noticed that we are all together now in a new Europe, and that decisions are taken at European level by shared sovereignty of many governments including the Irish government, which affect the situation in Northern Ireland substantially. Farming, for instance. If we can live together in agreed institutions in a new Europe, with Greeks, Italians, Spaniards, Portuguese, French and Germans, with whom we have greater differences, can we not do the same in Ireland?'[13]

This analysis sometimes sounds less a political objective, more a *cri de coeur*. John Hume has made it his life's work to educate and lead his own people, the Catholic Nationalists of Northern Ireland, and to convert the rival, larger community of Protestant Unionists from its iron-clad attitude that 'what we have, we hold'. Perhaps no one man can do that, however gifted. The gulf between the communities is too wide, and too deeply rooted in perceived versions of history and persecution.

Consciously or no, Hume set himself that task in the early days of the civil rights campaign, buoyed by a strong – almost messianic – self-belief and by the partial success of reforms wrung first from a reluctant Stormont and then from the British government. Hume's role in what is still called 'the peace process', despite there being no peace and no sign of progress as the Unionists consolidate their ascendancy in the wake of Drumcree, remains central. But it is difficult to imagine his vision of a New Ireland coming to fruition during his lifetime. If there is a tragic aspect to his life, it is that John Hume brought a rational mind to bear on an irrational situation. In Ulster, deep thought, generosity of spirit and a brilliant pedagogic style are not enough. The three decades that Hume has dedicated to the search for an historic compromise in Ulster have taken their toll. He has virtually no outside interests, other than a delight in his grandchildren that is plain to see. 'The job has become completely all-absorbing,' he admits. In the summer of 1996, soon after 'Drumcree 2', he paced the garden of his home in Donegal, staring across the grey expanse of Lough Foyle, and confessed to me that he was in the grip of a deep depression. It was worst in the mornings. It felt 'like a bereavement'. Perhaps it was a sense that his life's work would not, after all, yield the objective for which he had struggled so hard. Six months later, in the same place, he said things had not improved: 'It's like butterflies in the stomach, only fifty times worse ... It's not depression, but chronic anxiety – anxiety about everything, especially when I wake up in the morning.' A few weeks later, he announced that he would fight on. Not, like Margaret Thatcher, 'We fight on, we fight to win', but simply to reach agreement with the Unionists. 'We are not looking for victory or revenge.'

The general election of 1 May 1997 brought mixed fortunes for John Hume. He scored a convincing win over Sinn Fein in his own seat of Foyle, taking 52.5 per cent of the vote – up 8 per cent on the Forum elections the previous year. In a 71 per cent turnout, he received 25,109 votes to Mitchel McLaughlin's 11,445. Sinn Fein's share of the poll was down almost 2 per cent. However, his party did not fare so well elsewhere. Dr Joe Hendron lost West Belfast to Sinn Fein. Gerry Adams scored a humiliating victory over the SDLP, taking 25,662 votes (56 per cent of the poll) to Dr Hendron's 17,753 (39 per cent). Seamus Mallon and Eddie McGrady were returned for Newry and Armagh and South Down respectively. But Joe Byrne, a rising star in the SDLP, just failed to pick up the new constituency of Tyrone West, in substantial measure due to Sinn Fein's strong showing. And Martin McGuinness gained Mid Ulster for Sinn Fein, beating Hume's aide Denis Haughey into third place. The SDLP had gone down from four seats to three, and Sinn Fein went up from none to two – though in line with their policy of abstentionism, neither would take his seat at Westminster. Across the province, Hume's party increased its share of the vote only marginally from the 1992 general election, up half a per cent to 24 per cent. Sinn Fein's portion rose dramatically from 10 per cent to 16 per cent, making it the third largest party in terms of vote share.

An exuberant John Hume welcomed Tony Blair's landslide victory for Labour, which now had a Commons majority of 179 over all other parties at Westminster and predicted that the outcome would reinvigorate the peace process. 'Tony Blair will do it because the government that has just left was not a government at all for the last couple of years, because it had no majority. And therefore they only sat at the peace process.' He hoped that all parties would be present at talks on the future of Northern Ireland due to restart at Stormont on 3 June. 'Sinn Fein know that they can be at that table, if the IRA end their campaign completely and absolutely,' Hume urged, adding that he was ready to meet Gerry Adams if that would help bring about an IRA ceasefire. His deputy, Seamus Mallon, was less optimistic, saying the election outcome was 'a vote that gives a blank cheque to the IRA'.[14]

In government, Blair moved quickly. His first meeting with a foreign head of government was with Irish Prime Minister John Bruton, only a week after taking over the reins of office. And on 16

May, Blair paid a surprise visit to Belfast, bearing an olive branch for Sinn Fein: the offer of talks with government officials – the first since February 1996 – before an IRA ceasefire. His radical plan was 'one further effort' to get the Republican movement into the political process. 'My message to Sinn Fein is clear, and clear,' said the Prime Minister. 'The settlement train is leaving. I want you on that train. But it is leaving anyway. You cannot hold the process to ransom any longer. So end the violence, and end it now.' At the talks with officials, Sinn Fein would have to demonstrate that they were serious about wanting peace. 'If they are, I will not be slow in my response. If they are not, they can expect no sympathy or understanding. I will be implacable in my pursuit of terrorism.'[15] Hume had been informed by Dr Mo Mowlam, the new Northern Ireland Secretary, the previous night about Blair's initiative and what he was going to say. He was unstinting in his praise for the Prime Minister, calling his speech 'the most comprehensive' he had heard.

Gerry Adams quickly picked up the offer of talks, while holding out little hope of a cessation of violence. 'We have neither the responsibility, or the authority, or the ability to negotiate a ceasefire,' he warned.[16] The Sinn Fein President also accused Blair of 'a degree of crassness' in making a 'pro-Unionist speech'. The Prime Minister had made clear to his Belfast audience that Labour was no longer a 'persuader' for a united Ireland. Indeed, he declared: 'I believe in the United Kingdom. I value the Union. My agenda is not a united Ireland.' Almost thirty years after John Hume began his long march towards a New Ireland, the language had hardly changed.

Notes

ONE · DECISION TIME

1. John Boyle O'Reilly, quoted in *A New Ireland*, p. 21.
2. *Independent*, 21 December 1996.
3. David Trimble, interview, 12 December 1996.
4. Michael Ancram, interview, 11 December 1996.
5. *Belfast Telegraph*, 24 February 1993.
6. Edward Kennedy, Foreword to Hume, *A New Ireland*.
7. Private interview, Northern Ireland, 3 April 1996.
8. Hume, *A New Ireland*, p. 159.
9. BBC, *Inside Politics*, 21 December 1996.
10. *The Unionist*, Autumn 1996, p. 4.
11. Transcript, CNN, *Larry King Show*, 5 October 1994.
12. Drower, *John Hume Peacemaker*, p. 208.
13. Hume, *A New Ireland*, p. 97.
14. Quoted in Holland and Phoenix, *The Secret War*, p. 80.
15. Bennett, 'The Party and the Army'.
16. David Trimble, interview, 11 December 1996.

TWO · DERRY BOY

1. White, *John Hume*, p. 5.
2. Hume, *A New Ireland*, p. 24.

3. John Hume, interview, 2 June 1995.
4. J. W. Blake, *The War Years*, p. 9.
5. John Hume, interview, 2 June 1995.
6. Hume, *A New Ireland*, p. 267.
7. Neil McLaughlin, interview, 20 September 1995.
8. Quoted in White, *John Hume*, p. 9.
9. Eamonn McCann, interview, 8 April 1995.
10. O'Neill, *Autobiography*, p. 29.
11. John Hume, interview, 2 June 1995.
12. Eamonn McCann, interview, 8 April 1995.
13. McCann, *War and an Irish Town*, p. 16.
14. Ibid., p. 17.
15. John Hume, interview, 2 June 1995.
16. Neil McLaughlin, interview, 20 September 1995.
17. Professor Liam Ryan, interview, 23 September 1995.
18. *The Graduate*, Maynooth, April 1995, p. 3.
19. White, *John Hume*, p. 22.
20. Hume, *A New Ireland*, p. 26.

THREE · THE TOWN I LOVE SO WELL

1. Transcript of *John Hume's Derry*, RTE, 1969.

2. John Hume, interview, 2 June 1995 (and ensuing quotes).
3. Hume, *Social and Economic Aspects of the Growth of Derry*.
4. White, *John Hume*, p. 34.
5. Michael Canavan, interview, 2 June 1995.
6. Viney, 'Journey North', *Irish Times*, 8 May 1964.
7. Ibid., 9 May 1964.
8. Hume, 'The Northern Catholic', *Irish Times*, 18 May 1964.
9. Quoted in White, *John Hume*, p. 39.
10. Curran, *Countdown to Disaster*, p. 34.
11. Paul Rose, interview, 19 July 1995.
12. *Derry Journal*, 6 August 1965.
13. Cland Wilton, interview, 21 September 1995.
14. Michael Canavan, interview, 2 June 1995.

FOUR · CIVIL RIGHTS, UNCIVIL TIMES

1. Tomlinson, *Housing*.
2. Feeney, *The Civil Rights Movement*, vol. 9, no. 2, p. 30.
3. Purdie, *Politics in the Street*, p. 93.
4. Campaign for Social Justice in Northern Ireland, *Londonderry*, p. 2.
5. McCann, *War and an Irish Town*, p. 34 and ff.
6. Eamonn McCann, interview, 8 April 1995.
7. Curran, *Countdown to Disaster*, p. 80.
8. John Hume, interview, 2 June 1995.
9. Gerry Fitt, interview, 12 July 1995.
10. *Irish Times*, 5 October 1968.
11. John Hume, interview, 2 June 1995.

12. Michael Canavan, 2 June 1995.
13. Eamonn McCann, interview, 8 April 1995.
14. McCann, *War and an Irish Town*, p. 47.
15. McLean, *The Road to Bloody Sunday*, p. 52.
16. McCann, *War and an Irish Town*, p. 49.
17. Curran, *Countdown to Disaster*, p. 112.
18. Cameron Report on Disturbances in Northern Ireland.
19. McLean, *The Road to Bloody Sunday*, p. 64.
20. John Hume, interview, 2 June 1995.
21. Quoted in Curran, *Countdown to Disaster*, p. 116.
22. McLean, *The Road to Bloody Sunday*, p. 68.
23. Cameron Report, p. 57.
24. McCann, *War and an Irish Town*, p. 57.
25. Purdie, *Politics in the Street*, p. 248.
26. Ibid.

FIVE · VIOLENCE BEGETS POLITICS

1. Callaghan, *A House Divided*, p. 15.
2. Curran, *Countdown to Disaster*, p. 130.
3. White, *John Hume*, p. 82.
4. Adams, *Free Ireland*, p. 45.
5. Hastings, *Ulster 1969*, p. 153.
6. Paddy Devlin, interview, 30 May 1995.
7. Devlin, *Straight Left*, p. 138.
8. Adams, *Free Ireland*, p. 51.
9. Devlin, *Straight Left*, p. 139.
10. Ibid., p. 140.
11. Paddy Devlin, interview, 30 May 1995.
12. White, *John Hume*, p. 102.

13. Bloomfield, *Stormont in Crisis*, p. 131.
14. Quoted in Kelly, *How Stormont Fell*, p. 33.
15. Ibid., p. 50.
16. Bloomfield, *Stormont in Crisis*, p. 146.
17. Campbell, *Edward Heath*, p. 427.
18. Moloney and Pollak, *Paisley*, p. 328.
19. Devlin, *Straight Left*, p. 166.

SIX · THE DEATH OF
STORMONT

1. Kelly, *How Stormont Fell*, p. 116.
2. McLean, *The Road to Bloody Sunday*, p. 125.
3. McCann et. al., *Bloody Sunday in Derry*, p. 20.
4. Quoted in White, *John Hume*, p. 120.
5. Devlin, *Straight Left*, p. 169.
6. Bloomfield, *Stormont in Crisis*, p. 160.
7. Whitelaw, *Memoirs*, p. 120.
8. Devlin, *Straight Left*, p. 176.
9. Quoted in White, *John Hume*, p. 131.
10. Ibid., p. 141.
11. Devlin, *Straight Left*, p. 199.
12. White, *John Hume*, p. 143.
13. Devlin, *Straight Left*, p. 205.
14. Fitzgerald, *All in a Life*, p. 217.
15. Quoted in Bew and Gillespie, *Northern Ireland*, p. 75.

SEVEN · POWER SHARED AND
LOST

1. Bloomfield, *Stormont in Crisis*, p. 147.
2. Rees, *Northern Ireland*, p. 25.
3. Quoted in Anderson, *14 May Days*, p. 36.

4. Rees, *Northern Ireland*, p. 68.
5. Anderson, *14 May Days*, p. 78.
6. Ibid., p. 99.
7. Pimlott, *Harold Wilson*, p. 634.
8. Rees, *Northern Ireland*, p. 82.
9. White, *John Hume*, p. 170.
10. Ibid., p. 171.
11. Rees, *Northern Ireland*, p. 90.
12. Fitzgerald, *All in a Life*, p. 243.
13. Quoted in Rees, *Northern Ireland*, p. 243.
14. Moloney and Pollak, *Paisley*, p. 333.
15. Ibid.
16. White, *John Hume*, p. 180.
17. Rees, *Northern Ireland*, p. 262.

EIGHT · LEADER

1. Quoted in White, *John Hume*, p. 89.
2. Fitzgerald, *All in a Life*, p. 348.
3. Devlin, *Straight Left*, p. 278.
4. John Hume, interview, 4 April 1996.
5. Ibid.
6. Fitzgerald, *All in a Life*, p. 333.
7. Gerry Fitt, interview, 12 July 1995.
8. Quoted in Benn, *Conflicts of Interest*, p. 433.
9. White, *John Hume*, p. 205.
10. Fitzgerald, *All in a Life*, p. 334.
11. Hume, 'The Irish Question, a British Problem'.
12. Bishop and Mallie, *The Provisional IRA*, p. 352.

NINE · HUNGER STRIKE

1. Beresford, *Ten Men Dead*, p. 15.
2. John Hume, interview, 4 April 1996.
3. Ibid.
4. White, *John Hume*, p. 220.

5. John Hume, interview, 4 April 1996.
6. Quoted in White, *John Hume*, p. 219.
7. O'Malley, *The Uncivil Wars*, p. 112.
8. Fitzgerald, *All in a Life*, p. 253.
9. John Hume, interview, 4 April 1996.
10. Ibid.
11. Beresford, *Ten Men Dead*, p. 319.
12. O'Malley, *The Uncivil Wars*, p. 124.
13. Thatcher, *The Downing Street Years*, p. 391.
14. John Hume, interview, 4 April 1996.
15. John Hume's address to SDLP annual conference, November 1981.
16. Thatcher, *The Downing Street Years*, p. 395.

TEN · THE ANGLO-IRISH AGREEMENT

1. White, *John Hume*, p. 244.
2. Arnold, *Haughey*, p. 218.
3. Hume, *A New Ireland*, p. 62.
4. Ibid., p. 63.
5. O'Brien, *The Long War*, p. 126.
6. White, *John Hume*, p. 249.
7. Hansard, 28 June 1983, cols. 507–10.
8. Hansard, 13 July 1983, cols. 927–30.
9. Thatcher, *The Downing Street Years*, p. 396.
10. Fitzgerald, *All in a Life*, p. 396.
11. *Derry Journal*, 10 February 1984.
12. Hume, *A New Ireland*, p. 63.
13. Fitzgerald, *All in a Life*, p. 525.
14. Ibid., p. 535.
15. Flackes and Elliott, *Northern Ireland*, p. 67.

16. Hume, *A New Ireland*, pp. 64ff.
17. Hansard, 22 November 1985, cols. 780–1.
18. Hume, *A New Ireland*, pp. 67–8.

ELEVEN · TALKING TO GERRY

1. John Hume, conversation with author, May 1996.
2. Adams, *Free Ireland*, p. 152.
3. John Hume, conversation with author, May 1996.
4. O'Brien, *The Long War*, p. 173.
5. Adams, *Free Ireland*, p. 188.
6. Hume, *A New Ireland*, p. 115.
7. John Hume's address to SDLP annual conference, Belfast, 9 November 1985.
8. Thatcher, *The Downing Street Years*, p. 405.
9. Coogan, *The Troubles*, p. 330.
10. Hansard, 9 November 1987, col. 26.
11. John Hume, interview, 4 April 1996.
12. Hume, *A New Ireland*, p. 115.
13. Hume to Adams, letter, 17 March 1988.
14. John Hume, interview, 5 April 1996.
15. Hansard, 21 March 1988, col. 28.
16. Hume, *A New Ireland*, p. 115.
17. Mallie and McKittrick, *The Fight for Peace*, p. 81.
18. Sean Farren, interview, 4 April 1996.

TWELVE · BREAKTHROUGH

1. *Londonderry Sentinel*, 8 February 1989.
2. 'Building the 1990s', John Hume's address to SDLP annual conference, Newcastle, 4 November 1989, p. 1.

3. *Irish Times*, October 1990, quoted in Bew and Gillespie, *Northern Ireland*.
4. Quoted in Mallie and McKittrick, *The Fight for Peace*, p. 112.
5. Ibid., p. 117.
6. Quoted in Bew and Gillespie, *Northern Ireland*, p. 274.
7. Ibid., p. 283.
8. Hume, *A New Ireland*, p. 116.
9. Quoted in McKittrick, *Endgame*, p. 265.
10. Hume, *A New Ireland*, p. 116.
11. *Irish News*, 26 April 1993.
12. *Independent on Sunday*, 2 May 1993.
13. Duignan, *One More Spin on the Merry-go-round*, p. 96.
14. Ibid., p. 98.
15. Hume, *A New Ireland*, p. 116.
16. Adams, *Free Ireland*, p. 212.
17. John Hume, interview, 4 April 1996.
18. Mallie and McKittrick, *The Fight for Peace*, p. 112.
19. Duignan, *One More Spin on the Merry-go-round*, p. 104.
20. Mallie and McKittrick, *The Fight for Peace*, p. 191.
21. Ibid., p. 214.
22. Alex Attwood, interview, 1 June 1995.
23. Mallie and McKittrick, *The Fight for Peace*, p. 129.

THIRTEEN · CEASEFIRE

1. Bishop Edward Daly, interview, 7 April 1995.
2. Quoted in Mallie and McKittrick, *The Fight for Peace*, p. 258.
3. Duignan, *One More Spin on the Merry-go-round*, p. 123.
4. Ibid., p. 304.
5. Senior Republican source quoted in O'Brien, op. cit., p. 320.

6. Duignan, *One More Spin on the Merry-go-round*, p. 149.
7. Hume, *A New Ireland*, p. 131.
8. *Independent*, 14 October 1994.
9. *Independent*, 2 February 1995.
10. *New Statesman*, 17 March 1995.
11. Coogan, *The Troubles*, pp. 391–2.
12. Hansard, 27 April 1995, cols 971–2.
13. Transcript, BBC, *Breakfast with Frost*, 22 August 1995.
14. *Independent*, 11 September 1995.
15. *Belfast Telegraph*, 28 November 1995.

FOURTEEN · WAR ONCE MORE

1. *News of the World*, 6 January 1996.
2. *Daily Telegraph*, 13 February 1996.
3. *Irish Voice*, New York, 5 March 1996.
4. *Belfast Telegraph*, 22 May 1996.
5. *Belfast Telegraph*, 22 May 1996.
6. *Daily Telegraph*, 1 June 1996.
7. Hansard, 13 June 1996, col. 410.
8. *New Statesman*, 16 August 1996.
9. *The Times*, 10 August 1996.
10. *Sunday Times*, 8 September 1996.
11. David Trimble, interview, 11 December 1996.
12. Transcript, BBC Radio 4, 'Today', 9 October 1996.
13. *Daily Telegraph*, 23 November 1996.
14. *Independent*, 30 November 1996.

FIFTEEN · WHAT FUTURE?

1. John Hume, interview, 3 January 1997.
2. Ibid.
3. Ibid.
4. *Daily Telegraph*, 8 February 1997.
5. *Fortnight*, 3 February 1997.
6. *Irish News*, 21 February 1997.

7. *Financial Times*, 28 February 1997.
8. *Sunday Independent*, 16 March 1997.
9. Quoted in Drower, *John Hume Peacemaker*, p. 11.
10. *New Statesman*, 6 December 1996.
11. *Irish Independent*, 4 January 1997.
12. John Hume, interview, 2 January 1997.
13. John Hume, interview, 3 January 1997.
14. *Irish Times*, 3 May 1997.
15. *The Times*, 17 May 1997.
16. *Independent on Sunday*, 18 May 1997.

Works Cited

Adams, Gerry (1995), *Free Ireland* (Dingle, Co. Kerry: Brandon).

Anderson, Ian (1994), *14 May Days* (Dublin: Gill and Macmillan).

Arnold, Bruce (1993), *Haughey* (London: HarperCollins).

Benn, Tony (1990), *Conflicts of Interest: Diaries 1977–80* (London: Hutchinson).

Bennett, Ronan, 'The Party and the Army', *London Review of Books*, 21 March 1996.

Beresford, David (1987), *Ten Men Dead* (London: Grafton).

Bew, Paul and Gordon Gillespie (1993), *Northern Ireland: A Chronology of the Troubles* (Dublin: Gill and Macmillan).

Bishop, Patrick and Eamonn Mallie (1988), *The Provisional IRA* (London: Corgi).

Blake, J. W. (1995), *The War Years, Derry 1939/45* (Derry: Heritage Library, Guildhall Press).

Bloomfield, Ken (1994), *Stormont in Crisis* (Dundonald: Blackstaff Press).

Callaghan, James (1973), *A House Divided* (London: Collins).

Cameron Report on Disturbances in Northern Ireland (1969), CMD532 (London: HMSO).

Campaign for Social Justice in Northern Ireland (1965), *Londonderry: One Man. No Vote* (Dungannon: CSJ).

Campbell, John (1993), *Edward Heath: A Biography* (London: Random House).

Coogan, Tim Pat (1995), *The Troubles* (London: Hutchinson).

Curran, Frank (1986), *Countdown to Disaster* (Dublin: Gill and Macmillan).

Devlin, Paddy (1993), *Straight Left* (Dundonald: Blackstaff Press).

Drower, George (1995), *John Hume Peacemaker* (London: Gollancz).

Duignan, Sean (1995), *One More Spin on the Merry-go-round* (Dublin: Blackwater).

Feeney, Vincent (1974), *The Civil Rights Movement in Northern Ireland*, Vol. 2, no. 2.

Fitzgerald, Garret (1991), *All in a Life* (London: Macmillan).

Flackes, W. D. and Sydney Elliott (1989), *Northern Ireland: A Political Directory* (Dundonald: Blackstaff Press).

Hastings, Max (1970), *Ulster 1969; The Fight for Civil Rights in Northern Ireland* (London: Gollancz).

Holland, Jack and Susan Phoenix (1996), *The Secret War Against Terrorism in Northern Ireland* (London: Hodder and Stoughton).

Hume, John (n.d.), *Social and Economic Aspects of the Growth of Derry, 1825–59*. Unpublished MA thesis.

—— (1964), 'The Northern Catholic', *Irish Times*, 18 and 19 May.

—— (1979), 'The Irish Question, a British Problem', *Foreign Affairs*, Winter 1979–80, pp. 300–13.

—— (1996), *A New Ireland* (Boulder, CO: Roberts Rinehart).

Kelly, Henry (1973), *How Stormont Fell* (Dublin: Gill and Macmillan).

McCann, Eamonn (1980), *War and an Irish Town* (London: Pluto Press).

McCann, Eamonn, Maureen Shiels and Bridie Hannigan (1992), *Bloody Sunday in Derry* (Dingle, Co. Kerry: Brandon).

McKittrick, David (1994), *Endgame* (Dundonald: Blackstaff Press).

McLean, Dr Raymond (1983), *The Road to Bloody Sunday* (Dublin: Ward River Press).

Mallie, Eamonn and David McKittrick (1996), *The Fight for Peace* (London: Heinemann).

Moloney, Ed and Andy Pollak (1994), *Paisley* (Dublin: Poolbeg Press).

O'Brien, Brendan (1995), *The Long War* (Dublin: O'Brien Press).

O'Malley, Padraig (1983), *The Uncivil Wars* (Boston, MA: Houghton Mifflin).

O'Neill, Terence (1972), *The Autobiography of Terence O'Neill* (London: Ruper Hart-Davis).

Pimlott, Ben (1993), *Harold Wilson* (London: HarperCollins).

Purdie, Bob (1990), *Politics in the Street* (Dundonald: Blackstaff Press).

Rees, Merlyn (1985), *Northern Ireland* (Dublin: Gill and Macmillan).

Thatcher, Margaret (1993), *The Downing Street Years* (London: HarperCollins).

Tomlinson, Mike (1980), *Housing: The State and the Politics of Segregation* (London: CSE Books).

Viney, Michael (1964), 'Journey North', *Irish Times*, 8 and 9 May.

White, Barry (1984), *John Hume: Statesman of the Troubles* (Dundonald: Blackstaff Press).

Whitelaw, William (1990), *The Whitelaw Memoirs* (London: Headline).

Index

Heath, Edward
  as leader of opposition 53
  becomes Prime Minister 95
  rapport with Faulkner 100
  internment crisis 105, 106, 107, 109
  abolition of Stormont 112–13
  Darlington Conference 118
  accession to EEC 120
  Sunningdale Agreement 124–5, 128, 137, 240
  general election (1974) 129–30
  loses Tory leadership 141
  Hume's view on 304
Hendron, Dr Joe 189, 203, 216, 241, 294, 300, 306
Heseltine, Michael 236
'Hillsborough Treaty' see Anglo-Irish Agreement
Holkerri, Harri 279
Homeless Citizens' League 59–60
Hone, Patricia see Hume, Pat
Howe, Geoffrey 172
Hughes, Brendan 168
Hume, Agnes (sister) 23
Hume, Aiden (son) 148
Hume, Aine (daughter) 148
Hume, Annie (mother) 21–3, 28
Hume, Annie (sister) 23
Hume, Harry (brother) 23
Hume, Jim (brother) 23
Hume, John
  rumours of candidacy for Irish presidency 1–2, 301–2
  career 2–3
  stress-related illnesses 3
  relationship with Gerry Fitt 3–4, 93, 94–5
  vision for Ireland 5–7
  training and experience as teacher 5–6
  work to rebuild economy of Derry 7–9
  battle to gain university status for Magee College 8, 48–52
  relationship with USA 9, 10–12
  relationship with Europe 9–10
  educational background 9–10
  young life in Derry 10
  MA thesis 10
  role in civil rights movement 11
  search for peace 12–13
  tipped to win Nobel Peace Prize (1995) 13–16
  support for Women's Peace Movment 15
  urges inclusion of Sinn Fein in peace process 18–19
  family background 20–5
  school education 24–9
  earliest political memory 25
  influence of Catholic Church 26–7
  studies for priesthood 30–3
  begins teaching career 34, 36
  love of Derry 35
  works on MA thesis 36–7
  sets up Derry Credit Union (1958) 38–9
  marries 39
  chairs Derry Housing Association 40
  writes script for A City Solitary 40–3
  writes keyhole article for Irish Times 43–8
  moves into politics 53–7
  makes Open Door film 55
  goes into smoked salmon business 57
  role in civil rights marches (1968) 63–76
  attempts to win reform on housing 63–4
  stands as Independent MP in Stormont elections (1969) 77–80
  states political principles 78–9
  chased by mob in Derry 81
  persuades Bogside residents to evacuate houses 82–3
  no longer chairman of CAC 84
  condemns riots 85
  asks government to ban Apprentice Boys March 86
  injured in battle for the Bogside (1969) 87–8
  walks out of Stormont 89
  relationship with Paddy Devlin 89–90, 93, 94–5
  escorts Callaghan through riot areas 90–1
  attempts to form coalition in Stormont 92–3
  role in formation of SDLP (1970) 93–5, 97–9
  general election (1970) 96
  calls for constitutional change 100–1
  investigates shootings by British Army 102
  withdrawal of SDLP from Stormont 102–4
  dismayed at imposition of internment 105
  arrested 105
  refuses to cooperate with Faulkner administration 106, 113
  launches Alternative Assembly 106
  talks with DUP 107
  targetted by terrorists 107–8
  opposes internment 109–11
  Bloody Sunday (1972) 111–12
  ends SDLP boycott of public office 114
  attempts to negotiate ceasefire 114–17
  discussions with Whitelaw on 'community government' 117–19
  writes Towards a New Ireland 118–19
  views on Europe 120
  urges boycott of referendum on the border (1973) 121
  involvement in Northern Ireland Assembly 122–4
  as Minister of Commerce in Executive 123, 131, 132–5, 138
  Sunningdale Conference and Agreement 124–6, 128–38, 137
  Ulster Workers' Council strike (1974) 132–7, 162
  refuses to resign from Executive 136
  Constutional Convention 139, 141, 144, 145
  decides to stand in general election (1974) 139–40
  alarmed at government deal with Sinn Fein 141
  remarks on RUC 142
  in talks to forge coalition 143
  Eileen Paisley calls 'a twister' 145
  works as unpaid constituency representative 148
  makes propaganda visit to USA 149–51
  made associate fellow at Harvard 150
  SDLP chairman criticizes 152–3
  stands for European parliament 152, 156, 157–8, 159
  appointed political adviser to EEC Commissioner 154
  Pope's visit to Ireland (1979) 158
  becomes leader of SDLP 159–60
  article for Foreign Affairs 160–4, 170
  attends 'Atkins Talks' 164–6
  Maze hunger strikes (1980) 168–71, 174–9
  Strategy for Peace policy document 170–1
  relationship with Fine Gael 172–3
  Anglo-Irish Inter-Governmental Council (1981) 180, 181–4
  achievements in European Parliament 181
  house is fire-bombed 183